EMT – Basic
Certification
Exam

2nd Edition

Greg Santa-Maria

THOMSON
ARCO

Australia • Canada • Mexico • Singapore • Spain • United Kingdom • United States

Dedication

This book is dedicated to the spirit of my friend, Neil Hyland,
who gave his life in the line of duty while responding to
another's call for help. — March 2, 1995

The following textbooks were referenced in the writing of this book:

American Academy of Orthopedic Surgeons. *Emergency Care and Transportation of the Sick and Injured.* 7th ed. Jones and Bartlett.
Henry, Mark C., and Edward R. Stapleton. *EMT Prehospital Care.* 2nd ed. Philadelphia: Saunders, 1997.
McSwain, Norman E., et al. *The Basic EMT: Comprehensive Prehospital Patient Care.* St. Louis: Mosby Lifeline, 1997.
O'Keefe, Michael F., et al., *Brady Emergency Care.* 8th ed. Upper Saddle River: Brady/Prentice Hall, 1998.

For more information, contact Peterson's, 2000 Lenox Drive, Lawrenceville, NJ 08648; 800-338-3282; or find us on the World Wide Web at: www.petersons.com/about

ISBN 0-7689-1412-4

Printed in the United States of America

10 9 8 7 6 5 4 3 2   05 04

Second Edition

ACKNOWLEDGMENTS

In writing this book, I tapped the resources, support, and assistance of many people. I watched what started out as a concept turn into an actual completed piece of work. After many hours of labor, I must acknowledge many people who, in one way or another, made this project possible.

To Denise, Dominick, and Samantha. Your encouragement and support are the only reason that this project ever got finished. You guys are my spirit, and my heart beats with and for you. I love you all always.

My writing experience and career would have never taken a successful turn had it not been for my medical director and friend Richard Westfal, M.D. His encouragement to pursue written projects and his selfless dedication to the field of emergency medicine was the catalyst for my beginning to write this text. In the same breath, I must mention Mr. Joseph Davis. Joe has been my mentor and my friend since I arrived at Saint Vincent's Hospital in New York City. His undying support and patience in my development as an educator has not gone unrecognized and never will.

A special and personal thanks to my Lakota Tiyospaye for teaching me that spiritual support is the greatest gift you can give. My sister, Steph Quickbear, who pointed me down the good road, Cal Thunderhawk (my Bro), and Regina (Brooklyn in da house!) Thunderhawk, for teaching me with actions and not words. Our all-night discussions are always lessons in true friendship and dedication, Pilamaya. (POC my Kolas)

Finally to my EMS partner and best friend, Howard Gelfman, for teaching me that it's not always good to just go "take a look," and that when your cup fills up with knowledge, by emptying it, you may gain more. You can never learn enough.

If I missed anybody, it is truly by oversight. Thank you.

CONTENTS

A CAREER IN EMERGENCY MEDICAL SERVICES

Congratulations on deciding to seek a career in Emergency Medical Services (EMS). You have taken the first step in a lifelong career of helping people in their most desperate times of need. As an EMS provider, you will witness and experience things that most of your family and friends will only experience on the evening news.

Consider the fact that in every city, in every state, there are Emergency Medical Technicians (EMTs) standing by to answer a call for help. These people, like you, are dedicated to a lifelong service to humankind. Your daily contribution to the preservation of life and, more importantly, the quality of life will long be remembered. The patient whose life you have touched forever will remember you long after you have forgotten about the call. There is no greater feeling of accomplishment than to arrive on the scene of an emergency and to breathe life back into a cardiac arrest patient or save the life of a child. There is also nothing worse than to arrive on the scene of an emergency and, despite your own best efforts, lose the patient to his or her illness or injury.

The life of an EMS provider is exciting, exhilarating, and heartbreaking— all at the same time. It takes a person who is committed to lifelong learning. There is no place in EMS for the person who completes an EMT program and shuts the door on learning. I have told each and every EMS student that I have had the honor to educate that completing his or her EMS program is just the beginning. I have told them that passing their exam does not make them an EMT or Paramedic. The real test is not on paper or in a classroom. The real test comes after they pass the course and examinations and are at work in the field. The dedication of the EMS personnel is tested every day on every call. Your ability to remain calm and retain your critical-thinking skills in the face of a sometimes disastrous situation is what makes you an EMS provider. Then and only then will you fall back on your education. Then and only then will your lifelong dedication pay off.

To meet the constant challenges of their profession, EMS providers must seek out new opportunities to learn. There are constant changes in the world of emergency medicine that must be addressed. EMS providers must stay on the cutting edge of technology while remaining compassionate and caring individuals. EMS providers must be advocates of patient care and stand up for the rights of their patients. You must remember that to your patients, you are a total stranger that they have entrusted their very lives to. EMS providers must reciprocate by maintaining the highest standard of skills and knowledge while also remaining compassionate and sensitive to the needs of the patient. These needs are not just medical, but they are also psychological.

As you read this book, keep these thoughts in mind. Keep in mind that for every hour that you review the information, you will be that much more prepared for the final examination—the rest of your career.

LEVELS OF CERTIFICATION

There are several levels of certification in the EMS system as you can see in the descriptions below. This is a general list since certification levels vary in many states. In addition, these states may have added other certification levels.

Lay Rescuer

A lay rescuer is usually the first person that comes into contact with a patient. The lay rescuer could be a professional, a family member, or a bystander who is trained in CPR or basic first aid. The actions of this person may be crucial to the survival of the patient. There are several organizations that provide training for lay rescuers. The best known are the American Heart Association and the American Red Cross. Local organizations may also provide lay rescuer training. These training programs are all offered with different curriculum. People who wish to become trained as a lay rescuer should contact a local emergency or first-aid squad for additional information.

Certified First Responder

Some cities and states will develop first responder programs for their regions. In New York City, for example, the Fire Department has trained their engine company personnel to the first responder level. First responder units respond to the emergency call with personnel who are trained in the administration of oxygen as well as basic airway and other lifesaving procedures. First responders may also be trained in defibrillation. Using an Automated External Defibrillator (AED), they may defibrillate patients in cardiac arrest within minutes of the emergency. These first responders may be responsible for saving hundreds of lives each year.

Emergency Medical Technician–Basic

The Emergency Medical Technician–Basic-level responder has completed a course using the National Highway Traffic Safety Administration-Department of Transportation guidelines (NHTSA-DOT). EMT–Basics are trained in recognition of and intervention in medical and trauma emergencies. This training encompasses airway management, scene assessment, medical (including the use of the Automated External Defibrillator), and trauma emergencies as well as pediatric and obstetric/gynecological emergencies. The EMT–Basic is also trained in assisted medication administration, which requires a basic knowledge of pharmacology, and may be trained in advanced airway management using the endotracheal tube. This level of training may be enhanced on a state-to-state basis.

Emergency Medical Technician–Intermediate

The training of the Emergency Medical Technician–Intermediate encompasses all the training of the Emergency Medical Technician–Basic, with several additional areas of study. The EMT–Intermediate (based on approval by the certifying state) can be trained in:

- advanced airway management using the endotracheal tube

- intravenous fluid administration

- medication administration (including medications for diabetic as well as cardiovascular emergencies)

Several states offer variations in this level of training based on regional needs.

Emergency Medical Technician–Paramedic

The Emergency Medical Technician–Paramedic is the highest level of training offered for field EMS providers. The EMT–Parametic completes an NHTSA-DOT–approved training program that includes a comprehensive knowledge in anatomy and physiology, pharmacology, cardiology, and trauma management. This course also contains detailed training in pediatrics. EMT–Paramedics are required to complete several hundred hours of clinical training (usually 1,400 hours or more) as well as a field internship. There are also various specialty areas that an EMT–Paramedic may have the option of pursuing. Some of these areas include critical care transport, pediatric transport, and air medical transport. The EMT–Paramedic usually operates in a well-equipped Mobile Intensive Care unit, which has the capability of operating as a one-bed emergency room. EMT–Paramedics administer a full spectrum of cardiac medications as well as medications for other medical emergencies. They are also trained in:

- advanced airway management using endotracheal tubes

- Needle Cricothyroidotomy kits

- pleural decompression kits

EMT–Paramedic training can be enhanced to meet the needs of a specific region, although the core curriculum remains constant.

The information provided in this section is a general overview of the training levels of EMS providers. For more comprehensive information, contact your state EMS office. The addresses, phone numbers, and Web sites of all state EMS offices are provided later in the book.

JOB DESCRIPTION OF THE EMT–BASIC

The following job description is a reprint from the NHTSA–DOT EMT–Basic Curriculum. It is the author's opinion that this description fully explains the requirements for EMT–Basic training.

CAREER REQUIREMENTS

Responds to emergency calls to provide efficient and immediate care to the critically ill and injured and transports the patient to a medical facility.

After receiving the call from the dispatcher, drives the ambulance to address or location given, using the most expeditious route, depending on traffic and weather conditions. Observes traffic ordinances and regulations concerning emergency vehicle operation.

Upon arrival at the scene of crash or illness, parks the ambulance in a safe location to avoid additional injury. Prior to initiating patient care, the EMT–Basic will also "size-up" the scene to determine that the scene is safe, the mechanism of injury or nature of illness, total number of patients and to request additional help if necessary. In the absence of law enforcement, creates a safe traffic environment, such as the placement of road flares, removal of debris, and re-direction of traffic for the protection of the injured and those assisting in the care of injured patients.

Determines the nature and extent of illness or injury and establishes priority for required emergency care. Based on assessment findings, renders emergency medical care to adult, infant, and child, and medical and trauma patients. Duties include, but are not limited to, opening and maintaining an airway, ventilating patients, and cardiopulmonary resuscitation, including use of automated external defibrillators. Provide prehospital emergency medical care of simple and multiple system trauma, such as controlling hemorrhage, treatment of shock (hypoperfusion), bandaging wounds, and immobilization of painful, swollen, and deformed extremities. Medical patients include: assisting in childbirth; management of respiratory, cardiac, diabetic, allergic, behavioral, and environmental emergencies; and suspected poisonings. Searches for medical identification emblem as a clue in providing emergency care. Additional care is provided based upon assessment of the patient and obtaining historical information. These interventions include assisting patients with prescribed medications, including sublingual nitroglycerin, epinephrine auto-injectors, and hand-held aerosol inhalers. The EMT–Basic will also be responsible for administration of oxygen, oral glucose, and activated charcoal.

Reassures patients and bystanders by working in a confident, efficient manner. Avoids mishandling and undue haste while working expeditiously to accomplish the task.

Where a patient must be extricated from entrapment, assesses the extent of injury and gives all possible emergency care and protection to the entrapped patient and uses the prescribed techniques and appliances for safely removing the patient. If needed, radios the dispatcher for additional help or special rescue and/or utility services. Provides simple rescue service if the ambulance has not been accompanied by a specialized unit. After extrication, provides additional care in triaging the injured in accordance with standard emergency procedures.

Complies with regulations on the handling of the deceased, notifies authorities, and arranges for protection of property and evidence at scene.

Lifts stretcher, placing in ambulance and seeing that the patient and stretcher are secured, continues emergency medical care.

From the knowledge of the condition of the patient and the extent of injuries and the relative locations and staffing of emergency hospital facilities, determines the most appropriate facility to which the patient will be transported, unless otherwise directed by medical direction. Reports directly to the emergency department or communications center the nature and extent of injuries, the number being transported, and the destination to assure prompt medical care on arrival.

Identifies assessment findings that may require communications with medical direction for advice and for notification that special professional services and assistance be immediately available upon arrival at the medical facility.

Constantly assesses patient en route to emergency facility, administers additional care as indicated or directed by medical direction.

Assists in lifting and carrying the patient out of the ambulance and into the receiving facility.

Reports verbally and in writing his observation and emergency medical care of the patient at the emergency scene and in transit to the receiving facility staff for purposes of records and diagnostics. Upon request, provides assistance to the receiving facility staff.

After each call, restocks and replaces used linens, blankets and other supplies, cleans all equipment following appropriate disinfecting procedures, makes careful check of all equipment so that the ambulance is ready for the next run. Maintains ambulance in efficient operating condition. Ensures that the ambulance is clean and washed and kept in a neat, orderly condition. In accordance with local, state, or federal regulations, decontaminates the interior of the vehicle after transport of patient with contagious infection or hazardous materials exposure.

Determines that vehicle is in proper mechanical condition by checking items required by service management. Maintains familiarity with specialized equipment used by the service.

Attends continuing education and refresher training programs as required by employers, medical direction, licensing, or certifying agencies.

Meets qualifications within the functional job analysis.

CLINICAL INTEGRATION

EMT–Basic students should integrate their classroom training with clinical internships. These internships are provided to all EMT–Basic students, regardless of their training program. It is important to note that clinical requirements vary from region to region. The recommended clinical interface for EMT–Basic students is to complete at least five patient history and physical assessments.

EMT–Basic students should take full advantage of their clinical time. EMS instructors should make it mandatory that EMT–Basic students attend a minimum of 20 hours of ambulance clinical as well as another 20 hours of emergency department Clinical. If the EMT–Basic program requires less clinical interaction, students should request to attend additional hours, which is usually allowed upon request.

Students should make every effort to interact with as many patients as possible during their clinical time. Student interaction should include the following:

PATIENT HISTORY AND PHYSICAL EXAMINATION

This interaction includes a discussion with the patient based on his or her current medical problem as well as a past medical history. The physical examination should be complete and follow the guidelines for the physical examination on the skill sheet in the appendix section of this book.

MEDICAL INTERVENTIONS

Students should observe any and all interventions and seek out the explanation behind these interventions. No EMT–Basic student should participate in interventions that are not clearly defined in his or her scope of practice.

AMBULANCE PREPARATION

Students on a field clinical should assist personnel with their duties regarding ambulance maintenance. They should check the vehicle's equipment and, if required, ask for an explanation as to what each piece of equipment is used for and how it is used. EMT–Basic students should always make themselves knowledgeable with the equipment locations in the event that it is needed in an emergency situation.

All interaction by EMT-Basic students should be documented on field clinical assessment forms. These forms are provided by instructors and should be filled out by students or their preceptors at the clinical site. Students should receive a copy of this form to evaluate their performance and work on any weak areas identified.

Chapter 1

ANATOMY AND PHYSIOLOGY REVIEW

INTRODUCTION TO THE REVIEW

In order for the EMT–Basic to gain an understanding of the pathophysiological processes that she will encounter in the field, she must first have an understanding of basic anatomy and physiology.

In general terms: anatomy is described as the study of structure of the human body, and physiology is the study of function of the human body. Unfortunately, the time allotment of an EMT–Basic curriculum does not allow for complete instruction in these areas. This section will serve as a review of basic anatomical structure and physiological function. The EMT–Basic student should realize that knowledge of anatomy and physiology is the foundation of understanding the function of his patient's disease process. This, in turn, will help him develop a rational approach to treatment based on his information gathering as well as his knowledge of disease and its presentation.

This section will be divided into three subsections:

Review of Topographic Anatomy

This review will cover widely accepted terminology for body locations. The knowledge of this section is imperative for several reasons. First, the EMT–Basic will need to understand these terms in order to communicate with other providers. Second, documentation is an important part of the patient chart; once delivered to the hospital, it should have clearly defined information. And last, the legal aspect of prehospital care almost requires the EMT–Basic to explain his patient's injury and illness based on accepted terminology of topographic anatomy.

Review of Anatomy and Physiology by Body System

As important as patient care itself is the knowledge of the working mechanisms of the human body. This section will cover anatomy and physiology based on body systems. It is important to remember that each body system works as part of the total functioning unit of the human body. In areas where an extremely relevant correlation exists between body systems, an explanation will be given of the relationship between these systems.

Review of Medical Terminology

This section will contain a list of medical terms, in glossary form, that the EMT–Basic student should have a wide knowledge of. These terms are the foundation of understanding human structure and function.

REVIEW OF TOPOGRAPHIC ANATOMY

The EMT–Basic should remember that most of the terminology of topographic anatomy is based on the anatomic position. This position is described below:

Anatomic Position

The anatomic position is described as the patient standing forward, facing the EMT–Basic; the patient's palms are facing the EMT–Basic.

The following chart will describe other positions in which the patient may be described as either being "found in," or "transported in."

Position	Description
Supine	Patient lying on back, face up
Prone	Patient lying on chest, face down
Fowlers	Patient seated with knees bent
Semi-Fowlers	Patient seated with knees straight
Trendelenburg	Patient in a lying position with head lower than feet
Shock Position	Patient in a lying position with legs elevated

The following chart describes descriptions of anatomical locations or references:

Position	Description
Anterior	Toward the front of the body
Posterior	Toward the rear of the body
Medial	Toward the midline
Lateral	Away from the midline
Proximal	A term used to describe two points of reference in relationship to the heart in terms of that which is closer to the heart. Example: The elbow is proximal to the wrist.
Distal	A term used to describe two points of reference in relationship to the heart in terms of that which is further from the heart. Example: The wrist is distal to the elbow.
Flexion	The act of bending an extremity
Extension	The act of straightening an extremity
Abduction	To move away from the body
Adduction	To move toward the body
Midline	An imaginary vertical line that is drawn through the body that separates it into right and left halves.
Axillary Line	An imaginary vertical line that runs on the lateral side of the body that separates the body into front and back halves.
Superior	A reference term used to describe position as it refers to the body in terms of that which is closer to the head. Example: The heart is superior to the liver.
Inferior	A reference term used to describe position as it refers to the body in terms of that which is closer to the feet. Example: The liver is inferior to the heart.

Position	Description
Unilateral	On one side of the body
Bilateral	On both sides of the body
Ipsilateral	On the same side of the body
Contralateral	On the opposite side of the body
Nipple Line	An imaginary horizontal line that is drawn across the nipple line of the chest. This can be an important landmark in chest injuries as well as spinal injuries.
Umbilicus	An imaginary horizontal line that is drawn across the level of the abdomen. This can be an important reference point regarding abdominal and spinal injuries.

COMMON PREFIXES AND SUFFIXES USED IN MEDICAL TERMINOLOGY

The following charts contain a list of common prefixes and suffixes that are used in everyday situations that the EMT–Basic will encounter. The first chart contains prefixes, and the second chart contains suffixes. The EMT–Basic should practice combining these prefixes and suffixes in order to develop a comprehensive knowledge of basic terminology. These terms are commonly used in the field of emergency medicine and should be used while communicating with other EMS professionals as well as with emergency department personnel.

Common Prefixes

Prefix	Meaning	Example	Explanation
a-	absence of	aseptic	absence of contamination
ab-	away from	abduction	movement away from
ad-	toward	adduction	movement toward
an-	without	anuria	without urine output
ante-	prior to	antepartum	prior to childbirth
bi-	two	bilateral	on both sides
brady-	slowed	bradycardia	slow heart beat
contra-	opposite	contralateral	on the opposite side
cyan-	blue	cyanosis	bluish appearance of skin
diplo-	double	diplopia	double vision
dys-	difficult	dyspnea	difficulty breathing
endo-	inside	endotracheal	inside the trachea
epi-	above	epidural	above the dura mater
erythro-	red	erythrocyte	red blood cell
exo-	outside	exocrine	the external secretion of a gland
hemi-	one side	hemiplegia	one-sided paralysis
hyper-	over	hyperextension	extreme extension of the neck
hypo-	under	hypoglycemia	low blood sugar
inter-	in between	intercostal	between the costal space
intra-	inside of	intravascular	in the vascular space

Prefix	Meaning	Example	Explanation
peri-	surrounding	pericardium	sac surrounding the heart
poly-	multiple	polyuria	frequent urination
post-	after	postpartum	after childbirth
quad-	four-sided	quadriplegia	paralysis of all four limbs
retro-	behind	retroperitoneal	behind the peritoneal cavity
supra-	above	supraventricular	above the ventricles
tachy-	rapid	tachypnea	rapid breathing
trans-	through	transected	went completely through

Common Suffixes

Suffix	Meaning	Example	Explanation
-algia	pain	neuralgia	pain along a nerve tract
-cide	caused death	suicide	killed self
-emesis	vomit	hematemisis	vomit blood
-emia	in blood	hypoglycemia	low sugar in blood
-genic	formed by	neurogenic	caused by nervous system
-ism	condition of	embolism	pulmonary embolism
-itis	swelling	hepatitis	swelling of the liver
-lysis	clearing/ reduction	dialysis	clearing of toxins
-megaly	enlarged	cardiomegaly	enlarged heart
-ostomy	an outlet	colostomy	outlet on colon
-otomy	cutting of	appendectomy	removal of the appendix
-plegia	paralysis of	hemiplegia	one-sided paralysis

THE SKELETAL SYSTEM

The skeletal system consists of 206 bones. This system provides the body with several important functions.

- Structure: Provides a framework for the body

- Protection: Protects vital organs

- Motion: Provides motion (along with the muscular system)

The skeletal system is broken down into two divisions: the axial skeleton, which consists of the skull, spinal column, and ribs, and the appendicular skeleton, which consists of all other bones in the body.

The Axial Skeleton

The Skull

The skull consists of several different structures, which, after several months of life, fuse together to form a protective shield for the brain. Sometimes known as the cranium, this term is inclusive of all of these structures. Although the brain is protected by these structures, it is not included as part of the structures of the cranial cavity.

There are four different parts of the skull, all of which the EMT–B should be familiar with. The first is the occipital region, which is located at the back of the head, just superior to the first cervical vertebrae. The frontal region (forehead) is located above the eyes. The parietal region is located at the top of the head between the frontal and occipital region, and the temporal region is located on the sides of the head, just above the ears.

The anatomical position of these regions is important for the identification of injury sites in head trauma patients. If the EMT–B has a knowledge of these areas, he will be able to transmit comprehensive information to the hospital regarding the patient's condition. Injury to these areas will alert the EMT–B to possible injury to underlying structures, such as the brain, which are contained within the cranial cavity.

The skull also consists of six major facial bones. The first major facial bone is the mandible, or lower jaw. The upper jaw, the maxilla, actually consists of two bones, one on the right and and one on the left hemisphere of the body. This is also true of the zygoma, or cheekbones. The nasal bone gives structure and protection to the nose (nares). The eyes, or eye sockets, are called orbits. These circular structures support the eyeball. The orbit is comprised of the shared borders of the frontal bone as well as the upper margin of the maxilla and zygoma bones.

Within the skull are several structures that are important for the EMT–Basic to understand. The ethmoid bone is in the frontal area and is positioned in the midline of the skull. This bone separates the right and left halves of the skull. The sphenoid bone is a butterfly-shaped structure located on the basilar skull above the maxilla. This bone has several bony protrusions that may cause brain injury in severe head trauma. The foramen magnum is a large opening in the base of the skull anterior to the occipital region. It is the foramen magnum that allows the spinal cord to pass through the skull and into the spinal column.

The Spinal Column

The main function of the spinal column is to provide structure and support to the body as well as protect the spinal cord. The spinal column, rib cage, and sternum form the thoracic cavity. This cavity is responsible for the shape of the chest and protection of the organs of the thoracic cavity. Running within the spinal column is an opening known as the spinal foramen. This structure, like the foramen magnum in the skull, allows the spinal cord to pass freely down the length of the spinal column. The bones of the spinal column are called vertebrae; each vertebrae is actually a separate bone that is joined together by ligaments and other tissue.

There are 33 spinal vertebrae in the spinal column. Each vertebrae is further broken down into sections. The chart below shows the section and number of vertebrae in each section.

Section	Number of Vertebrae
Cervical	7
Thoracic	12
Lumbar	5
Sacral	5 (fused)
Coccygeal	5 (fused)

The spinal column consists of specially shaped bones that allow anterior, posterior, and lateral bending as well as rotation. Spinal bones (with the exception of the first two cervical vertebrae) all consist of the following structures.

Section	Description
Body	Thick and disc-shaped, weight-bearing portion of the vertebrae
Articular process	A point of attachment for muscle anterior to the spinous process. Located on the right side
Spinous process	Posterior midline, bony prominence felt through the skin of the back
Transverse process	A point of attachment for muscle anterior to the spinous process. Located on the left side
Vertebral foramen	In the center of the body, allows passage of the spinal cord

Located between each vertebrae is a fibrous disc. These discs provide a strong joint as well as absorption of shocks on the spinal column. Between each vertebrae there are structures called the vertebral foramina. These foramina allow for nerves to pass through each section of vertebrae to allow innervation of different parts of the body. It is important to make a connection as to which nerves pass through at what level of vertebrae. There is a direct connection between these nerve passages, spinal cord damage, and levels of paralysis due to cord injury.

The first two cervical vertebrae are called atlas (C1) and axis (C2). Atlas and axis are shaped differently as to allow the base of the skull to sit properly on the spinal column. The atlas supports the skull, and the axis connects the atlas and skull structure to the rest of the spinal cord. Injury at this level of the spinal column with accompanied cord damage will ultimately result in death.

The thoracic spine, which is larger and stronger than the cervical spine, articulates with the ribs to form the thoracic area.

The lumbar spine, which is the strongest section of the spinal column, is larger and thicker than the other sections of the spinal column. This is primarily due to the fact that the lumbar spine supports the largest portion of the body weight. In a full-grown adult, it is in the lumbar region that the spinal cord ends in a structure called the cauda equina, which is a bundle of nerves that innervate the lower part of the body. This will be discussed later on in this section. The sacrum and coccygeal spine are fused sections of the spine. The sacrum is the posterior support for the pelvis and assists in forming the pelvic girdle. The coccygeal spine is the lowest portion of the spine, which projects below the pelvis with a series of spinous processes.

The Sternum
The sternum is a flat bone located in the midline in the anterior thoracic cavity. Also known as the breastbone, the sternum is made up of three sections of bones: the upper section, called the manubrium; the middle section, called the body; and the lower section, called the xyphoid process. During CPR, the hand is placed on the body of the sternum, avoiding the xyphoid process.

The Ribs
There are twelve pairs of ribs that make up the rib cage. The first seven pairs of ribs are connected directly to the sternum by cartilage. The remaining five pairs of ribs are called false ribs because they are not directly connected to the sternum. The last two pairs of ribs are called floating ribs, as they are not connected to the anterior portion of the rib cage. False ribs are attached posteriorly to the spine and anteriorly to cartilage, which then connects to the sternum. Floating ribs are connected posteriorly to the spine and float free anteriorly. Spaces between the ribs are called intercostal spaces. It is within these spaces that the EMT–Basic will witness intercostal retractions. Intercostal retractions are seen when a patient is suffering from difficulty breathing, and the intercostal muscles (located in these spaces) are working to expand and contract the chest wall to help breathing.

The Appendicular Skeleton
To give you a better understanding of the appendicular skeleton, the bones in this section will be described as they are found in the body. The description will begin with the upper appendicular skeleton and move on to the lower appendicular skeleton. Each bone discussed will be connected to the bone that directly precedes it.

The Scapula
The scapula is a flat, triangular bone that attaches posteriorly to the rib cage. The scapula forms the connecting point for the structures of the upper skeleton to the axial skeleton. Attaching to the scapula is the clavicle. This attachment point is called the acromioclavicular joint.

The Clavicle
The clavicle attaches to the scapula at the midaxillary line, then attaches to the sternum in the area of the manubrium, creating the sternoclavicular joint. This is also known as the collarbone. Collarbone fractures are very common in falls on the outstretched hand.

Bones of the Upper Arm and Hands
The humerus is the largest bone of the upper skeleton and is attached to the scapula at its head. The humerus attaches distally with the radius and ulna bones of the lower arm, creating the elbow joint. The radius runs along the thumb side of the arm, and, therefore, the term *radial pulse* is associated with the radial artery on that side of the lower arm.

The ulna runs along the "pinky" side of the lower arm, and both radius and ulna attach to the bones of the hand distally, creating the wrist. The bones of the hand from proximal to distal are the carpal bones, metacarpal bones, and phalanges (fingers).

The Pelvis

The pelvis is made up of several bones, forming a support structure and connecting point between the lower extremity and the spinal column. The bones of the pelvis include left and right halves. Each half includes the ilium, or upper half (hip bone); the ischium, or lower half (forming part of the attachment point for the femur); and the pubis bones. These bones attach posteriorly to the coccygeal spine, forming the pelvic girdle. Anteriorly, they are connected at the pubic symphysis.

The Femur

The femur is the largest bone in the body. It attaches to the pelvis at its proximal end or head. The attachment between the head of the femur and the shaft is called the greater trochanter. This attachment area becomes important to the EMT–Basic when treating elderly patients with hip fractures, as it is in this area where the fractures usually occur. The femur attaches distally to the bones of the lower leg, the tibia and fibula. Anteriorly at this connecting point sits the patella, or knee cap. This articulation point (connection point) is collectively called the knee.

The Tibia

The larger of the two bones of the lower leg, the tibia is known more commonly as the shinbone. This bone connects proximally to the knee joint and distally to the bones of the foot. The tibia supports body weight.

The Fibula

Like the tibia, the fibula connects proximally at the knee joint and distally to the bones of the foot. At its distal connection point, the anklebone is created.

Bones of the Foot

The bones of the foot, similar to the bones of the hand, are the tarsals, which connect to the talus (the connection point of the distal tibia and fibula), the metatarsals, and phalanges (toes).

THE MUSCULAR SYSTEM

The muscular system is a complex arrangement of tissue and chemical reactions beyond the scope of the EMT–B. This system will be covered briefly by touching the important points that will affect the EMT–B in her field interactions.

Muscles, with bone, provide body movement. The muscles contract and relax, causing parts of the body to move up and down, rotate, and move laterally and medially. Muscle tissue accounts for approximately half of the total body weight. There are three types of muscle tissue: skeletal muscle, cardiac muscle, and smooth muscle.

Skeletal Muscle

Skeletal muscle is muscle that is attached to the bones (skeleton). The primary function of skeletal muscle is to provide movement. Skeletal muscle is a voluntary muscle, meaning that it can be made to move at the person's need. In other words, a person moving his arm is using voluntary muscle to create movement.

Cardiac Muscle

Cardiac muscle is involuntary muscle. As its name suggests, most of the heart is made up of involuntary, or cardiac muscle. Cardiac muscle has a unique feature in that it can produce and conduct electrical stimulation. A good example of this is the cardiac conduction system. The cardiac conduction system is a pacemaker for the heart that creates the heartbeat. The ability of cardiac muscle to create electrical impulses is called automaticity. Simply stated, any part of the cardiac muscle can take over as a cardiac pacemaker should the normal system fail.

Smooth Muscle

Smooth muscle is specially developed muscle that is usually found in the walls of blood vessels and organs. It is generally considered involuntary muscle because it is not consciously controlled. The body controls smooth muscle in that it can facilitate peristalsis (the digestive process of physically moving food through the digestive system), blood vessel constriction and dilation, and other expansions and contractions that regulate bodily function.

THE BRAIN, SPINAL CORD, AND NERVES (NERVOUS SYSTEM)

A complex system, the nervous system controls all functions of the body. The brain is constantly taking in data from internal and external stimuli and reacting to it for the benefit of survival. Every day, the brain makes millions of unconscious decisions to maintain body temperature, increase or decrease breathing and heart rate, and react to outside threats.

A perfect example of the nervous system is to imagine yourself at an automated teller machine withdrawing cash. A man in a mask brandishing a gun and demanding money approaches you from behind. Suddenly you turn around, your heart is racing, your breathing increases, you begin to sweat, and you might become slightly nauseous. However, your vision is sharp and your mind is racing, weighing alternatives for your safety. All of these responses happened without your thinking. This is the brain and nervous system in action. The approach of the man with the gun and your initial response sets off a chain reaction of events within the nervous system.

The brain interprets the man with a gun as a threat. To respond to the threat, it signals the sympathetic nervous system to engage. Once the sympathetic nervous system is engaged, your heartrate increases, pupils dilate, breathing increases, and blood flow to the GI tract decreases and shifts to areas of importance, like to the muscles and nervous system, the heart, and the pulmonary system. This entire chain of events is known as the fight or flight mechanism, and it's all due to nervous system response to an event. Mostly unconscious, this response is just an example of the complexity of the nervous system.

The Brain

The human brain is one of the largest organs in the body. The average adult brain weighs approximately 3 to 3½ pounds. For our purposes, we will divide the brain into four smaller parts. The EMT–Basic should realize that the brain consists of multiple sub-parts.

The following chart will review the four parts of the brain and their basic functions:

Structure	Function	Description
Brain stem	Controls involuntary function	Controls heart rate, respiratory rate, swallowing, and coughing
Diencephalon	Sensory processing and body function control	Processes sensory information from the spinal cord; controls Autonomic NS; regulates hunger and thirst; regulates body temperature; regulates emotional response
Cerebrum	Largest portion of the brain; fine sensory control	Controls the five senses—hearing, vision, taste, touch, and smell; controls speech; controls personality
Cerebellum	Coordination of balance	Interprets signals from the body and brain that correct imbalances in balance; coordinates skilled motor activities like painting or skating

The brain is located in the cranial cavity, an enclosed cavity that is a sealed structure in normal adults. In newborns, the cranial cavity is not yet sealed but remains loosely bound for several months, usually sealing within eighteen months. There are several coverings that offer protection to the brain. Collectively, these coverings are called the meninges, which consist of three layers. The outermost layer is called the dura mater, the middle layer is the arachnoid layer, and the inner layer is called the pia mater.

Within the cavity, and between the pia and arachnoid mater, the brain is protected by cerebrospinal fluid. This fluid circulates throughout the brain and spinal cord. Cerebrospinal fluid serves two functions. Initially, the cerebrospinal fluid provides nourishment to the brain; secondly, it provides a protective barrier for the brain in the case of impact of the outer skull. For example, in a fall where a person hits his head, the cerebrospinal fluid cushions the shock, preventing injury. Without the cerebrospinal fluid, the brain would bounce off the hard interior surface of the skull and become damaged.

The Cranial Nerves

There are twelve pairs of cranial nerves located at the base of the brain and control. These nerves do not attach to the spinal cord but pass through different openings in the skull and perform motor and sensory functions.

The following chart describes the twelve cranial nerves and their functions:

Number	Name	Motor/ Sensory	Function
I	Olfactory	Sensory	Controls sense of smell; loss of this sense could indicate injury to this nerve.
II	Optic	Sensory	Controls vision; damages to structure of the eye, pathways in the brain, or orbital fractures may cause visual loss.
III	Oculomotor	Motor	Controls movement of the eyeball and eyelid; damage to this nerve may cause double vision as well as other multiple defects.
IV	Trochlear	Motor	Controls movement of the eyeball; damage to this nerve may cause double vision as well as other multiple defects.
V	Trigeminal	Both	Controls movement of the lower jaw; controls facial muscles involved in the act of eating
VI	Abducens	Motor	Controls lateral eye movement; controls eye movement looking outward or peripherally
VII	Facial	Both	Controls facial expressions; controls salivation and tearing
VIII	Vestibulocochlar	Sensory	Controls hearing; controls equilibrium
IX	Glossopharyngeal	Both	Controls salivation; controls taste
X	Vagus	Both	Controls Parasympathetic NS
XI	Accessory	Motor	Controls swallowing; controls head movement
XII	Hypoglossal	Motor	Controls tongue movement; controls sensory muscles of the mouth, which send signals through the sensory nerves to the brain; usually when eating, drinking, or engaging in other sensory activity

Nervous Systems

The body contains specialized systems of nerves that control messages from the brain to the body. There are two complex systems of nerves in the body. The central nervous system consists of the brain and spinal cord, while the peripheral nervous system consists of all other nerves. The autonomic nervous system is a branch of the peripheral nervous system. This system is further broken down into two systems, called the sympathetic and parasympathetic nervous systems. These systems control involuntary function.

These branches of the autonomic nervous system control whether or not there is an increase or a decrease of bodily function. Generally, the sympathetic nervous system controls the speeding up of the body functions. This includes increased heart rate, increased breathing, or the dilation of pupils. This is called the fight or flight response. The parasympathetic nervous system works in an opposite fashion, slowing down the body. The parasympathetic nervous system slows heart rate and breathing and increases the rate of peristalsis.

A good example of the parasympathetic nervous system at work is after a person eats a big meal. Suddenly, that person becomes sluggish and tired. This is due to a takeover of the parasympathetic nervous system coordinating digestion. It moves blood flow from the brain and other vital organs to absorb nutrients in the process of digestion. The decreased blood flow to other vital organs, although not dangerous, makes the person tired.

The Spinal Cord

The spinal cord passes through the foramen magnum in the skull and continues down through the spinal foramen. As the spinal cord passes down, nerves branch off through openings in the spinal column. These nerves control different motor and sensory activity. The nerves and their locations have a direct relation to paralysis after spinal cord injury; it is common to hear that a person who is paralyzed from the waist down had a spinal-cord injury at the level of the twelfth thoracic vertebrae. Patients paralyzed from the nipple line down have injury at the level of the first thoracic vertebrae.

The reflex arc is located in the spinal cord. Some impulses in the body do not generate a response from the brain; instead, it is controlled in the spinal cord. The reflex arc is a perfect example of the spinal cord creating a primitive motor response to an outside stimulation. An example of this is when a person is near a hot stove and accidentally places his hand on the flame. An impulse is sent through the nervous system to the spinal cord. This impulse is interpreted as a painful experience. The spinal cord, in response to this pain message, sends back a message to the arm, and in an involuntary motion, the response is for the hand to pull away from the source of the flame. This entire process happens instantaneously. The reflex arc decreases the size of the injury by interpreting the sensory signal and eliciting a motor response to avoid that pain source.

THE HEART

The heart, blood vessels, and blood all work together to support the body in its maintenance of homeostasis. In order to maintain homeostasis, all three of these components of the cardiovascular system must be operating properly.

The heart is a four-chambered pump. The upper chambers are called atria, while the lower chambers are called the ventricles. The heart is composed of a specially designed muscle called cardiac muscle, which is designed to generate electrical impulses. The heart can pump more than 3,000 gallons of blood a day.

There are two different systems through which the heart pumps blood. Coming from the right side of the heart, blood is pumped into the pulmonary circulation. Coming from the left side of the heart, blood is pumped into the systemic circulation. We will review these two systems separately.

The pulmonary circulation system begins when blood is pumped from the right ventricle into the pulmonary veins. The pulmonary veins carry deoxygenated blood from the heart and into the lungs, where it can be oxygenated. After the blood is oxygenated, it is returned to the heart by way of the pulmonary artery. The pulmonary artery returns blood to the left atria.

The systemic circulation begins in the left ventricle. Blood is pumped from the left ventricle and into the aorta. Once the blood leaves the left ventricle, it travels through the systemic circulation, supplying oxygen and nutrients to the body cells. Blood returns to the heart from the systemic circulation by way of the inferior and superior vena cava.

Within the heart, there are four separate chambers that are separated by valves. The valve between the right atria and the right ventricle is called the tricuspid valve. The valve between the left atria and left ventricle is called the bicuspid valve, or mitral valve. The valve between the right ventricle and the pulmonary circulation is called the pulmonic valve. The valve between the left ventricle and the systemic circulation is called the aortic valve. Blood returning to the heart fills the atria passively, and there are no valves returning from either the systemic or pulmonary circulation to the atria.

The heart is protected by a tough, non-elastic fibrous tissue called the pericardium. This layer of tissue serves several purposes. The first purpose is to provide protection to the heart muscle, and the second purpose is to prevent the heart from overstretching. The third purpose is to anchor the heart to the mediastinum. In some cases of severe chest trauma, the EMT–Basic should be aware that this sack could fill with blood due to a ventricular rupture.

BLOOD VESSELS

There are several types of blood vessels in the body. Each vessel performs a different function in regulating blood supply to the body. As blood leaves the left ventricle and moves into the systemic circulation, it is carried by all arteries, which then break down into smaller vessels called arterioles. Arterioles branch off into the body tissues and further break down into vessels called capillaries, vessels that are only one cell thick. Within the capillaries, gas exchange takes place as oxygen is delivered to the cells and carbon dioxide is removed from the cells. Nutrients are also delivered to the cells by way of the capillaries.

Just past the capillary level begins the return of blood flow back to the heart. Vessels coming off the capillaries and back to the heart begin as venoules. As the vessels expand in size, they turn into veins. As the venous return continues back toward the heart, the vessels expand in size until they reach the inferior and superior vena cava. The inferior and superior vena cava are the two largest veins in the body. These vessels are responsible for all blood returned to the heart. Both of these vessels return blood into the right atrium.

The EMT–Basic should be aware of the following physiological functions.

Arteries
Arteries carry oxygenated blood away from the heart.

Arterioles
Arterioles are smaller arteries that enter the organs and tissues.

Capillaries
Capillaries are vessels that are one cell thick where gas and nutrient exchange takes place.

Venoules
Venoules carry blood from the capillaries on its return trip to the heart.

Veins
Veins are larger vessels that ultimately return all blood to the heart.

The EMT–Basic should also know the following terms as they relate to the cardiovascular system.

Cardiac Output
Cardiac output is determined by the following formula:
Cardiac output = stroke volume × heart rate.

Stroke Volume
Stroke volume is defined as the amount of blood pumped from the heart in one beat.

Blood Pressure

Blood pressure is defined as stroke volume times peripheral vascular resistance.

The Blood

The blood consists of multiple elements that are essential to maintaining functions that support life. The following chart outlines elements of the blood and their functions.

Element	Function
Red blood cell	Red blood cells contain hemoglobin, which transports oxygen and carbon dioxide in the blood.
White blood cell	White blood cells are specialized cells that attack foreign substances as they circulate in the blood. They fight things like diseases and infection.
Platelet	Platelets are responsible for blood clot formation and vasospasm after injury has occurred.
Plasma	Plasma is the liquid portion of the blood that carries all the elements of the blood through the vascular system.

THE ENDOCRINE SYSTEM

The endocrine system coordinates functions of the body by releasing substances called hormones. These hormones are basically messengers that are delivered to the cells and then create different reactions in the body to help support homeostasis. The pituitary gland, pineal gland, parathyroid glands, thyroid gland, and adrenal glands are all part of the endocrine system.

The body also contains endocrine tissue that is contained in the organ systems. The most widely known organ to contain endocrine tissue is the pancreas. The pancreas secretes both insulin and glucogon, two important hormones that are responsible for the regulation of blood sugar in the body.

Insulin helps the body convert sugar into a form that is usable by the cells, while glucagon is responsible for breaking down stored sugars for use by the body as energy.

The EMT–Basic should be aware that the endocrine system is a very complex system that regulates multiple bodily functions. The functions listed above are those that will most commonly be encountered in dysfunction while in the field. Diabetic patients who have an insulin regulation problem will sometimes become unconscious from either hypoglycemia (low blood sugar) or hyperglycemia (high blood sugar), based on their levels of insulin.

Another important function of the endocrine system is the release of epinephrine and nor-epinephrine by the adrenal glands. Epinephrine and nor-epinephrine are the hormones that are responsible for an increase of heart rate and contraction, vasoconstriction, and pupil dilation. You may remember these as the responses of the sympathetic nervous system discussed earlier. During the fight or flight response, epinephrine and nor-epinephrine are secreted by the adrenal glands.

Finally, the endocrine system is also responsible for sexual development. The testicles produce testosterone, which help in male development, and the ovaries secrete estrogen and progesterone, which help in female development.

THE RESPIRATORY SYSTEM

The respiratory system is responsible for bringing oxygen into the body and eliminating carbon dioxide. It is important to realize the definitions of the following terms to fully understand the function of gas exchange.

Ventilation

Ventilation is the actual mechanical function of moving air into and out of the lungs. This process is affected by the diaphragm and the muscles of the chest wall. As a patient inhales, the diaphragm contracts and moves downward, and the chest muscles contract and move outward. This creates a larger area inside the chest wall, decreasing the pressure inside the lungs. As the pressure decreases, outside air is drawn into the lungs to stabilize it with the atmospheric pressure. Exhalation is produced by the diaphragm moving upward (expanding) and the chest muscles moving inward. This function increases the pressure inside the lungs, and the air is forced out.

Respiration

Respiration is an internal function that is often broken down into two categories: external respiration and internal respiration.

External respiration occurs when air is exchanged between the alveoli and the capillaries (gas exchange at the alveolar level). Oxygen is taken into the capillaries by the red blood cells that contain hemoglobin, and carbon dioxide is removed from the red blood cells and sent back into the lungs for expiration.

Internal respiration occurs at the tissue cellular level. Oxygen is delivered to the cells by the red blood cells. The red blood cells pick up the waste products of cellular respiration (carbon dioxide) and return them to the lungs during external respiration.

The respiratory system is broken down into two distinct sections: the upper respiratory system and the lower respiratory system. The upper respiratory system consists of the nose, pharynx, and their associated structures. The lower respiratory system consists of the larynx, trachea, bronchi, and lung tissue (including alveoli). The following chart refers to the structures of the respiratory system and their functions.

Structure	Function
Nose	Filters and moisturizes air; olfactory (smell) tissue in the nose allows the sense of smell.
Pharynx	Passageway for air, assists in voice function; balances air pressures between the ears and the throat
Larynx	The "voice box," a passageway between the laryngopharynx and the trachea
Epiglottis	A leaf-shaped structure that provides protection to the airway during swallowing; prevents aspiration of foreign bodies and liquids into the airway
Trachea	The trachea is made up of rings of cartilage and forms the air passage into the smaller airways. It divides into the right and left branches. This point of division is called the carina.

Structure	Function
Bronchi	There are two main bronchi that branch off from the trachea on the right and left side. The bronchi travel deeper into the lungs, bringing inhaled air into the lower airways.
Bronchioles	The bronchioles are the smallest part of the airway. The bronchioles attach the hard structure of the airway to the alveoli, where air exchange takes place.
Alveoli	The alveoli are structures shaped like bunches of grapes. A capillary membrane surrounds each alveolus, where the exchange of air and waste products takes place. This is the only place in the entire airway that air exchange can occur. Collapse of the alveoli is known as *atelectasis*.

The Lungs

Situated in the thoracic cavity, the lungs are separated in the center by the heart and other anatomical structures. Each lung works independent of one another so that if one lung gets damaged, the other lung will remain functional.

The lungs are divided into lobes; the right lung has three lobes and the left lung has two lobes. The heart, which sits predominantly on the left side, is located in a space created by the left lung, which has a sharper lower border at the midline to accommodate the heart. This is the reason that in the trachea, the left mainstem bronchus has a much more acute angle than the right mainstem.

Each lung is covered by a two-layered membrane called the pleura. These membranes serve to protect the lungs from injury and also create a smooth expansion and contraction of lungs during inspiration and expiration. As a two-layered membrane, the pleura has two parts: the visceral pleura, attached to the lung, and the parietal pleura, attached to the chest wall. In between these layers is a serous fluid that lubricates the layers to create that smooth expansion and contraction mentioned above. It is important to know that between these layers lies a potential space. In lung injury, this space may fill with air or blood, causing a pneumothorax or a hemothorax. The EMT–Basic should be aware of this possibility while caring for the patient with a chest injury, and lung sounds should be monitored frequently.

Within the lungs are the alveoli. The alveoli are rounded sacs (see previous table) that have a capillary membrane attached. Gas and waste product exchange take place at the level of this membrane. This process, known as external respiration, is essential for the maintenance of homeostasis. If there is impaired gas exchange for any reason, hypoxia will develop, and the patient may suffer permanent damage to the brain or other organs. This condition may even result in death.

The lungs have the capacity to contain a large volume of air. Normal total lung capacity is 6,000 ml of air, although normal tidal volume (the amount of air taken in during one breath) is about 500 ml of air. These numbers are important for the EMT–Basic to understand during assisted ventilation. While normal tidal volume is 500 ml, only about two thirds of that volume ever reaches the alveoli. The other one third remains in the structural components of the airway, which is called "anatomic dead space." During assisted ventilation, the adult bag-valve-mask device delivers 800 ml of air when properly used. Therefore, it is imperative that the EMT–Basic performs ventilatory assistance correctly and efficiently. This involves maintaining a proper mask seal, using proper ventilation techniques to achieve good ventilations, and attaching the device to an oxygen source.

THE GASTROINTESTINAL SYSTEM

The gastrointestinal system, also known as the digestive system, provides essential nutrients to the body. These nutrients are converted to various sources of energy as well as other components that are usable by the body. The breakdown of food is a two-step process. The first step is actual digestion, which is breaking food down into molecules that may be used by the body. The second step is absorption, where these molecules are actually absorbed by the body for use.

The digestive system is broken down into two distinct parts: the gastrointestinal tract and the alimentary canal. The gastrointestinal tract includes all of the organs and structures of the digestive system. The alimentary canal is the continuous tube that begins in the mouth and ends at the anal opening. The alimentary canal is the path that food takes during the digestive process.

Structures of the Digestive System and Their Classifications

Structure	Function	Classification
Mouth	Food is ingested into the mouth, beginning the digestive process.	Alimentary
Teeth	The teeth grind up food in a process known as mechanical digestion.	GI Tract
Tongue	The tongue moves food in the mouth to enable chewing, shapes the food, and forces it into the back of the mouth for swallowing.	GI Tract
Parotid Glands	Parotid glands produce saliva, which contains digestive enzymes and assists in mechanical digestion in the mouth by beginning to break food down.	GI Tract
Pharynx	The pharynx serves as a viaduct between the mouth and the esophagus.	Alimentary
Esophagus	A muscular tube that is mucous secreting and expands and contracts to move food down into the stomach. No digestive processes occur in the esophagus.	Alimentary
Stomach	The stomach serves as a holding area for digestion. Protein digestion takes place in the stomach. The stomach secretes digestive enzymes that further break food down. Once digestive enzymes are secreted, the stomach mixes them with the food and produces a substance called chyme, which is passed into the small intestine for further absorption.	Alimentary

Structure	Function	Classification
Small Intestine	The small intestine is approximantely 10 to 12 feet long and is responsible for most of the digestion and absorption of the body. It contains three parts: the duodenum, jejunum, and the ileum. The small intestine connects with the large intestine at the ileocecal valve.	Alimentary
Large Intestine	The final stages of digestion occur in the large intestine. Water absorption is finalized here, and the food now becomes more solid. Normal bacteria in the large intestine convert proteins into other substances for absorption and elimination.	Alimentary
Liver	The liver produces bile, which helps break down fats and metabolizes carbohydrates and proteins. It also removes toxins, stores glucose in the form of glycogen, and stores vitamins.	GI Tract
Gallbladder	The gallbladder stores bile produced by the liver. When needed, bile is excreted into the small intestine through the cystic duct.	GI Tract
Pancreas	The pancreas secretes digestive enzymes and hormones that regulate blood sugar.	GI tract
Anus and Rectum	The anus and rectum are the final holding areas for digested food. Highly muscular, the anus moves digested products into the rectum for elimination from the body.	Alimentary

The EMT–Basic should have an understanding that gastrointestinal emergencies are extremely hard to isolate and effectively diagnose and treat in the field. Due to the complexity of the structures and the multiple organs involved, there are many emergencies that will have the same medical presentation. The most common of these presentations is abdominal pain. The treatment of abdominal pain is best handled at the emergency department, where comprehensive imaging and medical testing can pinpoint the diagnosis. With a large number of these emergencies requiring surgical intervention, the EMT–Basic best serves the patient by providing a safe, comfortable ride to the emergency department while monitoring vital signs and treating the patient symptomatically to relieve pain and anxiety.

THE URINARY SYSTEM

The urinary system is another system that helps the body in waste elimination. The system is composed of two kidneys, two ureters, the bladder, and the urethra. The kidney's main function is to filter toxins out of the blood and send them to the bladder for excretion from the body. Kidneys are also responsible for maintaining blood volume, which in turn regulates blood pressure. They also assist in the regulation of the pH of the body, as they are one of the components of the buffer system of the body.

The kidneys are highly vascular organs and need a constant blood supply to avoid being damaged. This is especially pertinent information when the EMT–Basic is treating a patient in a state of hypoperfusion. Hypoperfusion will cause the body to shunt blood away from the kidneys to supply the heart, lungs, and brain. Without blood flow, the kidneys shut down, causing additional pathophysiological process in the trauma or hypovolemic patient. Patients who have kidney failure are in danger of contracting many different illness, due to the build-up of toxins in the blood.

Patients who have chronic kidney failure are treated by the use of hemodialysis. These patients are usually seen three times a week and are attached to a dialysis machine, which mechanically filters the blood through a highly technical process. Interaction with any patient who has a history of kidney failure should involve transport for further evaluation.

SUMMARY

The human body is a highly complex machine that consists of multiple organ systems and chemical reactions that are necessary to maintain a homeostatic balance. It is not uncommon for failure of one system to upset the balance of another or the entire organism as a whole. For example, failure of the respiratory system to properly deliver blood to the capillaries for distribution to the cells will result in multi-organ hypoxia and create cellular changes as they resort to alternate forms of respiration to produce energy needed for their survival.

The EMT–Basic should try to gain and retain as much knowledge as possible about the anatomy and physiology of the body systems as well as the pathophysiology of these systems. This understanding will help the EMT–Basic in properly assisting and treating the patient to offset the chain reactions that occur in the body during a period of illness or injury. This is not by any means an elective topic, and the information given in this text is only the tip of the iceberg as far as understanding these complex body systems. It is suggested that the EMT–Basic continue her education in this area, as the understanding of the structure and function of the body is tantamount in the understanding of the treatment of its disease processes.

GLOSSARY OF REQUIRED MEDICAL TERMS FOR THE EMT–BASIC

The following list is required vocabulary knowledge for the EMT–Basic. The EMT–Basic should be familiar with all of the terms on this list. Developing a comprehensive knowledge of these terms will assist the EMT–Basic in understanding some of the disease processes described by the term. Each term below is given a definition and an example of its use by the EMT–Basic.

A

abdomen   The area between the anatomical line of the rib margin and the pelvis.

abnormal   Not a normal finding, as in abnormal blood pressure.

absorbed   To pass through or set in. Some poisons are absorbed through the skin.

abuse   To treat improperly, as in child abuse.

accessory   Assist, an adjunct to. The patient was breathing with her accessory muscles.

accident   Not on purpose, a motor vehicle collision, or other trauma causing event.

airborne   Circulating in the air. Influenza is an airborne virus.

airway   Path of air as it enters the body. The trachea is part of the airway.

alert   Aware, awake, familiar with surroundings. The patient was alert on arrival.

aligned   In line, correctly matched up. The physician then aligned the bone.

alveoli   Sacs in the lung where gas exchange takes place. Oxygen and carbon dioxide are exchanged in the alveoli.

amniotic   Fluid within the sac protecting a fetus. The fetus is suspended in amniotic fluid.

amphetamine   A stimulant. The patient was experiencing a rapid pulse after taking an amphetamine.

amputation   Removal of a limb or other body structure. The patient rolled over in his vehicle, causing an amputation of the right leg.

analgesic   A pain reliever. The patient was given an analgesic to ease the pain of his fracture.

anaphylaxis   Severe allergic reaction. The patient was having airway problems due to anaphylaxis.

aneurysm   A ballooning of a blood vessel, usually an artery. The patient was diagnosed with an aortic aneuryrsm.

angina   Pain in the chest. The angina attack lasted five minutes.

angulated   On an angle. The fracture was angulated.

anti-shock   To prevent shock. The anti-shock trousers were applied.

anxiety   Fear, apprehension. He suffered from an anxiety attack.

aorta   Largest blood vessel in the body. The aorta branches into several smaller arteries.

appendicitis   Inflammation of the appendix.

arrest   To stop. The patient was in cardiac arrest.

artery   A blood vessel that carries blood away from the body. The pulmonary artery carries blood from the heart to the lungs.

asphyxia   To suffocate. The patient died from asphyxia due to a hanging.

aspirin   An analgesic. The patient stated he took one aspirin prior to our arrival.

assessment   To examine, or an examination. I did a complete patient assessment.

associated   Affiliated, related to. The associated signs and symptoms included pain and inability to move the extremity.

asthma   A reactive airway disease. The patient had an asthma attack.

atrium   An upper chamber in the heart. The right atrium receives blood from the superior and inferior vena cava.

audible   Able to be heard. The man had audible wheezing on our arrival.

authorization   Permission. We had authorization from medical control.

avulsion   Tearing away of. The accident caused an avulsion of the patient's facial skin.

axillary   The imaginary line that runs from the armpit to the hip. The gunshot was located in the axillary region.

B

BVM   Bag-Valve-Mask. An adjunct for ventilation. The patient was ventilated using a BVM.

bladder   Collection area. Urine is collected in the urinary bladder prior to excretion.

bleeding   A break in the integrity of the vascular system. The laceration had minimal bleeding.

blisters   Bubbles in the skin. The second-degree burn caused the injury site to develop blisters.

bloodborne   Circulating in the blood. HIV is a bloodborne virus.

bone   The tissue that makes up the skeletal system. Red blood cells are developed in the bone tissue.

bowel   Term used for lower intestine. The patient has a history of bowel obstruction.

brain   The control center of the central nervous system. The brain controls most of the functions of the body.

breathing   The act of ventilation. On arrival, the patient was breathing and had a pulse.

bruise   A swollen and discolored area resulting from injury. The area where the patient was struck developed a large bruise.

burn   Tissue damage resulting from heat energy transfer. The patient had a third-degree burn.

C

cannula   A device used to deliver oxygen. We placed a nasal cannula on the patient.

cardiac   Pertaining to the heart. We treated the patient under cardiac arrest protocols.

cardiogenic   Pertaining to the cardiovascular system. He was in cardiogenic shock.

carotid   An artery that branches off the aorta, supplying blood to the brain. We checked for a carotid artery.

caustic   Burning, irritating. The substance was caustic to the skin.

cavity   Anatomic space. The heart is located in the thoracic cavity.

cells   Basic unit of structure in the body. The heart is composed of specialized cells called cardiac cells.

cerebellum   A structure of the brain. The cerebellum is responsible for balance.

cerebrum   A structure of the brain. The cerebrum has multiple functions; one of these functions is control of sensory input.

cervical   A division of the spinal column. There are seven cervical vertebrae.

chamber   An anatomic space. The ventricle is a chamber in the heart.

chronic   Longstanding. Emphysema is a chronic problem brought on by years of smoking.

circulation   Movement from one place to another. The red blood cells deliver oxygen by way of circulation in the vascular system.

clavicle   Bone structure. The clavicle is sometimes known as the breastbone.

clotting   To cake up, coagulate. The blood contains clotting factors.

colon   The large intestine. The colon is divided into three sections: the ascending, transverse, and descending colon.

column   Line or division. The spinal column contains thirty-three vertebrae.

combustion   The ignition of flammable materials. Smoke inhalation is a direct result of poisoning from the products of combustion.

congestive   Causing congestion. The patient suffered from congestive heart failure.

consciousness   Level of awareness. I determined the patient's level of consciousness.

consent   Form of permission. There are several forms of consent. Actual, implied, and informed are just a few.

constriction   Tightening of. The patient was wheezing due to constriction of his airway.

contusion   Bruise. The patient had a contusion over his left eye.

convulsions   Seizures. The patient was in convulsions upon our arrival.

coronary   Pertaining to the heart. The heart is supplied with blood by the coronary arteries.

cranial   Pertaining to the skull. The cranial nerves are located at the base of the skull.

crepitus   Broken bone ends rubbing together. Crepitus makes a scratchy rubbing sound when the EMT–Basic is securing a fracture.

croup   A viral infection. Croup is characterized by a seal bark type of cough.

crushing   To crush, compressing. The injury caused crushing to the left arm.

cyanosis   Bluish appearance of the skin. The patient's appearance included central cyanosis.

D

depressant   A medication that slows down the body systems. Barbiturates are depressant drugs.

deviation   To change from normal. During a tension pneumothorax, the patient will develop tracheal deviation.

diabetes   A pancreatic disorder. Diabetes is a condition where the body does not produce insulin.

diaphoresis   Sweating. The patient was having chest pain and diaphoresis.

diffuse   Spread out over a large area. While assessing the patient's lungs, I noticed that he had diffuse wheezing.

dilation   To make larger, to expand. Certain medications cause pupil dilation.

dislocated   Not in its correct location. His left shoulder was dislocated.

dislodged   Shaken loose, removed. The food bolus became dislodged after we performed the Heimlich maneuver.

dispatched   Sent to, assigned. We were dispatched to the call at 1:30 pm.

distal   Furthest from, distant. The wrist is distal to the shoulder.

distention   Swollen, extended. Due to poor BVM ventilations, the patient suffered gastric distention.

dizziness   Vertigo, spinning sensation. Patients who suffer from high blood pressure may complain of dizziness.

dosage   Amount of or rate of administration. The patient was taking the correct dosage of medication.

dressing   Cover, barrier. Burns should always be covered with a sterile dressing.

drooling   Excessive salivation. One of the major signs of epiglotitis in pediatrics is excessive drooling.

dyspnea   Difficulty breathing. The patient having an MI may complain of dyspnea.

E

ectopic   Irregular, abnormal. An ectopic pregnancy occurs outside of the uterus.

edema   Fluid collection, swelling. Pedal edema is a collection of fluid at the ankles.

elbow   Joint at the middle of the arm. The elbow is made up of the distal humerus and the proximal radius.

elevated   Lifted higher than. Patients in shock should be transported with their legs elevated.

embolism   Particle, a piece of fat, bone. An embolism may break free from the lower extremities and cause a stroke or pulmonary artery blockage.

emergency   Acute situation, life threatening. Anaphylaxis is a true emergency.

emphysema   Obstructive pulmonary disease. Emphysema is characterized by decreased lung compliance.

epilepsy   Seizure condition. Many patients with epilepsy are treated with Tegretol and Phenobarbital.

exchange   To switch. Air exchange takes place in the alveoli.

exertion   To stress, increase demand. Angina is exacerbated by exertion.

exhalation   Releasing air from the lungs. Exhalation is a passive mechanism.

exposed   Left open, cleared away from. All severe trauma injuries should be exposed by the EMT–Basic.

extremities   Limbs, arms, legs. Most injuries to the extremities are not life threatening.

F

facial   Relating to the facial skin or bone structure. Patients with facial injuries may also have airway complications.

febrile   To have a fever. Rapid rise in temperature in small children may cause febrile seizures.

femur   Long bone, located in the upper thigh. Fractures of the femur may cause excessive blood loss.

fetus   Embryo. The fetus develops in the uterus.

fibrillation   Chaotic, unorganized cardiac rhythm. Ventricular fibrillation is the most common cardiac rhythm in the first few minutes of cardiac arrest.

flail   Free floating. A flail segment consists of three or more ribs broken in two or more places.

fluid   Solutions made of liquid or plasma. Dehydration causes loss of large amounts of body fluids.

foreign   Unrelated to, not part of. The patient had a foreign body in his eye.

fracture   To break. A skull fracture may be indicative of brain injury.

frostbite   Superficial cold injury. Limbs with frostbite should only be rewarmed after the danger of refreezing is gone.

frothy   Foamy, bubbly. Patients in pulmonary edema may present with frothy, blood-tinged sputum.

G

gallbladder   Digestive organ. The gall bladder stores digestive enzymes.

gamma   Radiation type. Gamma radiation has an extreme rate of penetration.

gastric   Relating to the stomach. The patient was ventilated improperly and developed gastric distention.

gastrointestinal   Relating to the digestive system. Abdominal pain commonly is a symptom of a gastrointestinal disorder.

geriatric   Aged, elderly. Geriatric patients may have no pain during a cardiac event.

glucose   Form of sugar. Unconscious diabetics are given glucose to increase blood sugar levels.

H

hazardous   Dangerous. The EMT–Basic must assess every scene for hazardous conditions.

headache   Pain in the head. The patient with a severe headache and altered mental status should be transported to the hospital rapidly.

heart   Pertaining to the heart, blood pump. The heart pumps blood to the cells through the cardiovascular system.

hemoglobin   Iron compound that transports oxygen. Hemoglobin is attached to red blood cells.

hemorrhage   Bleeding. Blunt abdominal trauma may cause serious internal hemorrhage, usually from the liver and spleen.

hepatitis   Inflammation of the liver caused by a virus. All EMS personnel should be vaccinated against Hepatitis-B.

history   Past events. Prior events related to a patient's medical event. The patient's history is one of the most important factors in diagnosis.

humerus   Long bone of the upper arm. Mid-shaft humerus fractures should be splinted to the body.

hypertension   Increased blood pressure. Hypertension may be caused by cardiovascular disease or head trauma.

hyperventilate   Rapid ventilation. Fast breathing. The EMT–Basic should hyperventilate the hypoxic patient.

hypoglycemia   Low blood sugar. The unconscious patient with a diabetic history should be suspected of being hypoglycemic until proven otherwise.

hypoperfusion   Lack of perfusion to the tissues. Shock causes hypoperfusion.

hypothermic   Low body temperature. The hypothermic patient should be handled gently to avoid cardiac arrest.

hypovolemia   Low blood volume. Blood loss, burns, or dehydration may cause hypovolemia.

hypoxic   Lacking oxygen. Patients with carbon monoxide poisoning present as severely hypoxic.

I

illness   Form of disease, acute or chronic. The EMT–Basic responds to the patient suffering from illness or injury.

immobilize   To maintain, strengthen. EMS personnel must immobilize cervical spine injuries to prevent additional damage.

impaired   Incorrect, not considered normal. Pulmonary contusions cause impaired gas exchange in the lungs.

implied   Suggested. The patient was treated under implied consent, meaning that if the patient were conscious, he would agree to treatment.

inadequate   Lacking, not enough. Hypovolemia causes inadequate tissue perfusion.

indication   Sign of, suggestion. Uneven pupils are an indication of brain injury.

induced   Made happen. The EMT–Basic induced vomiting in the poisoned patient.

infarction   Tissue death. Myocardial infarction is defined as death of heart muscle.

inflammation   Swelling. Peripheral edema causes inflammation around the ankles.

ingestion   Taken internally. Ingestion is one of the four forms of poisoning.

injury   To get hurt by an outside force. Determination of the mechanism of injury will assist the EMT–Basic in identifying potential problems.

inspiration   To take in. Inspiration is part of the process of ventilation.

insulin   A hormone. Insulin assists in the process of cellular sugar breakdown.

internal   Within the body. Many internal injuries will show no external signs of injury.

intestines   The gastrointestinal tract. Nutrients are absorbed in the intestines.

ipecac   Medication. Ipecac is used to induce vomiting.

irrigate   To wash, rinse. The EMT–Basic should thoroughly irrigate the eyes of a patient with chemical burns.

isolated   Alone, apart. Patients with infectious disease should be isolated from the general population.

J

joint   Area permitting movement, articulation of two bones. Most bone attachments form a joint, which allows movement.

K

kidney   Organ. The kidney is part of the urinary system. Urine is produced in the kidney.

L

labor   Process of childbirth. The EMT–Basic should be aware of the three stages of labor.

ligament   Connective tissue. The ligament connects bone to bone.

lining   Covering. The pleura is a lining of the lung.

liter   A unit of measure. The patient lost a liter of fluid.

liver   Organ. The liver is an organ in the digestive system.

lobe   Part of, appendage. The left lung has three lobes.

lucid   Aware, awake, and alert. Two or more seizures without a lucid interval is called status epilepticus.

lumbar   Division of the spine. There are five lumbar vertebrae.

lung   Organ. The lung is responsible for air exchange.

M

medical   Pertaining to medicine. Asthma is a medical emergency.

membrane   Tissue, coating. The mucous membrane covers the inside of the mouth.

meningitis   Inflammation of the meninges. Meningitis may be viral or bacterial.

metabolic   Pertaining to metabolism. Metabolic acidosis is caused by improper cellular respiration.

moistened   Made wet. Burns should be covered with a moistened dressing.

mucous   Body fluid. The oral cavity is covered by a mucous membrane.

muscle   Body tissue. Movement in the body is a direct result of muscular contraction and expansion.

myocardial   Referring to the heart muscle. A myocardial infarction is the death of cardiac muscle.

N

narcotic   Analgesic, pain medication. An opioid medication is considered a narcotic.

nasal   Nose, nares. Air is filtered in the nasal cavity.

nausea   Symptom, precursor to vomiting. Nausea is a major side effect of most medications.

negligence   To neglect. An EMT–Basic is guilty of negligence when he fails to care for a patient in an appropriate manner.

nerve   Pathway in the nervous system. A nerve delivers and sends messages to and from the brain and spinal cord.

neurogenic   Pertaining to the nervous system. Neurogenic shock causes blood vessel dilation.

nitrogen   A gas. The normal atmosphere is made up of 79 percent nitrogen.

non-rebreather   Oxygen mask. A non-rebreather, powered by 10 to 15 liters of oxygen can deliver almost 100 percent oxygen.

nostril   Structure of the nose. A nostril is also called a nare.

noxious   Dangerous, poisonous. The by-products of fire include noxious fumes.

numbness   Loss of feeling, parasthesia. A sign of spinal cord injury is numbness below the level of the injury.

O

obstructed   Blocked. A myocardial infarction is caused by a blocked coronary artery.

obvious   Plain, clear. The patient was in obvious pain.

onset   Beginning, start. The patient stated that his onset of chest pain was related to doing heavy work.

operation   Surgical procedure. Aortic aneurysms are repaired in a surgical operation.

order   Physician directive. Medical control may order you to transport immediately.

organ   Part of the body systems. The heart is an organ.

oriented   Aware. The patient should be oriented to place and time.

overdose   Taking too much medication. An overdose of opioids may cause respiratory arrest.

oxygen   Gas. Oxygen is a first line medication in the treatment of many illnesses and injuries.

P

pacemaker   Heart-rate controller. A pacemaker may be artificial or natural (SA node in the heart).

palpate   To feel. During a physical examination, the EMT–Basic should palpate as well as auscultate.

pancreas   Organ. The pancreas is an organ of many functions, one of which is to produce insulin.

paralyze   Stop or prevent movement. Injury to the spinal cord will paralyze a patient.

partial   Part of, a percentage. The patient suffered from partial paralysis.

pectoris   Chest. A patient with chest pain can be described with angina pectoris.

pedal   Pertaining to the foot and/or ankle. Right heart failure causes pedal edema.

pediatric   Child, infant. Pediatric patients should be assessed toe to head in non-emergent situations.

pelvis   Boney structure of the hip. The pelvis is actually a collection of bones that form the hip.

penetrate   To enter. A bullet that penetrates the body is commonly known as penetrating trauma.

penicillin   Medication. Penicillin is used as an internal anti-bacterial agent.

pericardial   Covering the heart. Blood collecting in the sac outside the heart is known as a pericardial tamponade.

peripheral   On the edges, outside. During trauma, the patient's peripheral pulse is a good indicator of perfusion.

peritonitis   Inflammation of the peritoneum. The patient with a penetrating wound in the abdomen may develop peritonitis.

physician   Doctor. The EMT–Basic works under the license of a physician.

placenta   Organ. The placenta develops during pregnancy to supply the fetus with blood and nutrients.

pleura   Covering. The coverings of the lungs are known as the pleura.

pleuritis   Inflammation of the pleura. A rubbing sound on auscultation of the lungs indicates pleuritis.

pneumothorax   Air in the chest cavity. The chest trauma patient may develop a tension pneumothorax.

poisoning   Toxicological illness. Poisoning occurs when a foreign substance enters the body, causing cellular reaction.

position   Placement. The patient with dyspnea should be transported in a sitting position.

preceding   Before, prior. Part of a patient assessment is to obtain information on the events preceding the illness or injury.

pregnancy   Condition. Pregnancy is a normal condition in which a woman is carrying a fetus.

premature   Before its time, early. Premature ventricular beats can be treated with oxygen administration.

pressure   Stress, weight. To stop bleeding, pressure should be applied to an open wound.

previous   Past, prior to. The patient may have a previous episode of an illness exacerbation.

primary   First, most important. The primary survey is always the most important aspect of trauma care.

prolonged   Delayed, extended. The patient's transport may be prolonged due to road conditions, weather, or other reasons.

prone   Position. The prone position is lying face down.

psychogenic   Pertaining to psychological factors. Psychogenic shock is a mental condition that produces physical symptoms related to a traumatic event. These forms of shock are self-correcting.

pulmonary   Lungs and airway. Chest injury may result in pulmonary contusion.

pulsating   Beating, pulsation of a body part. Abdominal aortic aneurysms present with a pulsating mass in the abdomen.

pulse   Heartbeat, distal. The pulse is a wave formed by the movement of blood through an artery.

pumping   Beating. Cardiogenic shock is caused by ineffective pumping of blood by the heart.

pupillary   Pertaining to eyes. The shock patient will have delayed pupillary reaction.

Q

quadrant   Abdominal section. The liver is located in the upper right abdominal quadrant.

R

radiating   Moving to. A patient with coronary disease may have chest pain radiating to the arm or jaw.

radius   Bone. The radius is the distal bone of the arm along the thumb side of the arm.

rapid   Fast, quick. Shock may cause a rapid pulse.

rate   Speed. Taking a pulse determines the heart rate.

reaction   Response to. A person may have a serious reaction to a bee sting. This is known as anaphylaxis.

record   Document. All findings become a part of a patient's permanent record.

redness   Discoloration. An area of redness and swelling may indicate a fracture.

reduce   Make less. Applying pressure to an injury will reduce bleeding.

referred   Radiation to another area. Injuries to the liver and spleen may cause referred pain in the shoulders.

refill   Restock. A patient may need to refill a prescription.

reflex   Response. Touching a hot item will cause the person to pull away from it. This is due to the reflex arc.

relieved   Taken away, eliminated. Administration of oxygen relieved the patient's chest pain.

remove   Taken out, extracted. The EMT–Basic should not remove an impaled object.

resistance   Force, pressure against. The EMT–Basic may meet resistance when applying a splint.

respiratory   Pulmonary. Asthma, emphysema, and bronchitis are all respiratory diseases.

respond   React. A patient may or may not respond to treatment.

restlessness   Agitation, anxiety. Restlessness is an early sign of hypoperfusion.

results   Effects. The results of treatment should be well documented.

resuscitate   Revive, intervene. The patient who wishes no medical intervention will have a "Do Not Resuscitate" order.

retina   Anatomical structure of the eye. The rods and cones of the retina aid in vision.

retractions   Muscle activity. The patient with difficulty breathing will usually have intercostal retractions.

return   Regain, come back. The goal of CPR is to gain a return of pulses and respirations.

rewarm   Bring to normal body temperature. A frostbitten limb should be rewarmed as soon as possible.

ruptured   Broken. Abdominal trauma may result in a ruptured spleen, causing massive internal bleeding.

S

sacral   Spinal column division. The sacral bones consist of five fused vertebrae.

safety   Protection. The EMT–Basic has a high priority to ensure personal safety.

scalp   Tissue of the head. Scalp lacerations tend to bleed profusely.

scapula   Bone structure. The scapula is the bony protrusion on the superior, posterior part of the thoracic cavity.

scene   Location. Scene safety is the highest priority in response to a call.

sealed   Closed. Open chest wounds are sealed with an occlusive dressing.

secondary   As a result of. A patient may develop pulmonary edema secondary to an MI.

section   Part of. An MRI will show a cross-section of the body in a transverse cut.

sedentary   Slow, non-active. A sedentary lifestyle is a precursor to cardiac disease.

seizure   Acute medical condition. A seizure is caused by a chaotic firing of neurons in the brain.

sensation   Feeling, sense. Part of the patient assessment is to assess movement and sensation in all four extremities.

septic   Toxic, poisoned. A major infection in the body can lead to septic shock.

severe   Critical, major. Anaphylaxis is a severe, life-threatening emergency.

shallow   Superficial. A patient with a major chest injury may develop shallow respirations.

shellfish   Food. Allergies to shellfish are a major cause of anaphylaxis.

shivering   Shaking, tremors. Shivering is an early sign of hypothermia.

shock   Hypoperfusion. Shock is defined as inadequate tissue perfusion, or hypoperfusion.

shortness   Lack of, less. Dyspnea is another term for shortness of breath.

significant   Major, pertinent. Unequal pupils are a significant finding in a patient with head injuries.

signs   Effects, findings. The patient should be evaluated for associated signs and symptoms.

site   Area, location. The EMT–Basic should adequately describe the injury site in his transmission to the receiving hospital.

skull   Cranium. The skull is the collective term used for the bones of the head.

social   Personal, habit. A patient's social history is a pertinent part of the medical history.

solid   Consisting of matter, not hollow. The liver and spleen are considered solid organs.

spleen   Organ. The spleen assists in immune system development.

splint   Support. The EMT–Basic should always check for a distal pulse after the application of a splint.

spontaneous   At once, immediate. Automatic defibrillation may precipitate spontaneous circulation.

spread   Move, grow larger. The rash from chicken pox will begin on the trunk and spread to the extremities.

stabilized   Equaled, perfused. The patient who maintains homeostasis after treatment is considered stabilized.

stages   Parts, sections. A grand mal seizure has three stages: aura, tonic clonic, and post-ictal.

sterile   Clean. Sterile gloves should be used for invasive procedures.

sternum   Breastbone. The sternum is the anterior attachment for the ribs.

stiff   Hard, uneasily moved. Sprains and strains will result in stiff joints.

stimulant   Substance that increases metabolism. Cocaine is a stimulant.

stomach   Organ. The stomach is responsible for extraction of some nutrients in the digestive process.

stool   Solid waste. Stool production is the final phase of digestion.

stress   Anxiety, pressure. The EMT–Basic should be aware of stress reactions after particularly emotional calls.

stroke   CVA. A stroke may have three different causes: hemorrhagic, embolic, and thrombotic.

struck   Hit. The EMT–Basic should be aware of the mechanism of injury in a patient struck by a vehicle.

subcutaneous   Below the cutaneous layer of the skin. A patient with significant chest trauma may develop subcutaneous emphysema.

substance Chemical, medication. Morphine is a controlled substance.

substernal Below the sternum. Patients with cardiac conditions usually complain of substernal chest pain.

suction Remove, apply vacuum to. The EMT–Basic should suction blood or vomitus from a patient's airway during the primary survey.

sudden At once, acute. An aortic aneurysm is characterized by a sudden onset of tearing pain between the shoulders.

suffering In pain. The job of the EMT–Basic is to ease suffering.

surface On top. A first-degree burn is isolated to the surface layer of the skin, causing redness.

survey Inspection. The primary survey is designed to detect and correct life-threatening conditions as they are exposed.

suspect Think, evidence points to. When a patient has severe facial trauma, one may suspect cervical spine trauma as well.

sustained Continued, prolonged. During resuscitation, the patient may remain in sustained ventricular fibrillation.

swallowing Taking internally. Swallowing gasoline may cause respiratory complications.

swelling Inflammation. Swelling is associated with soft tissue injury.

symptoms Complaints. Symptoms are what the patient states they are feeling—headache, chest pain, or nausea.

syndrome Disease process, a collection of signs. Cushings syndrome is an indicator of increasing intercranial pressure.

syrup Medication type. Certain medications are supplied in a syrup form; syrup of ipecac is an example.

systolic Contraction of the heart. The systolic blood pressure is relative to ventricular output.

T

tablets Medication type. Patients with angina may need to be assisted in taking nitroglycerine tablets.

tachycardia Rapid pulse. The patient in shock will present with decreased blood pressure and tachycardia.

tachypnea Rapid breathing. Anxiety and fear will produce tachypnea.

tamponade To apply pressure. To control external bleeding, the EMT–Basic should apply direct pressure to the wound—this will tamponade the bleeding.

temperature Measurement of heat. Hypothermia is caused by a decrease in body temperature.

tendons Connective tissue. Tendons connect muscle to bone.

tension Pressure, stress. Air trapped in the chest cavity will cause pressure on the heart and lungs. This is known as a tension pneumothorax.

thickness Degree of penetration. A third-degree burn is considered a full-thickness burn.

thoracic Pertaining to the chest cavity. The heart and lungs lie within the thoracic cavity.

tibia Bone of the lower leg. The tibia forms the knee joint proximally and runs medial down the leg to form the ankle joint distally.

tingling Numbness, loss of sensation. Patients with hyperventilation syndrome may complain of tingling in the extremities.

tissues Foundation of body structure. All organs in the body are made up of specialized tissue.

tracheal Regarding the trachea. Insertion of a breathing tube into the lungs is called endotracheal intubation.

traction Opposite force, stretch. The EMT–Basic must apply traction to a fractured femur.

transverse Through at a horizontal angle. A transverse fracture is a fracture that runs horizontally through a bone.

trauma Injury to the body. The patient who has injuries to more than one organ system is referred to as a multi-system trauma patient.

U

umbilical Lifeline. The developing fetus is fed and oxygenated through the umbilical cord.

unconscious Not awake, loss of consciousness. The unconscious trauma patient must be assessed for severe head injury.

unequal Different sized. Patients with severe head trauma may present with unequal pupils.

unseal Remove a seal. If, after an occlusive dressing is applied the patient develops dyspnea, the EMT–Basic should unseal the occlusive dressing.

unstable Critical, not homeostatic. The decompensated shock patient is considered unstable.

uterus Reproductive organ. The fertilized egg attaches to the uterus to develop.

V

vacuum Suction, opposite pressure. The EMT–Basic should be sure that there is proper vacuum in the suction unit.

vagina Female birth structure, canal. During childbirth, the baby travels through the vagina and is delivered.

vapor Mist, off-gassing. Certain medications are delivered in vapor form.

vascular With veins and arteries. The liver is an extremely vascular organ; therefore, it will cause a large amount of blood loss when injured.

vehicle Means of transportation. May be an automobile, ambulance, or a method of administration.

vein Blood vessel that returns blood to the heart. Deoxygenated blood is returned to the heart in a vein.

ventilate Mechanical movement of air in and out of the lungs. It is good to hyperventilate the hypoxic patient.

ventricular From the ventricles. Ventricular tachycardia may have a pulse or be pulseless.

verbal Spoken, communicated. EMS personnel may receive verbal orders from their base station physician.

vertebrae Spinal bone. There are twelve thoracic vertebrae.

vessels Transport structures for blood. Arteries and veins are called blood vessels.

vicinity In the area, nearby. The patient with penetrating injuries in the vicinity of the heart should be monitored for pericardial tamponade.

virus   Illness, may be airborne (influenza) or bloodborne (HIV, Hepatitis); not responsive to antibiotics.

vital   Essential. Normal blood pressure is vital to the sustenance of life; therefore, it is a vital sign.

vomitus   Vomit, stomach contents. The head injury patient may present with projectile vomitus.

W

wound   Injury. Any external injury that causes bleeding or swelling is referred to as a wound.

Chapter 2

REVIEW QUESTIONS WITH RATIONALES

This section will cover the objectives set forth in module 1 of the NHTSA curriculum for the EMT–Basic.

HOW TO USE THIS SECTION

In the following section, you will be reviewing multiple-choice questions. These questions are categorized based on objectives that are outlined in the NHTSA-DOT, EMT–Basic Curriculum.

It is suggested that you answer these questions in a test format. In other words, it is suggested that you take out a blank sheet of paper, number it, then try and answer the questions. After you complete each section, match your answers to the answer key for that section, noting any incorrect answers. Once you have graded your answers, you may refer to the rationales for each answer or, only the answers that were incorrect. It is suggested, however, that the student review rationales for every answer, as the rationales will have additional information from which the student may benefit.

In addition, you may want to do additional research into a specific topic by referring to it in your textbook or one of the textbooks used as a reference for this review guide.

An examination is an evaluation tool. To be certified or licensed in the Emergency Medical Services field, a student must satisfactorily complete their final evaluation. On that premise, students should evaluate themselves, identify weak areas, review them, and then retake the section review test afterward. This type of self-evaluation, if used correctly, will assist the EMT–Basic student in scoring higher on the final certification examinations.

Take your time, sit back, and begin your evaluation. Any questions you have should be written down and researched through textbooks, or you may ask your senior instructor for an explanation of specific questions that may not be clearly answered by your personal research.

INTRODUCTION TO EMERGENCY MEDICAL CARE

1. Which of the following is NOT a component of the EMS system?

    (A) 911 dispatcher
    (B) First responders
    (C) Emergency department staff
    (D) All of the above are correct.

2. The EMT–Basic may provide all of the following patient interactions EXCEPT

    (A) detailed physical assessments.
    (B) ventilation using a bag-valve-mask ventilator.
    (C) field administration of medications in cardiac arrest.
    (D) spinal immobilization.

3. Which of the following is the primary responsibility of the EMT–Basic?

    (A) Patient care
    (B) Patient transport
    (C) Patient safety
    (D) Personal safety

4. The definition of quality improvement is

    (A) the review of system aspects that need improvement based on an identified problem.
    (B) the identification of a possible problem and its correction before it surfaces.
    (C) a medical director review of patient call reports.
    (D) an EMT–Basic documentation of patient interactions.

5. The ultimate responsibility for patient care is at the discretion of

    (A) the EMT–Basic on scene.
    (B) the physician medical director.
    (C) advanced-level providers on-scene (if applicable).
    (D) the emergency department staff.

THE WELL-BEING OF THE EMT–BASIC

1. Many EMS calls can cause a stress reaction in the EMT–Basic. However, there are specific calls that have a higher incidence of stress reaction. Of the following calls, which would have the highest incidence of stress for the EMT–Basic?

    (A) A 75-year-old cardiac patient, who feels better after assisted medication
    (B) A 3-year-old child who is unconscious and not breathing after being struck by an automobile
    (C) A 50-year-old male with an amputated hand
    (D) A 17-year-old female who has overdosed on Tylenol

2. You are a new EMT–Basic, and you have been placed with an experienced partner. After a few quiet tours, you notice that your partner seems uninterested in work, is very irritable with you, complains of difficulty sleeping, and hardly ever eats anything. You consider this a sign of what?

   (A) Your partner may be having a cumulative stress reaction.
   (B) Your partner is having an acute stress reaction.
   (C) Your partner does not like new EMT–Basics.
   (D) You disregard these actions, thinking that some people are just like this.

3. Of the following, which is not a good example of stress reduction practices?

   (A) Maintaining a properly balanced diet
   (B) Going out for drinks after each shift
   (C) Exercising
   (D) Following a regimen for relaxation

4. You respond to a call for a patient with difficulty breathing. Upon your arrival, you find a 38-year-old male who has been coughing for two weeks and complaining of night sweats and low-grade fever. During your assessment, you notice that other people in the house also have the same type of cough and fever. Your scene assessment reveals the possibility that this patient may be suffering from

   (A) chronic bronchitis.
   (B) a communicable disease.
   (C) an Asthma attack.
   (D) influenza.

5. Gloves should be worn when treating which of the following patients?

   (A) A 45-year-old male patient with AIDS that has been vomiting blood
   (B) A 75-year-old female complaining of excessive vomiting
   (C) A 15-year-old female who has a laceration to her right lower leg
   (D) All of the above

6. You respond to an overturned tanker truck. There is no placard on the truck, but you notice a milky blue liquid on the ground that has the distinct odor of onions. The driver of the truck is lying on the ground in this unidentified substance. You should do all of the following EXCEPT

   (A) approach the driver carefully and rapidly extricate him, being careful not to step in the puddle of liquid.
   (B) request a HAZ-MAT response team to extricate and decontaminate the driver.
   (C) set up a triage area in the event that this incident produces more than one patient.
   (D) set up a treatment area and await decontaminated patients for treatment.

7. You arrive at the scene of a shooting inside a tavern. On your arrival, you notice two large crowds who are obviously still fighting with each other. An intoxicated male approaches you frantically, telling you that his friend is inside and was shot in the chest. Your initial actions are to

    (A) take your equipment inside and attempt to access the patient.
    (B) request immediate police assistance and do not enter the tavern until they arrive.
    (C) ask the male to have his friends provide you protection.
    (D) have the patient brought out to you by his friends.

MEDICAL/LEGAL/ETHICAL

1. Responding to an emergency call, assessing, and providing treatment and transport are all part of the EMT–Basic's

    (A) response to consent.
    (B) scope of practice.
    (C) liability.
    (D) treatment protocol.

2. The definition of expressed consent is

    (A) consent to treat a refusing patient by court order.
    (B) treatment of an unconscious patient.
    (C) treatment of a patient after they have made an informed decision to be treated.
    (D) forcibly treating a patient even though they refuse care.

3. The definition of implied consent is

    (A) consent to treat a refusing patient by court order.
    (B) treatment of an unconscious patient.
    (C) treatment of a patient after they have made an informed decision to be treated.
    (D) forcibly treating a patient even though they refuse care.

4. You are on the scene of a diabetic call. On your arrival, the family had already administered glucose paste and the patient is now coming around. You identify yourself and explain to the patient why you are there. The patient allows a full assessment but refuses transport to the hospital. You should do all of the following EXCEPT

    (A) explain the risks of refusal of transport.
    (B) explain to the patient that they may contact the emergency service if the problem happens again.
    (C) obtain a patient signature on the refusal form, as well as a witness signature.
    (D) None of the above.

5. You respond to a call for a 21-year-old patient with hyperventilation syndrome. On your arrival, the patient is adamantly refusing an assessment. You tell her that it is necessary and do your assessment against her will, even though she keeps telling you to leave her alone. You may be found guilty of

   (A) assault.
   (B) battery.
   (C) negligence.
   (D) abandonment.

6. You and your partner are on the scene of a minor car accident and treating one patient who will require stitches at the local hospital. You hear on the EMS radio that there is a patient shot two blocks away, and the police are asking for an ambulance forthwith. You tell the patient you are treating to seek alternate transport to the hospital and respond to the shooting. You may be charged with

   (A) assault.
   (B) battery.
   (C) negligence.
   (D) abandonment.

7. You are treating a patient for a possible fractured ankle. You and your partner arrive at the hospital and ask the patient to hop over to the wheelchair. In doing so, the patient falls and injures his arm. You may be guilty of

   (A) assault.
   (B) battery.
   (C) negligence.
   (D) abandonment.

8. You transport several children to the hospital after an incident in the school cafeteria produced a toxic gas. When you arrive at the emergency department, you notice a film crew standing there. The newsperson is asking the names and conditions of the children. You freely give the names and conditions. You have done which of the following?

   (A) Breached patient confidentiality
   (B) Committed negligence
   (C) Committed abandonment
   (D) Treated under false implied consent

9. When responding to a crime scene, the first responsibility is

   (A) providing care to any injured parties.
   (B) maintaining the scene evidence.
   (C) questioning bystanders about the perpetrator.
   (D) securing the scene until police arrive.

VITALS/SAMPLE

1. All of the following are considered vital signs EXCEPT

    (A) blood pressure.
    (B) motor function.
    (C) pulse rate.
    (D) respiratory rate.

2. Respiratory rate is assessed by

    (A) counting breaths for 15 seconds and multiplying by four.
    (B) counting breaths for 30 seconds and multiplying by two.
    (C) counting breaths for a full 60 seconds.
    (D) counting full chest rises for 60 seconds.

3. You are assessing a patient's respirations. You notice that there is stridor, nasal flaring, and accessory muscle use; the patient is sitting in a tripod position. You can state that the patient has _____ breathing.

    (A) regular
    (B) shallow
    (C) labored
    (D) rapid

4. Pulse rate is assessed by

    (A) counting impulses for 30 seconds and multiplying by two.
    (B) counting impulses for 15 seconds and multiplying by four.
    (C) counting breaths for a full 60 seconds.
    (D) counting full chest rises only for 60 seconds.

Match the following skin color presentations to their possible causes.

5. cyanosis

    (A) liver abnormalities
    (B) inadequate oxygenation
    (C) impaired perfusion status
    (D) heat exhaustion

6. jaundice

    (A) liver abnormalities
    (B) inadequate oxygenation
    (C) impaired perfusion status
    (D) heat exhaustion

7. pallor

    (A) liver abnormalities
    (B) inadequate oxygenation
    (C) impaired perfusion status
    (D) heat exhaustion

8. flushing

    (A) liver abnormalities
    (B) inadequate oxygenation
    (C) impaired perfusion status
    (D) heat exhaustion

9. Cool and clammy skin is a sign of _____ , while hot and dry skin is s sign of _____ .

   (A) shock. . . heat exposure
   (B) fever. . . heat loss
   (C) cold exposure. . . heat exposure
   (D) fever. . . heat loss

10. When assessing for normal capillary refill, you should see blood return to the blanched extremity in _____ seconds; longer blood return times indicate _____ .

   (A) 4 seconds. . . hypertension
   (B) 4 seconds. . . poor circulation
   (C) 2 seconds. . . hypertension
   (D) 2 seconds. . . poor circulation

11. You respond to a call for an unconscious patient. On your arrival, you find a 28-year-old male unconscious on the floor. His girlfriend states that he was fine and then just passed out. Your assessment reveals constricted pupils. You suspect this patient has overdosed on

   (A) barbiturates.
   (B) alcohol.
   (C) narcotics.
   (D) benzodiazepines.

12. Your patient is unconscious after being struck on the head with a lead pipe. In a patient with severe head injury, you would expect his pupils to be unreactive or

   (A) unequal.
   (B) constricted.
   (C) dilated.
   (D) unaffected.

13. During assessment, you shine your penlight in the patient's eye. You would expect the pupils to respond by

   (A) dilating unilaterally.
   (B) dilating bilaterally.
   (C) constricting unilaterally.
   (D) constricting bilaterally.

14. Contraction of the left ventricle and its resulting blood flow reading is known as

   (A) diastolic blood pressure.
   (B) systolic blood pressure.
   (C) arterial pressure.
   (D) positive pressure.

15. The blood pressure that signifies the relaxation stage of the ventricles is known as

   (A) diastolic blood pressure.
   (B) systolic blood pressure.
   (C) arterial pressure.
   (D) positive pressure.

16. What are the two different ways to obtain a patient's blood pressure?

   (A) Inspection and palpation
   (B) Inspection and auscultation
   (C) Auscultation and palpation
   (D) Auscultation and percussion

17. All of the following are symptoms EXCEPT

   (A) headache.
   (B) nausea.
   (C) vomiting.
   (D) chest pain.

18. Which of the following is not a sign?

   (A) Obvious deformity of an extremity
   (B) Vomiting
   (C) Dilated pupils
   (D) Abdominal pain

19. All of the following are components of the SAMPLE history EXCEPT

   (A) medication.
   (B) allergies.
   (C) signs and symptoms.
   (D) pulse rate.

LIFTING AND MOVING PATIENTS

1. Lifting and moving a patient using your body properly is defined as

   (A) body mechanics.
   (B) physical mechanics.
   (C) body lift technique.
   (D) efficient lifting.

2. All of the following are elements of an effective lift EXCEPT

   (A) keeping the back straight.
   (B) lifting with the legs.
   (C) shifting weight on the lift to compensate for balance.
   (D) keeping the weight near your body.

3. You need to transport a stable patient with chest pain down several flights of stairs. Which of the following devices is best suited for this carry?

   (A) Scoop stretcher
   (B) Long backboard
   (C) Stair chair
   (D) Wheeled stretcher

4. When carrying a patient using a stair chair, a third EMS provider should be used as a spotter. Where should the spotter be positioned?

   (A) The top of the stairs above the carry, looking down and advising the crew of obstacles
   (B) The bottom of the stairs below the carry, looking up and advising the crew of obstacles
   (C) Directly behind the person at the lowest point of the carry, hand on their back, directing the carry
   (D) On the side of the patient, between the carriers, steadying the chair

5. You and your partner must do a carry down two flights of stairs. Upon opening your stair chair, you notice that it is broken. You do not have time to wait for another unit. Your partner approaches the patient from the rear, places her arms under the patient's arms, and grabs his wrist. You grab the patient under the knees. This type of lift is known as a(n)

   (A) extremity lift.
   (B) two-person patient drag.
   (C) clothing drag.
   (D) patient chair lift.

6. All of the following are examples of emergency moves EXCEPT

   (A) extremity lift.
   (B) sheet drag.
   (C) blanket drag.
   (D) clothing drag.

7. The draw sheet method, direct ground lift, and direct carry are all examples of

   (A) emergency moves.
   (B) non-emergency moves.
   (C) long-range carrying techniques.
   (D) trauma patient carries.

8. You are the first arriving unit on the scene of a house fire with a report of trapped occupants. Your partner runs into the house to try to get the people out. After several minutes, your partner appears in the doorway and falls backward unconscious. Which of the following methods would be the best way to extricate your partner from this situation?

   (A) The fireman's carry
   (B) Extremity carry to a stair chair
   (C) Scoop stretcher
   (D) Long spine board

9. Your patient is a 46-year-old female who has been extricated from a motor vehicle and is unconscious. Her vital signs are BP 90/60, pulse 120, and respirations 22. The patient has gone through the windshield, and there is a high index of suspicion of spinal injury. What would be the most therapeutic position for transport of this patient?

   (A) On a scoop stretcher with head elevated
   (B) On a long spine board with the legs elevated 12 inches
   (C) On a long spine board with the foot end of the board elevated 12 inches
   (D) On a soft wheeled stretcher in Trendelenburg position

10. You are transporting an unconscious patient who is extremely intoxicated. Which of the following positions would be the best position for transport of this patient?

   (A) Trendelenburg
   (B) Semi fowler
   (C) Fowler
   (D) Recovery

ANSWER SHEET

Chapter 2: A Career in Emergency Medical Services

Introduction to Emergency Medical Care

1. Ⓐ Ⓑ Ⓒ Ⓓ   4. Ⓐ Ⓑ Ⓒ Ⓓ
2. Ⓐ Ⓑ Ⓒ Ⓓ   5. Ⓐ Ⓑ Ⓒ Ⓓ
3. Ⓐ Ⓑ Ⓒ Ⓓ

The Well-Being of the EMT–Basic

1. Ⓐ Ⓑ Ⓒ Ⓓ   5. Ⓐ Ⓑ Ⓒ Ⓓ
2. Ⓐ Ⓑ Ⓒ Ⓓ   6. Ⓐ Ⓑ Ⓒ Ⓓ
3. Ⓐ Ⓑ Ⓒ Ⓓ   7. Ⓐ Ⓑ Ⓒ Ⓓ
4. Ⓐ Ⓑ Ⓒ Ⓓ

Medical/Legal/Ethical

1. Ⓐ Ⓑ Ⓒ Ⓓ   4. Ⓐ Ⓑ Ⓒ Ⓓ   7. Ⓐ Ⓑ Ⓒ Ⓓ
2. Ⓐ Ⓑ Ⓒ Ⓓ   5. Ⓐ Ⓑ Ⓒ Ⓓ   8. Ⓐ Ⓑ Ⓒ Ⓓ
3. Ⓐ Ⓑ Ⓒ Ⓓ   6. Ⓐ Ⓑ Ⓒ Ⓓ   9. Ⓐ Ⓑ Ⓒ Ⓓ

Vitals/SAMPLE

1. Ⓐ Ⓑ Ⓒ Ⓓ   6. Ⓐ Ⓑ Ⓒ Ⓓ   11. Ⓐ Ⓑ Ⓒ Ⓓ   16. Ⓐ Ⓑ Ⓒ Ⓓ
2. Ⓐ Ⓑ Ⓒ Ⓓ   7. Ⓐ Ⓑ Ⓒ Ⓓ   12. Ⓐ Ⓑ Ⓒ Ⓓ   17. Ⓐ Ⓑ Ⓒ Ⓓ
3. Ⓐ Ⓑ Ⓒ Ⓓ   8. Ⓐ Ⓑ Ⓒ Ⓓ   13. Ⓐ Ⓑ Ⓒ Ⓓ   18. Ⓐ Ⓑ Ⓒ Ⓓ
4. Ⓐ Ⓑ Ⓒ Ⓓ   9. Ⓐ Ⓑ Ⓒ Ⓓ   14. Ⓐ Ⓑ Ⓒ Ⓓ   19. Ⓐ Ⓑ Ⓒ Ⓓ
5. Ⓐ Ⓑ Ⓒ Ⓓ   10. Ⓐ Ⓑ Ⓒ Ⓓ   15. Ⓐ Ⓑ Ⓒ Ⓓ

Lifting and Moving Patients

1. Ⓐ Ⓑ Ⓒ Ⓓ   5. Ⓐ Ⓑ Ⓒ Ⓓ   8. Ⓐ Ⓑ Ⓒ Ⓓ
2. Ⓐ Ⓑ Ⓒ Ⓓ   6. Ⓐ Ⓑ Ⓒ Ⓓ   9. Ⓐ Ⓑ Ⓒ Ⓓ
3. Ⓐ Ⓑ Ⓒ Ⓓ   7. Ⓐ Ⓑ Ⓒ Ⓓ   10. Ⓐ Ⓑ Ⓒ Ⓓ
4. Ⓐ Ⓑ Ⓒ Ⓓ

ANSWERS TO CHAPTER 2

Introduction to Emergency Medical Care	The Well-Being of the EMT–Basic	Medical/Legal/Ethical	Vitals/SAMPLE		Lifting and Moving Patients
1. D	1. B	1. B	1. B	11. C	1. A
2. C	2. A	2. C	2. B	12. A	2. C
3. D	3. B	3. B	3. C	13. D	3. C
4. A	4. B	4. D	4. A	14. B	4. C
5. B	5. D	5. B	5. B	15. A	5. A
	6. A	6. D	6. A	16. C	6. A
	7. B	7. C	7. C	17. C	7. B
		8. A	8. D	18. D	8. A
		9. A	9. A	19. D	9. C
			10. D		10. D

RATIONALES FOR THE ANSWERS

Introduction to Emergency Medical Care

1. **The correct answer is (D).** Since all three choices are components of the EMS system, the correct answer is (D), none of the above. The components of the EMS system consist of the following:

   1. patients
   2. public citizens who call 911 and/or provide initial care
   3. 911 dispatcher
   4. first responders (fire, police, or other EMS agency)
   5. EMS personnel (EMT–B, EMT–I, EMT–P)
   6. emergency department staff
   7. allied heath personnel

   All of the above components have a direct interaction with the patient once the patient enters into an EMS system.

2. **The correct answer is (C).** The EMT–Basic may provide non-invasive procedures in patient care. There are circumstances in which the EMT–Basic may assist in medication administration. These circumstances include assistance with the patient's own prescribed medication in asthma, angina, and anaphylaxis. The EMT–Basic does not administer cardiac arrest medications.

3. **The correct answer is (D).** Although all of these answers are responsibilities of the EMT–Basic, his primary responsibility is to assure his own personal safety as well as the safety of his partner. If the EMT–Basic enters an unsafe situation, there is a possibility of injury or death.

4. **The correct answer is (A).** The true definition of quality improvement is a review of system aspects that need improvement based on an identified problem. Choice (B) in this question refers to quality assurance. Choices (C) and (D) are components of the quality improvement process.

5. **The correct answer is (B).** The EMT–Basic works as an extension of the physician medical director. The medical director assumes responsibility for all patient treatments in the field that are initiated by the EMT–Basic within the system for which he has oversight. In the field, the highest level of provider is in charge of patient care; however, it is still the medical director who is ultimately responsible for patient care.

The Well-Being of the EMT–Basic

1. **The correct answer is (B).** It is imperative that the EMT–Basic understand that illness and injury know no age boundaries. The circumstances outlined in question 6 reflect calls from the routine to the highly stressful incident. The serious injury of a child always carries a high stress factor for the EMT–Basic. The EMT–Basic should be aware of the signs of acute and cumulative stress reactions.

2. **The correct answer is (A).** EMS personnel may suffer from a cumulative stress reaction at any time. Usually, these reactions are precipitated by a current event or serious call; however, they may just exacerbate as in this question, with a slow and steady onset. Your responsibility is to your partner's well-being. You should discuss these signs and symptoms with your partner or your supervisor to ensure that your partner may receive treatment for a cumulative stress disorder.

3. **The correct answer is (B).** There are many ways for an EMT–Basic to reduce stress; however, constant alcohol consumption is not effective in stress reduction. In fact, alcohol consumption and abuse may worsen the condition. For stress relief, the EMT–Basic should set aside time for relaxation, exercise, and proper diet.

4. **The correct answer is (B).** A key indicator that this patient has a communicable disease is the fact that there are others on the premises that suffer from the same symptoms. Most communicable diseases present with a low-grade fever and cough, and many of them present with some form of rash. It is in the best interest of the EMT–Basic to use respiratory protection on this type of call. This will reduce the incidence of disease spread to EMS providers.

5. **The correct answer is (D).** The EMT–Basic should wear gloves on any call where there is a chance that he may come in contact with blood or body fluids. It is a good idea to get into the habit of wearing gloves on all calls. In situations where there is a large amount of bleeding, the EMT–Basic should wear protective gowns, which provide a blood protection barrier. This protective clothing will limit exposure to blood and body fluids.

6. **The correct answer is (A).** The EMT–Basic should never put herself in harm's way under any circumstances. A hazardous materials incident has the potential to produce numerous patients due to product contact in any of its chemical states. The EMT should immediately request assistance, identify and isolate contaminated patients without becoming contaminated herself, and set up a triage and treatment area to receive patients after they are decontaminated.

7. **The correct answer is (B).** The aspect of scene safety falls into this situation. You have a patient inside a tavern where two groups of people are fighting. You are not aware of the status of the patient—or if anyone in the crowd is armed with a weapon. In the interest of your safety, entry should not be made. In this case, a request for bystander assistance is unavailable. You cannot request civilian protection, and you cannot request that someone else bring the patient out to you because you do not know the extent of his injuries. You must immediately request police assistance to control this situation.

Medical/Legal/Ethical

1. **The correct answer is (B).** The EMT–Basic's scope of practice is a well-defined definition that encompasses response, treatment, and transport of all emergency patients within her response area. Treatment protocols outline specific treatments for a given condition. Liability on the part of the EMT–Basic results from her failure to act within her scope of practice.

2. **The correct answer is (C).** Expressed consent is the treatment of patients after they make an informed decision, sometimes called informed consent. These patients have had their assessment and treatment plans outlined to them, and they have agreed to be treated.

3. **The correct answer is (B).** Implied consent occurs when the patient is unconscious. The EMT–Basic will treat under implied consent based on the theory that if the patient were conscious, he would agree to being treated.

4. **The correct answer is (D).** All of the answers are appropriate in this case; thus, the answer is choice (D), none of the above. In the case of a refusal of treatment, the EMT–Basic should complete a full assessment and inform the patient of the potential risks of not pursuing additional care. In addition—and if the EMT–Basic decides that additional treatment is necessary—medical control should be contacted for assistance. If the patient still refuses, then the EMT–Basic must secure a signed refusal from the patient as well as a witness. Finally, the patient should be given options to call back should he need assistance.

5. **The correct answer is (B).** Touching any patient against her will may bring up a charge of battery. If a fully conscious and aware patient states that she does not want assistance, the EMT–Basic should try to convince her verbally that she should be treated. If the patient still refuses, then the EMT–Basic should refrain from any physical examinations and contact medical control for additional assistance.

6. **The correct answer is (D).** Once you make contact with any patient and begin treatment, you are responsible for that patient until the emergency department staff takes over care. If you begin treatment and leave before a provider of equal or higher training takes over for you, you are guilty of abandonment.

7. **The correct answer is (C).** An EMT–Basic may be guilty of negligence if he fails to provide proper treatment to any patient already being treated. In this scenario, the EMT–Basic was negligent because these three rules were broken:

    - The EMT–Basic had a duty to act because the patient had an injury and requested assistance.

    - The standard of care was not provided because the patient was made to hop to a wheelchair rather than be transported on a stretcher.

    - The actions of the EMT–Basic caused harm to the patient because the patient fell, sustaining additional injury.

8. **The correct answer is (A).** Patient confidentiality is an important issue. EMT–Basic personnel should never release names and patient conditions to anyone other than emergency personnel or emergency department staff. Delivering information to the press is a breach of patient confidentiality.

9. **The correct answer is (A).** The EMT–Basic has a primary responsibility to care for the patient. Although the EMT–Basic should take careful measures not to disturb possible evidence, the first priority is human life. There should be no questioning of bystanders about the crime unless it involves the kinematics of the patient's injury. The EMT–Basic may not remain on the scene for police arrival if the patient is critical. The EMT–Basic should be aware that she should not enter a crime scene until police have secured the scene. This is not always the case when you are called to a private residence for an injury or assault patient. You may be unaware that a crime has been committed until after patient contact.

Vitals/SAMPLE

1. **The correct answer is (B).** Vital signs are defined in the field as blood pressure, pulse rate and quality, respiratory rate and quality, and skin color, temperature, and moisture. Although motor function is assessed, it is not considered a vital sign.

2. **The correct answer is (B).** To assess respiratory rate, the EMT–Basic should count breaths for at least 30 seconds and multiply that number by two.

3. **The correct answer is (C).** Nasal flaring, accessory muscle use, and positioning are all significant signs of labored breathing.

4. **The correct answer is (A).** To assess pulse rate, the EMT–Basic should count impulses for at least 30 seconds and multiply that number by two.

5. **The correct answer is (B).**

6. **The correct answer is (A).**

7. **The correct answer is (C).**

8. **The correct answer is (D).**

9. **The correct answer is (A).** The patient in shock will present with cool or cold, clammy skin; they may also have peripheral cyanosis. Patients with heat exposure (heat stroke) will present with hot and dry skin.

10. **The correct answer is (D).** Capillary refill is an effective, rapid perfusion test in infants and children. It is easily performed by squeezing a fingernail and counting the seconds before blood returns to the nail bed. Any time over 2 seconds may indicate poor perfusion status.

11. **The correct answer is (C).** The EMT–Basic should always suspect narcotic overdose in the unconscious patient with constricted pupils. This suspicion should be elevated when it is associated with shallow and slow breathing.

12. **The correct answer is (A).** Due to the kinematics of brain injury, injury to the brain will cause bleeding on the injured side of the brain. This, in turn, will put pressure on the optic nerve on the injured side, causing unequal pupils.

13. **The correct answer is (D).** Normal pupil response to light is constriction. In the normal patient, both pupils will respond, regardless of which eye the light is placed in front of. Any other response may be considered abnormal.

14. **The correct answer is (B).** When the heart contracts, blood is forced out into the aorta and out to the rest of the body. When we assess blood pressure, the systolic pressure, or top number, is a measurement of the pressure in the vessel during contraction.

15. **The correct answer is (A).** The diastolic blood pressure measurement is taken during ventricular relaxation. This reading relates the pressure that remains in the arteries while the heart is at rest.

16. **The correct answer is (C).** The EMT–Basic may obtain a blood pressure using two different methods. When using a stethoscope, the pulsations are counted from the moment you begin to hear them right up until they begin to disappear; this is known as auscultation. Palpation is done by placing the fingers on the pulse point in the wrist or the brachial artery.

17. **The correct answer is (C).** A symptom is something that a patient feels, or a complaint. Headache, nausea, and chest pain are all common patient complaints.

18. **The correct answer is (D).** A sign is something that the EMT–Basic will physically see. Extremity deformities, obvious injuries, pupil dilation, and vomiting are all visible signs. All signs should be documented on the patient call report.

19. **The correct answer is (D).** Pulse rate is not a component of the SAMPLE history. Pulse rate is part of the physical examination and not a part of the patient's history.

    SAMPLE stands for

    > S = Signs/Symptoms
    > A = Allergies
    > M = Medications
    > P = Past history
    > L = Last meal
    > E = Events leading up to current emergency

Lifting and Moving Patients

1. **The correct answer is (A).** Properly using your body, including proper stance and determination of the weight of the patient, is called body mechanics. The EMT–Basic should survey any and all lifts prior to lifting the patient to determine the possibility of injury.

2. **The correct answer is (C).** During a patient lift, the weight should never be shifted. Shifting weight during a lift may cause you to become off balance and subsequently drop the patient or cause injury to yourself. The EMT–Basic should be sure of the lift, including balance, before attempting it.

3. **The correct answer is (C).** When carrying patients down several flights of stairs, especially older buildings with narrow staircases, the stair chair is the carrying device of choice. The stair chair allows for tight turns and narrow hallways and staircases to be negotiated with relative ease.

4. **The correct answer is (C).** The spotter should always be behind the person at the lowest point of the carry. This person almost always has her back toward the patient and turned away from the carry itself. The spotter will then become a pair of eyes for the person at the bottom of the carry. The spotter may also advise the entire carry crew of obstacles, turns, and narrow hallways in advance. This will add to communication and smooth movement down the staircase.

5. **The correct answer is (A).** The extremity lift is an excellent technique for moving a patient short distances and when you have no other transport device. This is a commonly used lift for moving a patient from the floor to the wheeled stretcher, stair chair, or other device in a non-traumatic situation.

6. **The correct answer is (A).** The extremity lift is a non-emergent lift. Emergency moves are used in situations where the EMT–Basic may be in danger of personal injury, such as fires, unstable structures, and other hazardous situations. These moves are not indicated in non-dangerous situations, as they may cause additional injury to the patient.

7. **The correct answer is (B).** All of the above moves are non-emergency moves that are designed to facilitate a non-trauma patient's movement onto a stretcher. These moves should never be used on a patient with suspected spinal trauma, for fear of increasing the injury.

8. **The correct answer is (A).** In this situation, the fireman's carry is the best method of extrication. The fireman's carry is a one-person operation, which takes only seconds to initiate. The extremity carry, scoop stretcher, and long spine board are all two-person operations, which are time consuming given the situation.

9. **The correct answer is (C).** In any patient who has a suspected spinal injury and hypotension, the foot end of the long spine board should be elevated. This way, the patient is elevated as a unit. Elevation of only the legs could cause additional spinal movement and create additional damage. Soft-wheeled stretchers are not indicated, as they do not provide a stable spinal support.

10. **The correct answer is (D).** The unconscious patient who has no traumatic injury should be transported in the recovery position. The recovery position allows for management of the airway and prevents aspiration in the event that the patient vomits.

Chapter 3

AIRWAY

BASIC AIRWAY
About This Section

This section will test your knowledge about the indications for and use of basic airway adjuncts. Airway management is the front line of defense in the treatment of all illness and injury. You should practice this section until you are proficient in the knowledge needed to perform these skills.

1. All of the following are structures of the respiratory system EXCEPT

    (A) trachea.
    (B) alveoli.
    (C) esophagus.
    (D) pharynx.

2. The exchange of oxygen and carbon dioxide takes place in the

    (A) trachea.
    (B) alveoli.
    (C) bronchus.
    (D) epiglottis.

3. Of the following, which is not a sign of adequate breathing?

    (A) Abdominal movement
    (B) Equal chest rise and fall
    (C) Muscular retractions in the ribs
    (D) Audible breath sounds

4. You respond to a patient in respiratory distress. On your arrival, you find a 67-year-old male who has a respiratory rate of 32, nasal flaring, and shallow, irregular respirations. All of these findings are indicative of

    (A) normal respiratory patterns.
    (B) inadequate breathing.
    (C) choking.
    (D) proper ventilation.

5. Which of the following is not a cause of inadequate breathing?

    (A) Pulmonary edema
    (B) Allergic reactions
    (C) Airway obstruction
    (D) All of the above are causes of inadequate breathing.

6. The head tilt–chin lift airway maneuver can be used in all of the following patients EXCEPT

   (A) a patient who is choking.
   (B) a patient with chest pain.
   (C) a patient struck by an automobile.
   (D) a patient suffering an allergic reaction.

7. You are assigned to a motor vehicle accident on the interstate. On your arrival, you find a 22-year-old male who is unconscious after being ejected from the vehicle. The initial airway maneuver of choice for the patient would be the

   (A) head tilt–chin lift.
   (B) insertion of an oropharyngeal airway.
   (C) jaw thrust maneuver.
   (D) chin pull.

8. The EMT–Basic should never suction a patient for longer than _____ seconds.

   (A) 5
   (B) 10
   (C) 15
   (D) 20

9. While suctioning a patient, suction should be applied

   (A) during insertion of the catheter.
   (B) while advancing the catheter.
   (C) after the catheter is in place.
   (D) while removing the catheter.

10. All of the following adjuncts are used in artificial ventilation EXCEPT the

    (A) bag-valve-mask device.
    (B) non-rebreather mask.
    (C) pocket face mask.
    (D) flow restricted oxygen powered ventilation device.

11. The pocket face mask with supplemental oxygen may deliver up to _____ percent oxygen to the non-breathing patient.

    (A) 35
    (B) 50
    (C) 85
    (D) 100

12. The bag-valve-mask ventilation device with a reservoir may deliver up to _____ percent of oxygen to the non-breathing patient.

    (A) 35 to 45
    (B) 50 to 60
    (C) 75 to 85
    (D) 95 to 100

13. In order to ensure proper ventilation, the rescuer must deliver more than _____ milliliters of air using a bag-valve-mask device.

   (A) 500
   (B) 600
   (C) 700
   (D) 800

14. You are treating an unconscious patient using an oropharyngeal airway. Proper insertion of this device includes all of the following EXCEPT

   (A) measurement of the device from the corner of the mouth to the tip of the earlobe.
   (B) opening of the mouth using crossed finger technique.
   (C) inserting the airway along the curvature of the mouth.
   (D) checking that the flange properly rests on the patient's lips after insertion.

15. Your seizure patient requires an airway device. Which of the following airway adjuncts would be appropriate, based on the fact that the patient's mouth is clamped shut due to the seizures?

   (A) Oropharyngeal airway
   (B) Nasopharyngeal airway
   (C) Endotracheal tube
   (D) Bag-valve-mask device

16. To ensure proper size, the nasopharyngeal airway is measured from

   (A) the angle of the jaw to the corner of the mouth.
   (B) the corner of the mouth to the edge of the nostril.
   (C) the edge of the nostril to the angle of the jaw.
   (D) the nostril to the top of the ear.

Match the following oxygen cylinder sizes to their appropriate capacity:

17. D cylinder

   (A) 625 Liters
   (B) 350 Liters
   (C) 6,500 Liters
   (D) 3,000 Liters

18. E cylinder

   (A) 625 Liters
   (B) 350 Liters
   (C) 6,500 Liters
   (D) 3,000 Liters

19. M cylinder

   (A) 625 Liters
   (B) 350 Liters
   (C) 6,500 Liters
   (D) 3,000 Liters

20. The non-rebreather mask can deliver approximately what percent of oxygen when attached to a delivery system at 12 to 15 liters per minute?

   (A) 35 to 45
   (B) 45 to 55
   (C) 80 to 90
   (D) 100

21. The nasal cannula can provide varied oxygen concentrations. Which of the following liter flow/liter-per-minute combinations correctly describes the capabilities of the nasal cannula?

   (A) 1 to 6 liters, delivering 24 to 44 percent oxygen
   (B) 2 to 10 liters, delivering 24 to 44 percent oxygen
   (C) 10 to 12 liters, delivering 80 to 90 percent oxygen
   (D) 15 liters, delivering 100 percent oxygen

22. Your 82-year-old cardiac patient is complaining of difficulty breathing and chest pain. As you begin to administer oxygen through a non-rebreather mask, the patient fights the mask, saying it is too confining. You

   (A) tell the patient they must keep the mask on, regardless of their complaint.
   (B) begin ventilations with a bag-valve-mask ventilator.
   (C) remove the mask and apply a nasal cannula for comfort.
   (D) remove the mask and disregard oxygen administration.

ADVANCED AIRWAY

About This Section

The advanced airway module in the national standard curriculum is an optional module and is not required as part of the original EMT–Basic program. In order to provide the EMT–Basic with a full review of possible course materials, it has been included in this study guide. If the advanced airway module was not included in your original program, you should take the time to refer to your textbook chapter on advanced airway before attempting to answer these questions.

1. The trachea divides into two branches. The bifurcation point at which the branches form is called the

   (A) larynx.
   (B) carina.
   (C) right mainstem bronchus.
   (D) left mainstem bronchus.

2. The leaf-shaped structure that protects the airway is called the

   (A) trachea.
   (B) carina.
   (C) epiglottis.
   (D) vallecula.

3. The vocal cords are a primary anatomic structure to identify during endotracheal intubation. The vocal cords are located in the

   (A) pharynx.
   (B) carina.
   (C) larynx.
   (D) epiglottis.

4. The anatomical structure that is located posterior to the trachea and that is commonly the location of an improperly inserted endotracheal tube is known as the

   (A) carina.
   (B) right mainstem bronchus.
   (C) left mainstem bronchus.
   (D) esophagus.

5. All of these are anatomical differences between the pediatric airway and the adult airway EXCEPT which of the following?

   (A) The pediatric airway is more supple than the adult airway.
   (B) The tongue in the pediatric patient is larger.
   (C) The cricoid cartilage is the widest part of the airway.
   (D) Due to a smaller trachea, the pediatric patient is more prone to foreign body airway obstruction.

6. All of the following are benefits of endotracheal intubation EXCEPT

   (A) prevents aspiration.
   (B) allows direct ventilation without need of a mask seal.
   (C) facilitates deep airway suctioning.
   (D) does not elicit a gag reflex in the conscious patient.

7. Which of the following is not a complication of esophageal intubation?

   (A) Slowing of the heart rate
   (B) Esophageal rupture
   (C) Intubation of the right mainstem bronchus
   (D) Prevention of aspiration

8. Laryngoscope blades come in several different styles. The straight blade is also known as the _____ blade, while the curved blade is known as the _____ blade.

   (A) macintosh.. miller
   (B) miller..macintosh
   (C) fiber optic..miller
   (D) fiber optic..macintosh

9. In order from smallest to largest, what is the correct size of a laryngoscope blade?

   (A) 0, 1, 2, 3, 4
   (B) 4, 3, 2, 1, 0
   (C) 8, 6, 4, 2
   (D) 2, 4, 6, 8

10. All of these statements about the use of a stylet are true EXCEPT which of the following?

   (A) The stylet is used to increase the rigidity of the endotracheal tube.
   (B) After insertion, the tube/stylet should be shaped with a slight anatomical bend.
   (C) The tip of the stylet should protrude from the end of the endotracheal tube by approximately .5 inches.
   (D) The stylet can be lubricated to ease removal after intubation.

11. The typical size endotracheal tube for the adult male patient is _____, while the typical size endotracheal tube for a newborn is _____.

   (A) 8.0 to 8.5..3.0 to 3.5
   (B) 6.0 to 6.5..5.0 to 5.5
   (C) 2.0 to 2.5..9.0 to 9.5
   (D) 3.5 to 4.5..8.5 to 9.5

12. The commonly accepted formula for sizing an endotracheal tube in a child is

   (A) (Age + 3) × 6.
   (B) (Age + 16) ÷ 4.
   (C) (Height + Age) × 4.
   (D) (Weight + Height) × 6.

13. Which of the following is not a step in the placement of the endotracheal tube in an adult patient?

   (A) Prepare all equipment before attempting the insertion.
   (B) Insert the laryngoscope into the patient's mouth.
   (C) Sweep the tongue from right to left, and hold the mouth open with the blade.
   (D) Blindly insert the endotracheal tube, watching the area of the cricoid cartilage for a bump.

Questions 14 to 17 are based on the following scenario.

You and your partner are dispatched to a private residence for a patient with difficulty breathing. On your arrival, you find a 26-year-old male who has become unconscious. The family states that the patient is asthmatic and was having difficulty breathing before he passed out. Your assessment reveals that the patient has a pulse and is breathing at about 6 breaths per minute, has poor chest rise, and peripheral cyanosis.

14. Your first intervention would be to

   (A) open the airway, insert an OPA, and begin ventilations using a bag-valve-mask device.
   (B) immediately begin CPR.
   (C) immediately perform endotracheal intubation on the patient.
   (D) place a non-rebreather mask on the patient.

15. While ventilating the patient with a bag-valve-mask device, you notice that the ventilation is not producing adequate chest rise. Your next intervention would be to

    (A) hyperventilate as adequately as possible and perform endotracheal intubation.
    (B) remove the OPA, and insert an NPA.
    (C) increase your oxygen liter flow.
    (D) attach the patient to the AED for evaluation.

16. After you insert the endotracheal tube, you notice that you are not hearing lung sounds and that the patient is becoming centrally cyanotic. Your partner auscultates the abdomen and states that he hears air in the stomach during ventilations. What would be your next step in the management of this patient?

    (A) Continue ventilations, because asthmatics sometimes have silent chests
    (B) Remove the endotracheal tube and immediately reinsert the endotracheal tube
    (C) Remove the endotracheal tube, hyperventilate the patient using the bag-valve-mask device, then attempt endotracheal intubation again
    (D) Remove the endotracheal tube and transport using only the bag-valve-mask device

17. You have inserted the endotracheal tube for a second time, and your partner confirms bilateral lung sounds. Your next priority would be to

    (A) secure the endotracheal tube in a proper fashion.
    (B) begin immediate transport and secure the endotracheal tube en route.
    (C) reassess the patient status, and then secure the endotracheal tube.
    (D) ventilate the patient with 1 breath every 6 seconds.

18. All of the following are indicators of proper endotracheal tube placement EXCEPT

    (A) bilateral breath sounds on ventilation.
    (B) vomitus inside the endotracheal tube.
    (C) carbon dioxide detector indication.
    (D) visualization of the endotracheal tube passing through the vocal cords.

ANSWER SHEET

Chapter 3: Airway

Basic Airway

1. Ⓐ Ⓑ Ⓒ Ⓓ	6. Ⓐ Ⓑ Ⓒ Ⓓ	11. Ⓐ Ⓑ Ⓒ Ⓓ	16. Ⓐ Ⓑ Ⓒ Ⓓ	21. Ⓐ Ⓑ Ⓒ Ⓓ
2. Ⓐ Ⓑ Ⓒ Ⓓ	7. Ⓐ Ⓑ Ⓒ Ⓓ	12. Ⓐ Ⓑ Ⓒ Ⓓ	17. Ⓐ Ⓑ Ⓒ Ⓓ	22. Ⓐ Ⓑ Ⓒ Ⓓ
3. Ⓐ Ⓑ Ⓒ Ⓓ	8. Ⓐ Ⓑ Ⓒ Ⓓ	13. Ⓐ Ⓑ Ⓒ Ⓓ	18. Ⓐ Ⓑ Ⓒ Ⓓ	
4. Ⓐ Ⓑ Ⓒ Ⓓ	9. Ⓐ Ⓑ Ⓒ Ⓓ	14. Ⓐ Ⓑ Ⓒ Ⓓ	19. Ⓐ Ⓑ Ⓒ Ⓓ	
5. Ⓐ Ⓑ Ⓒ Ⓓ	10. Ⓐ Ⓑ Ⓒ Ⓓ	15. Ⓐ Ⓑ Ⓒ Ⓓ	20. Ⓐ Ⓑ Ⓒ Ⓓ	

Advanced Airway

1. Ⓐ Ⓑ Ⓒ Ⓓ	6. Ⓐ Ⓑ Ⓒ Ⓓ	11. Ⓐ Ⓑ Ⓒ Ⓓ	16. Ⓐ Ⓑ Ⓒ Ⓓ
2. Ⓐ Ⓑ Ⓒ Ⓓ	7. Ⓐ Ⓑ Ⓒ Ⓓ	12. Ⓐ Ⓑ Ⓒ Ⓓ	17. Ⓐ Ⓑ Ⓒ Ⓓ
3. Ⓐ Ⓑ Ⓒ Ⓓ	8. Ⓐ Ⓑ Ⓒ Ⓓ	13. Ⓐ Ⓑ Ⓒ Ⓓ	18. Ⓐ Ⓑ Ⓒ Ⓓ
4. Ⓐ Ⓑ Ⓒ Ⓓ	9. Ⓐ Ⓑ Ⓒ Ⓓ	14. Ⓐ Ⓑ Ⓒ Ⓓ	
5. Ⓐ Ⓑ Ⓒ Ⓓ	10. Ⓐ Ⓑ Ⓒ Ⓓ	15. Ⓐ Ⓑ Ⓒ Ⓓ	

ANSWERS TO CHAPTER 3

Basic Airway		Advanced Airway	
1. C	12. D	1. B	10. C
2. B	13. D	2. C	11. A
3. C	14. C	3. C	12. B
4. B	15. B	4. D	13. D
5. D	16. C	5. C	14. A
6. C	17. B	6. D	15. A
7. C	18. A	7. D	16. C
8. C	19. D	8. B	17. A
9. D	20. C	9. A	18. B
10. B	21. A		
11. B	22. C		

RATIONALES FOR THE ANSWERS

1. **The correct answer is (C).** The esophagus is a structure of the gastrointestinal system.

2. **The correct answer is (B).** Oxygen and carbon dioxide exchange, commonly referred to as gas exchange, takes place in the alveoli. The alveoli are sac-shaped structures that have a membrane that is one cell thick. These membranes are adjacent to capillaries, and the gas exchange occurs at this level.

3. **The correct answer is (C).** Muscle retractions, known as intercostal retractions, are signs of increased work of breathing. Patients most commonly seen with these retractions are those in severe respiratory distress.

4. **The correct answer is (B).** Increased respiratory rates, nasal flaring, pursed lip breathing, and shallow, irregular respirations are all sign of inadequate breathing.

5. **The correct answer is (D).** Inadequate breathing may be caused by a number of ailments, including pulmonary edema, chest pain, asthma, bronchitis, and head injuries.

6. **The correct answer is (C).** The head tilt-chin lift should never be used on any patient who may be suspected of having a cervical spinal injury.

7. **The correct answer is (C).** The jaw thrust maneuver is indicated for all unconscious patients who may have a cervical spinal injury. Although an oropharyngeal airway may eventually be indicated, it is not an initial airway maneuver.

8. **The correct answer is (C).** A patient should never be suctioned for longer than 15 seconds. Long periods of suctioning can cause the patient to become hypoxic. Patients who require suctioning will require high-flow oxygen and possible assisted ventilations after the procedure is completed. When possible, the patient should be hyperventilated prior to suctioning.

9. **The correct answer is (D).** Suction should be applied while removing the catheter. Long applications of suctions may result in hypoxia.

10. **The correct answer is (B).** Artificial ventilation is the process of manually forcing air into the patient's lungs. The bag-valve-mask, pocket face mask, and flow-restricted oxygen-powered ventilation device are all designed to deliver pressures great enough to produce artificial ventilation. The non-rebreather mask will not develop high pressures to ensure adequate ventilation and should never be used.

11. **The correct answer is (B).** The pocket face mask, when attached to an oxygen supply, can deliver up to 50 percent oxygen to the patient. The pocket face mask alone relies on the expired oxygen of the rescuer, which is normally 16 percent.

12. **The correct answer is (D).** The bag-valve-mask with supplemental oxygen can deliver almost 100 percent oxygen; this is based on the device having an oxygen reservoir. If the device lacks a reservoir, the percent of oxygen delivery falls to nearly 50 percent.

13. **The correct answer is (D).** The American Heart Association recommends that the patient being ventilated with a bag-valve-mask device should receive at least 800 milliliters of air during each ventilation. Improper delivery will result in poor patient oxygenation.

14. **The correct answer is (C).** The oropharyngeal airway is inserted upside down along the palate until resistance is felt. After the EMT–Basic feels resistance, the airway is gently rotated 180 degrees to ensure proper placement. Insertion along the curvature of the mouth may result in obstruction of the airway by the tongue.

15. **The correct answer is (B).** The nasopharyngeal airway is the airway of choice in patients who have no access to the mouth. In cases of seizure and oral trauma, it may be impossible to insert an oral airway, including an endotracheal tube. The airway of choice would be a nasopharyngeal airway. The bag-valve-mask device is not an airway adjunct, but it is a ventilation device.

16. **The correct answer is (C).** The nasopharyngeal airway should be measured from the nostril to the angle of the jaw. An improperly sized airway may result in kinking from over insertion as well as improper ventilation.

17. **The correct answer is (B).**

18. **The correct answer is (A).**

19. **The correct answer is (D).**

Rationale for questions 20, 21, and 22
Oxygen tanks are produced in several capacities. The D and E cylinders are usually portable, with the D tank being most popular. The M cylinder is used for a fixed onboard oxygen system.

20. **The correct answer is (C).** The non-rebreather mask can deliver oxygen concentrations as high as 80 to 90 percent when properly hooked up and at the proper liter flow.

21. **The correct answer is (A).** The nasal cannula will deliver a prescribed amount of oxygen based on the liter flow. At 1 liter, the cannula delivers 24 percent oxygen; at 6 liters, it delivers 44 percent oxygen.

22. **The correct answer is (C).** When a patient feels confined using a non-rebreather mask, the EMT–Basic should first attempt to calm the patient's fears about the mask and its confining qualities. If that approach fails, the EMT–Basic should remove the mask and apply a nasal cannula. In this instance, the patient is still receiving oxygen and is feeling less anxious about the mask.

Advanced Airway

1. **The correct answer is (B).** The bifurcation point of the trachea is the carina. The carina is where the right and left mainstem bronchi branch off into the right and left lungs.

2. **The correct answer is (C).** The epiglottis is a leaf-shaped structure above the laryngeal opening. The epiglottis acts like a flap during swallowing, closing off the trachea to foreign bodies such as foods and liquids. The vallecula is the space between the base of the tongue and the epiglottis; this space is important during endotracheal intubation since when the macintosh blade is used, its proper placement is in the vallecula.

3. **The correct answer is (C).** The vocal cords are located in the trachea. During endotracheal intubation, the landmark that is used for endotracheal tube insertion is the vocal cords. The endotracheal tube is inserted between the vocal cords. Visualization of the tube passing through the vocal cords is the best indicator of proper intubation.

4. **The correct answer is (D).** The esophagus is an organ of the gastrointestinal system that lies directly posterior to the trachea. In improper intubations, the endotracheal tube is passed into the esophagus. The EMT–Basic can easily detect improper insertion by assessing the patient's lung sounds; if lung sounds are absent after insertion, the endotracheal tube has been improperly inserted into the esophagus. Esophageal intubation is a common error made during intubation; however, if the EMT–Basic can identify this error, all that needs to be done is to remove the endotracheal tube and hyperventilate the patient prior to the next attempt.

5. **The correct answer is (C).** The cricoid cartilage is the narrowest part of the airway in the pediatric patient. Pediatric endotracheal tubes are uncuffed for this reason. Due to the narrow airway, the pediatric endotracheal tube uses the narrow cricoid cartilage to seal itself. The EMT–Basic should keep in mind that several different size endotracheal tubes should be on hand prior to attempting the intubation.

6. **The correct answer is (D).** In a conscious patient, the endotracheal tube will elicit a gag reflex in the patient. The benefits of endotracheal intubation are great, due to the fact that the airway is completely isolated. The EMT–Basic may deliver ventilations without a mask seal, allowing for better tidal volume and better oxygenation.

7. **The correct answer is (D).** One of the main uses of the endotracheal tube is that it prevents aspiration. During a prolonged intubation attempt, the patient may develop a slow heart rate due to vagus nerve stimulation. In addition, improper placement of the stylet may cause esophageal or tracheal tear, resulting in subcutaneous emphysema. The most common complication of endotracheal intubation is right mainstem bronchus intubation. This occurs when the endotracheal tube is inserted too deeply and becomes placed too low in the trachea. The indicator of right mainstem bronchus intubation is absence of lung sounds on the left side of the chest. To correct this problem, the EMT–Basic should slowly back the endotracheal tube out of the trachea while assessing left-sided lung sounds.

8. **The correct answer is (B).** The straight laryngoscope blade is the miller blade, and the curved laryngoscope blade is the macintosh blade. Fiber-optic blades do exist, but they are supplied in both styles of laryngoscope blades.

9. **The correct answer is (A).** Laryngoscope blades, regardless of style, are sized from smallest (0) to largest (4).

10. **The correct answer is (C).** The stylet should never protrude from the end of the endotracheal tube; this will almost always result in tracheal tearing. When inserting the stylet, the EMT–Basic should ensure that the tip does not protrude past the end of the cuff area.

11. **The correct answer is (A).** The average adult male will accept an endotracheal tube that is sized at 8.0 to 8.5, while the newborn infant will usually accept a 3.0 to 3.5 endotracheal tube size. It is suggested by more than one source to have an assortment of endotracheal tubes on hand during an intubation.

12. **The correct answer is (B).** The most common formula is (Age + 16) divided by 4. There are other methods for sizing pediatric endotracheal tubes: one is by matching the size of the patient's little finger to the size of the endotracheal tube, and the other is to use the Broselow tape. The Broselow tape has become a commonly accepted tool for treatment of pediatric patients.

13. **The correct answer is (D).** Endotracheal tubes are never blindly inserted. The laryngoscope is inserted, and the vocal cords are visualized the entire time during the attempt. The EMT–Basic should see the endotracheal tube pass the vocal cords to ensure proper placement.

14. **The correct answer is (A).** Basic life support procedures always take precedence over the more time-consuming advanced management procedures. The EMT–Basic should always attempt resuscitation using basic procedures. In addition, part of the skill of endotracheal intubation requires that the patient be hyperventilated prior to the intubation attempt.

15. **The correct answer is (A).** In many cases of asthma, the EMT–Basic will find ventilation difficult. That, combined with poor mask seal, can result in inadequate ventilation of an already hypoxic patient. The EMT–Basic should now perform endotracheal intubation for more precise airway control.

16. **The correct answer is (C).** After an unsuccessful attempt at endotracheal intubation, the patient should always be hyperventilated to ensure adequate oxygenation. The EMT–Basic should never reinsert an endotracheal tube without prior oxygenation. Transport without another attempt can be detrimental to patient outcome in this case, due to the fact that ventilations with the bag-valve-mask device were not highly effective.

17. **The correct answer is (A).** After proper insertion and confirmation of bilateral lung sounds, the highest priority is the securing of the endotracheal tube. The EMT–Basic should remember that maintenance of the airway is the highest priority in patient care. The securing of the endotracheal tube will ensure that this will not be displaced during movement and transport.

18. **The correct answer is (B).** Vomitus inside of the endotracheal tube is an indicator of esophageal intubation. The endotracheal tube should isolate the trachea from gastric contents. If the EMT–Basic sees vomitus inside the endotracheal tube, they should immediately stop ventilations, remove the endotracheal tube, suction, and hyperventilate the patient. After this is done, another attempt at endotracheal intubation can be made.

Chapter 4

ASSESSMENT

SCENE SIZE-UP

1. You are dispatched to an accident that involves a gasoline tanker and a car. On your arrival, you see several patients lying in the street. Your initial action is to

   (A) approach the patients and begin triage.
   (B) contact the dispatcher for additional resources.
   (C) ensure that the scene is safe for you and your partner to operate.
   (D) block access to the scene from civilian traffic.

2. All of the following are important aspects of pre-arrival dispatch information EXCEPT

   (A) the status of the patient as described by the caller.
   (B) any possibility of specialized equipment needs.
   (C) possibilities of violent activity on the scene.
   (D) name of the patient's private physician.

3. You are assigned to a multi-vehicle accident that involves a tour bus. You arrive at the scene to find approximately twenty patients with different types of injuries that range from minor to serious. You have determined the scene is safe. Your next action should be to

   (A) begin immediate treatment of the seriously injured patients.
   (B) contact dispatch for additional resources.
   (C) begin triage of all patients.
   (D) set up a treatment area.

4. All of the following are common injury or illness mechanisms encountered by the EMT–Basic EXCEPT

   (A) anaphylactic shock.
   (B) chest trauma secondary to blunt force.
   (C) elderly head injury due to a fall.
   (D) difficulty breathing due to myocardial infarction.

INITIAL ASSESSMENT

1. Which term best describes the EMT–Basic's assessment of the patient's living conditions, appearance, and complaints?

   (A) The SAMPLE history
   (B) Chief complaint
   (C) General impression
   (D) Initial assessment

2. You arrive at the scene to find that a 53-year-old patient was struck by a motor vehicle. Your assessment reveals that the patient does not readily answer questions; however, he responds to you shouting, "Are you ok?" What is this patient's classification on the AVPU scale?

   (A) Alert
   (B) Voice responsive
   (C) Pain responsive
   (D) Unresponsive

3. When assessing a patient, all of the following methods are used to assess a patient's airway EXCEPT

   (A) jaw thrust maneuver.
   (B) listening to the patient speak.
   (C) listening to lung sounds.
   (D) visual inspection of the upper airway.

4. Your assessment of a trauma patient finds that the patient suffered severe trauma to the lower jaw after a fall. Due to your findings, you begin to immobilize the patient's cervical spine. Your decision to do this is based on which of the following statements?

   (A) Cervical spine immobilization should be done on all trauma patients.
   (B) Trauma to the lower jaw is immobilized with a cervical collar.
   (C) Using a cervical collar assists in moving the patient to a soft stretcher.
   (D) It is protocol.

5. All of the following are assessment methods for patient breathing EXCEPT

   (A) watching the chest for rise during inspiration.
   (B) auscultating lung sounds.
   (C) assessing the patient for accessory muscle use.
   (D) suctioning the airway.

6. You are assessing a patient with asthma. During your assessment, the airway is clear and the lungs have equal expansion. Breath sounds are clear bilaterally due to the fact that the patient has self-treated with an aerosol medication prior to your arrival. Your treatment of the patient should include

   (A) self-assisting the patient with additional medication.
   (B) administration of maintenance oxygen and transport.
   (C) release of the patient on scene due to total relief.
   (D) request for ALS assistance since there is nothing more you can do.

7. Wheezing, gasping, accessory muscle use, and stridor are all signs of

   (A) adequate breathing.
   (B) inadequate breathing.
   (C) asthma.
   (D) airway obstruction.

8. Your patient is unresponsive, with inadequate respirations at a rate of 32 breaths per minute. You should immediately

   (A) provide 100 percent oxygen using a non-rebreather mask.
   (B) ventilate the patient with a bag-valve-mask device and supplemental oxygen.
   (C) perform obstructed airway maneuvers.
   (D) consider contacting ALS for advanced interventions.

9. In assessing the pulse in a conscious adult or child, the EMT–Basic would use which of the following pulse points?

   (A) Carotid
   (B) Femoral
   (C) Radial
   (D) Brachial

10. In assessing the pulse in an infant, the EMT–Basic would use which of the following pulse points?

    (A) Carotid
    (B) Femoral
    (C) Radial
    (D) Brachial

11. Capillary refill may be effectively assessed in which of the following patients?

    (A) Adults and children
    (B) Adults and infants
    (C) Infants and children
    (D) Adults only

12. During the initial assessment, the EMT–Basic will assess the patient for external bleeding. The primary reason this is done is

    (A) to detect and correct large volumes of blood loss.
    (B) to evaluate the area of injury.
    (C) to establish criteria for blood transfusions at the hospital.
    (D) The EMT–Basic does not assess for blood loss.

13. All of the following are abnormal findings in skin assessment EXCEPT

    (A) warm and pink.
    (B) pallor.
    (C) cyanotic.
    (D) ashen.

Questions 14 and 15 pertain to the following paragraph.
You and your partner respond to an accident where a car has run into a tree. On your arrival, patient 1 is a 24-year-old male, unconscious and breathing at 36 times a minute. His airway is clear, and he has a pulse of 120. His skin appears pale and diaphoretic. Patient 2 is a 26-years-old female. She is complaining of pain in the neck and chest. Her pulse is 104, respirations are 20, and skin is warm and dry.

14. Based on your general impression, how would you prioritize patient 1?

    (A) High
    (B) Medium
    (C) Low

15. Based on your general impression, how would you prioritize patient 2?

    (A) High
    (B) Medium
    (C) Low

PHYSICAL EXAMINATION: MEDICAL

1. Which of the following is not a component of the history of present illness?

    (A) Onset of illness
    (B) Quality
    (C) Severity
    (D) Pertinent past history

2. Place the following in the correct order in which you would assess a conscious patient.

    1. SAMPLE history
    2. Vital signs
    3. Focused physical examination
    4. History of present illness

    (A) 1, 2, 3, 4
    (B) 4, 1, 3, 2
    (C) 3, 1, 2, 4
    (D) 2, 4, 1, 3

3. Place in correct order the steps in assessing the unconscious patient.

    1. SAMPLE history
    2. Vital signs
    3. Rapid physical examination
    4. History of present illness

    (A) 3, 4, 1, 2
    (B) 4, 1, 3, 2
    (C) 3, 1, 2, 4
    (D) 3, 2, 4, 1

4. A patient with no known prior history is complaining of difficulty breathing. Your assessment reveals wheezing in all lung fields. The difference between this patient and a patient with a known history is

(A) the patient with a known history does not require a physical examination.
(B) the patient with no known history will not have a prescribed medication that you could assist in its administration.
(C) the patient with a known history will not need ambulance transport.
(D) the patient with no known history will generally respond better to oxygen.

PHYSICAL EXAMINATION: TRAUMA

1. Which of the following is not an indication for trauma center diversion?

(A) Death of a passenger in the same vehicle
(B) Ejection from the vehicle
(C) Isolated extremity fracture
(D) Vehicle rollover

2. In using the DCAP-BTLS assessment mnemonic, which of the following terms is not associated with this assessment?

(A) Death
(B) Contusions
(C) Burns
(D) Lacerations

3. Place in the correct order the steps in assessing the trauma patient with significant mechanism of injury.

1. SAMPLE history

2. Rapid trauma assessment

3. Reconsider mechanism of injury

4. Vital signs

(A) 3, 2, 4, 1
(B) 2, 4, 3, 1
(C) 1, 2, 3, 4
(D) 4, 1, 2, 3

4. Place in the correct order the steps in assessing the trauma patient with no significant mechanism of injury.

1. Chief complaint
2. Focused assessment of complaint area
3. Vital signs
4. SAMPLE history

(A) 3, 2, 4, 1
(B) 2, 4, 3, 1
(C) 1, 2, 3, 4
(D) 4, 1, 2, 3

DETAILED PHYSICAL EXAMINATION

1. Which of the following best describes the difference between the detailed physical examination of the trauma patient and the medical patient?

   (A) There is no difference between these examinations.
   (B) The detailed physical examination of the medical patient always consists of a head to toe examination.
   (C) The detailed physical examination of the trauma patient always consists of a head to toe examination.
   (D) The detailed physical examination of the medical patient and the trauma patient differ in that the medical patient will require a much more intensive physical examination.

2. As you assess a patient from a motorcycle collision, you would start at the head and look for which of the following signs of injury?

   (A) Tenderness
   (B) Deformities
   (C) Abrasions
   (D) All of the above

3. In a medical patient complaining of severe headache, which of the following detailed assessments would probably produce the most beneficial information?

   (A) Respiratory system evaluation
   (B) Neurological evaluation
   (C) Cardiopulmonary examination
   (D) Abdominal examination

4. Choose the statement below that best describes the detailed physical examination.

   (A) The detailed physical examination is done on all patients.
   (B) The detailed physical examination is done only on critical patients with obvious life-threatening injuries.
   (C) The detailed physical examination is done on patients who may have hidden signs of illness or injury that were not uncovered during the initial examination.
   (D) The detailed physical examination is done at the discretion of the medical director in charge of the service.

ON-GOING ASSESSMENT

1. All of the following are components of the on-going assessment EXCEPT

   (A) re-evaluation of airway, breathing, and circulation.
   (B) re-evaluation of vital signs.
   (C) evaluation of treatments and responses.
   (D) initial information gathering on the patient's history.

2. During the on-going assessment of your patient, you notice that the patient's blood pressure has dropped from 110/70 to 90/58. Because of this pertinent finding, you should

   (A) continue your current mode of treatment.
   (B) completely re-assess your interventions, as you may have omitted something.
   (C) advise your partner to speed up the transport.
   (D) administer oxygen to the patient.

COMMUNICATIONS

1. Which of the following is not a responsibility of the EMS dispatcher?

   (A) Prioritizing incoming emergency calls
   (B) Selecting and assigning the appropriate EMS units to an emergency
   (C) Selecting the appropriate receiving hospital
   (D) Assisting callers with emergency medical instructions

2. In using radio communications, which of the following would best describe the transmission of radio messages?

   (A) Radio transmission should be concise and directly to the point.
   (B) Radio transmission should be comprehensive reports that outline all information about the call.
   (C) Radio transmissions should include the patient's name and other personal information.
   (D) Radio transmission should include "ten-codes" as well as the verbal definition of them after they are transmitted.

3. Which of the following best details the proper order for delivering a verbal report over the air?

   (A) Unit ID, receiving hospital and ETA, age and sex of patient, chief complaint, history of present emergency, findings, treatments, responses
   (B) Patient's name, complaint, ETA to hospital, patient past history, allergies, and medications
   (C) Unit ID, patient's name, complaint, treatment and response, ETA to hospital
   (D) Unit ID, receiving hospital, complaint, findings, treatment, and response

4. While assigned to an emergency call, you must make several radio communications. Which of the following is not included in communicating with the dispatcher?

   (A) Acknowledgement of the assignment
   (B) Arrival at the scene
   (C) Information gathering techniques on scene
   (D) Arrival at the hospital

5. Your patient is an elderly male who has fallen in a park. On your arrival, you notice that the patient is wearing hearing aids in both ears and is speaking very loudly. In your communication with this patient, you should

   (A) speak normally, as the hearing aids should allow the patient to hear your questions.
   (B) speak slowly and clearly while facing the patient.
   (C) shout loudly into the patient's ear, to ensure that he will hear you.
   (D) contact the dispatcher for a specialty responder who knows sign language.

6. The most important aspects in communicating with pediatric patients include all of the following EXCEPT

   (A) allowing the child to remain with his parents.
   (B) allowing the child to have his favorite toy close by.
   (C) not telling a child if a procedure will cause pain or discomfort.
   (D) remaining honest with the child throughout the duration of the call.

7. You are assigned to a 75-year-old man with difficulty breathing. On your arrival, you find that the man's family is greatly concerned for his well-being. The patient is stable, with bilateral wheezing and a long history of emphysema. He states that his medications are not working and that he wants to go to the hospital. A family member approaches you during treatment and inquires as to his condition. An appropriate response would be to

   (A) tell the family member that you cannot divulge the patient's condition.
   (B) have your partner or police remove the family member to another room, to avoid them interfering with care.
   (C) advise the family member, in a concise fashion, the patient's condition and your plan of action.
   (D) advise the family member that they will have to ask the doctor at the hospital for information.

DOCUMENTATION

1. All of the following are components of the minimum data set EXCEPT

   (A) chief complaint.
   (B) vital signs.
   (C) perfusion status.
   (D) therapeutic interventions.

2. You respond to a 67-year-old male who states that he did not call the ambulance. His daughter is at the scene and states that she called because her father was up all night complaining of chest pain. When you question the patient, he states that he is not going to the hospital. All of the following are appropriate actions in the scenario EXCEPT

   (A) allow the patient to sign a refusal and leave.
   (B) request to do a physical examination of the patient just to "be sure" that he is ok.
   (C) after examining the patient, explain your findings and the need for further evaluation at the hospital.
   (D) document all findings, discussions with the patient, and alternatives offered to the patient, and have the patient and a witness sign the document.

3. You are reviewing the call report from the last run. You notice that your partner entered three sets of vital signs, and you are only aware that one set was taken. When you ask your partner about it, he states that although he only took one set of vital signs, he added additional sets to "make it look better." As a patient care provider, you should

   (A) change the report personally.
   (B) forget about the issue, as it makes no difference.
   (C) discuss the issue with your partner, advise him that it is illegal to falsify documentation, and request that he revise the report.
   (D) take your vehicle out of service, as you cannot work with this person anymore.

4. During your proofreading of a patient-care report, you notice that you have made an error in documenting in the narrative section. You should

   (A) leave the error as is, as it is minor.
   (B) start a new report, making sure that you write correctly this time.
   (C) draw a line through the error, write in the correction, and initial the correction.
   (D) completely cross out the error and write the correct line next to or above it.

ANSWER SHEET

Chapter 4: Assessment

Scene Size-Up

1. Ⓐ Ⓑ Ⓒ Ⓓ   3. Ⓐ Ⓑ Ⓒ Ⓓ
2. Ⓐ Ⓑ Ⓒ Ⓓ   4. Ⓐ Ⓑ Ⓒ Ⓓ

Initial Assessment

1. Ⓐ Ⓑ Ⓒ Ⓓ   6. Ⓐ Ⓑ Ⓒ Ⓓ   11. Ⓐ Ⓑ Ⓒ Ⓓ
2. Ⓐ Ⓑ Ⓒ Ⓓ   7. Ⓐ Ⓑ Ⓒ Ⓓ   12. Ⓐ Ⓑ Ⓒ Ⓓ
3. Ⓐ Ⓑ Ⓒ Ⓓ   8. Ⓐ Ⓑ Ⓒ Ⓓ   13. Ⓐ Ⓑ Ⓒ Ⓓ
4. Ⓐ Ⓑ Ⓒ Ⓓ   9. Ⓐ Ⓑ Ⓒ Ⓓ   14. Ⓐ Ⓑ Ⓒ
5. Ⓐ Ⓑ Ⓒ Ⓓ   10. Ⓐ Ⓑ Ⓒ Ⓓ   15. Ⓐ Ⓑ Ⓒ

Physical Examination: Medical

1. Ⓐ Ⓑ Ⓒ Ⓓ   3. Ⓐ Ⓑ Ⓒ Ⓓ
2. Ⓐ Ⓑ Ⓒ Ⓓ   4. Ⓐ Ⓑ Ⓒ Ⓓ

Physical Examination: Trauma

1. Ⓐ Ⓑ Ⓒ Ⓓ   3. Ⓐ Ⓑ Ⓒ Ⓓ
2. Ⓐ Ⓑ Ⓒ Ⓓ   4. Ⓐ Ⓑ Ⓒ Ⓓ

Detailed Physical Examination

1. Ⓐ Ⓑ Ⓒ Ⓓ   3. Ⓐ Ⓑ Ⓒ Ⓓ
2. Ⓐ Ⓑ Ⓒ Ⓓ   4. Ⓐ Ⓑ Ⓒ Ⓓ

On-Going Assesment

1. Ⓐ Ⓑ Ⓒ Ⓓ
2. Ⓐ Ⓑ Ⓒ Ⓓ

Communications

1. Ⓐ Ⓑ Ⓒ Ⓓ   5. Ⓐ Ⓑ Ⓒ Ⓓ
2. Ⓐ Ⓑ Ⓒ Ⓓ   6. Ⓐ Ⓑ Ⓒ Ⓓ
3. Ⓐ Ⓑ Ⓒ Ⓓ   7. Ⓐ Ⓑ Ⓒ Ⓓ
4. Ⓐ Ⓑ Ⓒ Ⓓ

Documentation

1. Ⓐ Ⓑ Ⓒ Ⓓ   3. Ⓐ Ⓑ Ⓒ Ⓓ
2. Ⓐ Ⓑ Ⓒ Ⓓ   4. Ⓐ Ⓑ Ⓒ Ⓓ

ANSWERS TO CHAPTER 4

Scene Size-Up	Initial Assessment	Physical Examination		Detailed Physical Examination	On-Going Assessment	Communications	Documentation
		Medical	Trauma				
1. C	1. C	1. D	1. C	1. C	1. D	1. C	1. D
2. D	2. B	2. B	2. A	2. D	2. B	2. A	2. A
3. B	3. C	3. D	3. A	3. B		3. A	3. C
4. A	4. A	4. B	4. C	4. C		4. C	4. C
	5. D					5. B	
	6. B					6. C	
	7. B					7. C	
	8. B						
	9. C						
	10. D						
	11. C						
	12. A						
	13. A						
	14. A						
	15. C						

RATIONALES FOR THE ANSWERS

Scene Size-Up

1. **The correct answer is (C).** The initial action of the EMT–Basic in any situation is to ensure scene safety. The EMT–Basic should do a scene survey from inside the vehicle prior to taking any actions in a rescue attempt. This applies not only to accidents, but also to all incidents. After the scene is considered safe, the EMT–Basic should call for additional resources and, if necessary, block civilian traffic from entry.

2. **The correct answer is (D).** The EMT–Basic should utilize pre-arrival dispatch data as an integral part of scene size-up. Information gathered prior to arrival is extremely helpful in assisting the EMT–Basic in knowing what equipment may be needed, if police or firefighters are needed on scene, or if the scene would actually be safe to enter. The name of the patient's physician is important but will not have any impact in the acute phase of patient care.

3. **The correct answer is (B).** Upon arrival of a mass casualty incident, the first arriving crew should immediately request additional assistance. A mass casualty incident is defined as any incident that overwhelms the resources of a given system. If you were to remain on the scene without assistance, you would become overwhelmed in a relatively short period of time. After scene safety, resource requests should follow immediately.

4. **The correct answer is (A).** Anaphylactic shock is a relatively uncommon occurrence. The EMT–Basic should be acutely aware that anaphylaxis is a true emergency—but a rare one. Some of the more common mechanisms are head injury due to trauma, chest and abdominal injuries, chest pain, and difficult breathing as well as multiple minor injuries.

Initial Assessment

1. **The correct answer is (C).** The EMT–Basic should complete a full physical examination on every patient; however, the general impression of a patient, or his or her condition, is usually formed within minutes of arrival. The EMT–Basic should evaluate the scene, including patient's living conditions, as well as the patient's appearance (affect) and complaints.

2. **The correct answer is (B).** This patient, due to his response to your shouting, is classified as verbally responsive, or V on the AVPU scale. If a patient is awake and answering questions, he would be considered A on the scale. Pain-responsive patients are considered P. Finally, unresponsive patients are considered U on the AVPU scale.

3. **The correct answer is (C).** When assessing a patient's airway, the EMT–Basic should use a jaw thrust maneuver, visually inspect the airway, and look for anything that may endanger it. If the patient is awake, the airway may be easily assessed by speaking to the patient. If the patient is speaking normally, it is a good sign that there is no airway compromise. Listening to lung sounds is an assessment tool; however, it is used to assess breathing, not airway.

4. **The correct answer is (A).** Any patient who has been designated a trauma patient during the initial assessment should be immobilized with a cervical collar. The cervical collar does not immobilize injury to the lower jaw; however, lower jaw injury is a good indicator that a large amount of energy was expended to the patient's head. This is indicative of cervical spinal injury. The cervical collar does not assist patient movement, especially of a trauma patient, to a soft stretcher.

5. **The correct answer is (D).** Suctioning of the airway is part of airway assessment, not breathing assessment. To assess a patient's breathing, the EMT–Basic should watch for equal chest rise, inspect the chest for any obvious injuries, and auscultate the lungs for injury indicators such as absent breath sound or wheezes, rales, and rhonchi.

6. **The correct answer is (B).** Many times, asthma patients call for ambulances then begin self-treatment. The EMT–Basic, after completing a history and physical, should provide supplemental oxygen and transport the patient for further evaluation at a hospital.

7. **The correct answer is (B).** Any abnormal respiratory sounds may be signs of inadequate breathing. The EMT–Basic should be aware of respiratory deficiencies and intervene to correct the breathing difficulty.

8. **The correct answer is (B).** This patient is a prime candidate for bag-valve-mask ventilation. The EMT–Basic should begin immediate ventilations for the unconscious patient with inadequate breathing. ALS may be requested, but it is not your immediate intervention. Airway management is especially important in pediatric patients, who commonly suffer cardiac arrest secondary to respiratory insufficiency.

9. **The correct answer is (C).** In assessment of a pulse in a conscious and stable adult or child, the EMT–Basic would use the radial pulse. Located at the wrist of the patient, the radial pulse is the most easily accessible pulse point. In the adult patient, a radial pulse indicates a systolic blood pressure of higher than 80mmHg.

10. **The correct answer is (D).** In an infant, the brachial pulse is the most appropriate pulse point. The EMT–Basic may feel a radial pulse; however, infants' arms contain more fat than an adult and may prevent the pulse from being felt. The brachial pulse is stronger and, therefore, easier to assess.

11. **The correct answer is (C).** Capillary refill is an effective way to assess patient perfusion in infants and children. In adults, there are factors other than hypovolemia that may alter capillary refill. In assessing capillary refill, the EMT–Basic will gently press on the top of the patient's nail bed, and blood flow should return to the area within two seconds. Any return after two seconds should be considered abnormal.

12. **The correct answer is (A).** Assessment of the patient for external blood loss is part of the initial assessment. The EMT–Basic should detect and correct any major blood loss before continuing to other parts of the assessment.

13. **The correct answer is (A).** Most patients will present with warm and pink skin. Pink skin is a sign of good perfusion, and warmth is generated to the skin by blood vessels. A patient with pallor, cyanosis, or ashen skin should alert the EMT–Basic to a problem.

14. **The correct answer is (A).** Patient 1 is a high-priority patient. This patient must receive immediate airway and ventilatory control as well as a complete initial assessment and immediate transport.

15. **The correct answer is (C).** Patient 2 is exhibiting no signs of hypoperfusion. She is conscious and stable and has no external signs of trauma. Based on the condition of patient 1, she should be transported rapidly but with a detailed physical examination performed.

Physical Examination: Medical

1. **The correct answer is (D).** In gathering information for the history of present illness, the EMT–Basic can use the mnemonic OPQRST. This stands for

   Onset
   Provocating factors
   Quality
   Radiation
   Severity
   Time

   Pertinent past history is gathered after the history of present illness under the SAMPLE history.

2. **The correct answer is (B).** The correct order in assessment of a conscious patient starts with the history of present illness, the SAMPLE history, physical examination, and vital signs.

3. **The correct answer is (D).** The correct order in assessment of an unconscious patient is different from the conscious patient. It is important to do a rapid physical assessment first, and then obtain a set of vital signs. After the vital signs are assessed, the family may be questioned as to the history of present illness and SAMPLE history.

4. **The correct answer is (B).** When the EMT–Basic is treating a patient with a known history, that patient will more than likely have a prescription medication. The EMT–Basic may assist that patient in taking his medication, therefore beginning the treatment process. In a patient with no known history, there is no medication on hand to assist the patient, and the EMT–Basic should, in this case, administer oxygen and transport the patient to definitive care.

Physical Examination: Trauma

1. **The correct answer is (C).** An isolated extremity fracture is not a significant mechanism of injury. Significant mechanism of injury is any circumstance that may lead to a life-threatening condition. Patients with significant mechanism of injury should receive a thorough, detailed physical examination.

2. **The correct answer is (A).** The DCAP-BTLS mnemonic reminds the EMT–Basic what to assess during a rapid physical assessment. The terms are as follows: deformities, contusions, abrasions, punctures/penetrations, burns, lacerations, and swelling. The term *death* is not associated with the DCAP-BTLS assessment.

3. **The correct answer is (A).** The correct assessment priority in a patient with significant mechanism of injury is to reconsider the mechanism of injury, begin a rapid trauma assessment, and obtain vital signs and a SAMPLE history.

4. **The correct answer is (C).** In the patient with no significant mechanism of injury, the EMT–Basic should use a different approach to patient assessment. This approach begins with obtaining a chief complaint, doing a focused assessment of any area of complaint, proceeding to vital signs, and obtaining a SAMPLE history.

Detailed Physical Examination

1. **The correct answer is (C).** The detailed physical examination of the trauma patient always requires that the patient be assessed from head to toe, due to the fact that the EMT–Basic would not be aware of hidden injury without a thorough assessment. Medical patients require a vectored physical that targets the patient's complaint. For example, a patient complaining of chest pain would not require a thorough examination of the head and neck, but a complete cardiopulmonary assessment is necessary.

2. **The correct answer is (D).** Assessment of the trauma patient would encompass all of the above mentioned injury markers. In addition, the EMT–Basic should assess for deformities, lacerations, burns, punctures, penetrating trauma, and any other injury that may occur from that particular mechanism of injury.

3. **The correct answer is (B).** Patients complaining of severe headache will usually be suffering from a neurological impairment. Assessment of this patient would include a complete neurological examination, including blood pressure and pulse rate. Blood pressure and pulse rate findings may demonstrate an increase in intracranial pressure.

4. **The correct answer is (C).** The EMT–Basic should perform a detailed physical examination on all patients who may have hidden injuries or signs of illness. This examination can, and sometimes will, be omitted for several reasons, such as the following:

   - The EMT–Basic has already diagnosed the patient's current problem and is treating it with positive results.

   - The patient requires critical airway, breathing, or circulatory intervention that does not allow time for a detailed examination.

On-Going Assessment

1. **The correct answer is (D).** The on-going assessment is completed on a patient so that the EMT–Basic can evaluate the patient status after interventions. This examination also serves to allow the EMT–Basic to re-assess all critical areas of her initial assessment and compare findings and vital signs to the initial baselines established during an initial examination. The initial patient history is gathered during the initial examination process and is not a component of the on-going assessment; however, the EMT–Basic is encouraged to talk to a conscious patient during the entire call. Frequent conversation may uncover and clarify pieces of the patient history that were previously left uncovered.

2. **The correct answer is (B).** If during your on-going assessment the patient's condition worsens, the EMT–Basic should re-assess the previous interventions and re-evaluate critical areas of the initial assessment. Obtaining baseline vital signs during the initial assessment creates a reference point for patient status evaluation after treatment. If the patient status is deteriorating, then additional interventions may be needed, including the request for ALS assistance.

Communications

1. **The correct answer is (C).** The EMS dispatcher is responsible for choices (A), (B), and (D), as well as other aspects of emergency medical dispatch; however, it is the responsibility of the EMT–Basic at the scene of the assignment to make the determination as to which hospital would best treat the patient's condition. The assessment of the EMT–Basic, as well as the response to treatment by the patient, will determine if the patient should be transported to a specialty center or the nearest receiving hospital. This responsibility cannot be handled by the EMS dispatcher.

2. **The correct answer is (A).** When communicating with the dispatcher, the EMT–Basic should use concise and direct radio messages. These messages should include only pertinent information that the dispatcher will need to document the call and assign additional emergency responders. Comprehensive radio reports are unnecessary and only serve to confuse all parties, as well as prevent other units from reporting to the dispatcher. The patient's personal information should never be transmitted over the air. There are multiple agencies (news, personal, etc.) that can have access to the emergency frequencies by the use of scanners. The patient's right to privacy should be protected at all times. The use of ten-codes should be used only if all parties are well versed in their definitions. Defining the ten-code after its transmission only serves to extend the transmission.

3. **The correct answer is (A).** The verbal report over the air should be a concise but detailed report that consists of the following information: Unit ID, receiving hospital and ETA, age and sex of patient, chief complaint, history of present emergency, findings, treatments, and responses. This information will be passed on to the receiving hospital in order to ensure that they are prepared to receive and treat the patient in an appropriate fashion.

4. **The correct answer is (C).** While on assignment, the EMT–Basic should be informing the dispatcher of his status every time it changes. These status reports should be delivered when assigned, on arrival at the emergency, en route to the hospital (includes verbal report), on arrival at the hospital, and when the unit is available after the call is complete. The EMT–Basic is also responsible for informing the dispatcher if they will be out of service for any other reasons; these reasons may include restocking, cleaning, refueling, tour change, etc.

5. **The correct answer is (B).** Patients who are hard of hearing will sometimes create a difficult situation when communicating. The EMT–Basic should speak slowly and clearly while facing the patient. Most patients with hearing problems can read lips and make out the words, as long as you are looking at them. Shouting in the patient's ear is inappropriate and may cause the patient to become apprehensive. Normally, hearing aids will allow the patient to hear well enough to understand you; however, there are cases when these will be ineffective. The use of sign language is an effective tool, provided all parties are knowledgeable in using it.

6. **The correct answer is (C).** It is of the utmost importance to inform the pediatric patient of all procedures that are being conducted and whether or not they will cause the child pain or discomfort. In not remaining totally honest with the child, the EMT–Basic will lose the trust of the child and render himself ineffective in the treatment of the patient. Children should be allowed to remain with a parent, and their favorite toy should accompany them, if requested. A demeanor of total honesty with the pediatric patient will develop a trusting atmosphere in which the EMT–Basic may perform his duties with a cooperative patient.

7. **The correct answer is (C).** Family members of elderly patients will show genuine concern for their beloved parent or grandparent. It is the responsibility of the EMT–Basic to inform them of the patient's condition as well as the treatment plan of the patient. In many cases, these family members will be the primary caretaker of the elderly patient. These caretakers will need to know the patient's information in order to contact the primary physician or other health-care workers. In addition, the family may be a wealth of information concerning the patient's history.

Documentation

1. **The correct answer is (D).** The "minimum data set" includes all information that is collected during initial patient contact. This information should be well documented on the prehospital care report. The components of the minimum data set include patient chief complaint, level of consciousness, blood pressure, perfusion status, skin condition (color, temperature, and moisture), heart rate, and respiratory rate. Therapeutic interventions are not part of the minimum data set; however, they should be documented on the prehospital care report.

2. **The correct answer is (A).** The EMT–Basic should never allow a patient to sign a refusal of treatment and leave without first attempting to examine the patient and convince them that they need medical care. The patient should receive a complete history and physical, with all necessary evaluations and assessments done based on the history of present illness. After this evaluation, all findings and outcomes should be discussed with the patient. If the patient still refuses, the EMT–Basic may elect to contact medical control for assistance or accept the refusal. All refusals should be well documented.

3. **The correct answer is (C).** The primary responsibility of the EMT–Basic is to the patient. Inaccurate patient care reports, or those that have been falsified, will shed improper information in the on-going treatment of the patient. If it was documented that a medication was given that was actually not given, the patient may not receive that medication at the hospital. The EMT–Basic should advise her partner that the form should be changed to reflect the pertinent information correctly and follow through to ensure that the information is changed.

4. **The correct answer is (C).** The EMT–Basic, upon finding an error in documentation, should draw a single line through the error and write the correction above the crossed-out error. In most cases, it is an error in word use that may be confusing to the hospital staff. You should never leave an error in place, as it may confuse patient care. In addition, completely crossing out the error may raise suspicions that something was omitted purposely.

Chapter 5

MEDICAL

In this section, the EMT–Basic will review study questions from module 4 of the NHTSA EMT–Basic curriculum. Since the medical section covers a wide array of information on medical emergencies that the EMT–B may encounter in the field, you should take plenty of time to review the questions in this section. It is advised that any question that is not fully understood be researched further in your basic textbook.

PHARMACOLOGY

1. All of the following medications may be carried on a basic life support unit EXCEPT

   (A) epinephrine.
   (B) activated charcoal.
   (C) oral glucose.
   (D) oxygen.

2. The EMT–Basic may assist the patient in taking all of the following medications EXCEPT

   (A) epinephrine.
   (B) nitroglycerin.
   (C) oxygen.
   (D) metered dose inhalers.

3. Match the following routes of administration to their proper definition.

1. Intravenous	(A) Into the muscle
2. Sublingual	(B) Into the bone
3. Intramuscular	(C) Beneath the skin
4. Subcutaneous	(D) Into the vein
5. Intraosseous	(E) Under the tongue

4. All of the following are necessary for the correct administration of a medication to a patient EXCEPT

   (A) correct medication.
   (B) correct dose.
   (C) correct route.
   (D) correct needle size.

RESPIRATORY

1. List, in the proper order, the structures of the respiratory system.

   (A) Nose, pharynx, larynx, trachea, bronchi, alveoli
   (B) Nose, larynx, pharynx, bronchi, trachea, alveoli
   (C) Nose, bronchi, larynx, pharynx, trachea, alveoli
   (D) Nose, bronchi, alveoli, pharynx, larynx, trachea

2. Rapid respiratory rate, diminished breath sounds, unequal chest expansion, and tripod positioning are all signs of

   (A) adequate breathing.
   (B) inadequate respiration.
   (C) heart attack.
   (D) asthma attack.

3. Which of the following is the medication of choice to treat the patient with breathing difficulty?

   (A) Epinephrine
   (B) Metered dose inhalers
   (C) Nitroglycerin
   (D) Oxygen

4. You respond to a call for a patient with difficulty breathing. On your arrival, you find a 27-year-old male who has a bluish coloration of the skin. Your assessment reveals an open airway and a respiratory rate of 6 breaths per minute. The proper device to deliver oxygen and ensure adequate breathing would be

   (A) a nasal cannula at 4 liters of oxygen per minute.
   (B) a non-rebreather mask at 8 liters of oxygen per minute.
   (C) a bag-valve-mask ventilator with oxygen reservoir and assisted ventilations.
   (D) a metered dose inhaler followed by 100 percent oxygen via non-rebreather.

5. Your conscious patient with adequate ventilations is complaining of difficulty breathing. In which position should this patient be transported?

   (A) Lying down with legs elevated
   (B) In a position that is comfortable to the patient
   (C) Sitting forward with knees flexed
   (D) On her side, to facilitate airway management

6. All of the following are signs of adequate air exchange EXCEPT

   (A) unequal chest expansion.
   (B) regular rhythm.
   (C) rate between 12 and 20 breaths per minute.
   (D) equal, clear breath sounds.

7. You are treating a pediatric patient who is in need of oxygen; however, the child is fighting the mask on her face. You should

(A) immobilize the patient and continue administration of oxygen.
(B) deliver oxygen by holding the mask in front of the child's face.
(C) discontinue oxygen administration.
(D) have the parent hold the child's arms down to facilitate use of the mask.

8. An episodic disease that causes breathing difficulty and can range from mild to severe is

(A) emphysema.
(B) chronic bronchitis.
(C) asthma.
(D) epiglottitis.

CARDIAC

1. A progressive condition that causes poor blood flow to the heart by blocking coronary arteries with calcium and fat deposits is called

(A) myocardial infarction.
(B) angina pectoris.
(C) atherosclerosis.
(D) ischemia.

2. The major difference between angina pectoris and myocardial infarction is

(A) the pain in myocardial infarction is always brought on by exertion.
(B) the duration of the pain in myocardial infarction is shorter than that of angina pectoris.
(C) the duration of the pain in angina pectoris is shorter and self-correcting after rest.
(D) the pain of myocardial infarction is usually relieved by administration of nitroglycerin.

3. Which of the following describes tachycardia?

(A) Heart rate below 100 beats per minute
(B) Heart rate above 100 beats per minute
(C) Heart rate less than 60 beats per minute
(D) Heart rate between 60 and 100 beats per minute

4. Which of the following describes bradycardia?

(A) Heart rate below 100 beats per minute
(B) Heart rate above 100 beats per minute
(C) Heart rate less than 60 beats per minute
(D) Heart rate between 60 and 100 beats per minute

5. Your patient is a 67-year-old female with chest pain that occurred at rest. The duration of the pain has been approximately 45 minutes, and she has had no relief with her medications. Chest pain of this type is indicative of

(A) angina pectoris.
(B) myocardial infarction.
(C) upper respiratory infection.
(D) influenza.

6. Which of the following would be most effective in the first few minutes of treatment of the cardiac arrest patient?

   (A) CPR
   (B) Attachment of an AED and rhythm analysis
   (C) Ventilation
   (D) Transport

7. Which of the following best describes the difference between a semi-automatic defibrillator and a fully automatic defibrillator?

   (A) The fully automatic defibrillator advises a shock and prompts the user to deliver it.
   (B) The semi-automatic defibrillator will deliver a shock on its own after advising all clear.
   (C) The fully automatic defibrillator will deliver a shock on its own after advising all clear.
   (D) A semi-automatic defibrillator will not analyze ventricular fibrillation automatically.

8. Which of the following cardiac rhythms, when producing a pulse, would generate a shock-advised message from an AED?

   (A) Ventricular fibrillation
   (B) Ventricular tachycardia
   (C) Pulseless electrical activity
   (D) Asystole

9. In treating a patient in cardiac arrest with an AED and CPR, when should you begin to consider transport?

   (A) After 6 shocks have been delivered
   (B) After 3 shocks have been delivered
   (C) Only after ALS care has arrived
   (D) Only after the patient regains a pulse

10. During the analyze mode of AED use, CPR should be

    (A) interrupted, to allow the AED to analyze the rhythm.
    (B) continued, as it will not interfere with the analyze phase.
    (C) interrupted, but ventilations continued.
    (D) continued, however at a slower rate.

11. Based on standards of care using an AED, three shocks are initially delivered in rapid succession without a pulse check. Please choose the appropriate rationale for this treatment.

    (A) Rapid successive shocks are more effective in treating ventricular fibrillation; the AED will determine if the rhythm is still able to be defibrillated.
    (B) Regardless of return of pulses, three shocks should be delivered.
    (C) The AED will deliver three shocks regardless of rhythm, once it analyzes a shockable rhythm.
    (D) It is up to the EMT–Basic to continue after the first defibrillation.

12. While transporting a patient complaining of chest pain, he becomes unconscious and has no pulse. Which of the following procedures should be followed?

    (A) CPR and ventilations should begin immediately and transport continued.
    (B) The AED should be attached and set to analyze while transport continues.
    (C) The AED should be attached and set to analyze and the driver told to stop the vehicle.
    (D) CPR should be performed for one minute in a stopped vehicle, then the AED attached.

13. After attaching the AED, it analyzes and delivers 3 successive shocks. A pulse is checked and found to be present; however, the patient is deeply unconscious. The EMT–Basic should

    (A) place the AED back in analyze mode to be sure that the rhythm has returned.
    (B) remove the AED, support ventilations and obtain baseline vital signs, and continue transport.
    (C) contact the dispatcher and request ALS (since the patient now has a pulse) and await their arrival.
    (D) contact medical direction for nitroglycerin administration.

14. All of the following patients are candidates for AED use, with the exception of

    (A) a 75-year-old male with no pulse.
    (B) an 87-year-old female who has just gone into cardiac arrest.
    (C) a 6-year-old drowning patient with no pulse.
    (D) a 52-year-old man with no cardiac history who is pulseless and not breathing.

15. You are on the scene of an elderly cardiac patient in cardiac arrest and the ALS crew has just arrived. Your AED has just delivered one shock and is in the process of analyzing for a second shock. Since the ALS crew has arrived, what should you do with your AED?

    (A) Leave it alone and allow it to continue analyzing the patient
    (B) Disconnect it and allow the ALS crew to attach their manual defibrillator
    (C) Hand over its operation to the ALS crew
    (D) Ask the ALS crew what they would like you to do with your AED

16. Why is it necessary to inspect the AED prior to each shift?

    (A) Operational checks at the beginning of each shift ensure that the AED is fully charged and functional.
    (B) The AED should not be checked unless it has been used during the previous shift.
    (C) It is not necessary to check it before each shift, as long as the previous shift states that it is operational.
    (D) None of the above

17. You are manning a first-aid office at the town pool when you get notified of a cardiac arrest in the locker room. You respond to the locker room with the AED. All of the following initial assessment steps are pertinent to the single rescuer AED procedure EXCEPT

(A) check for responsiveness.
(B) check for breathing.
(C) administer two breaths.
(D) activate EMS.

18. You respond poolside to a cardiac arrest and attach your AED but notice that the patient is lying in a wet area. Treatment of this patient should include

(A) analyzing and defibrillating the patient where he is lying, as the electricity will not be affected by the water.
(B) moving the patient to a dry area, then attaching the AED.
(C) drying the area with a towel to absorb excess water that may interfere with the delivered energy.
(D) You cannot attach the AED to this patient because he was wet.

19. It is essential for the EMT–Basic to have medical direction when it applies to cardiac patients. Why?

(A) There may be the need for medical control to assist medication administration.
(B) The medical director may order the EMT–Basic to administer medications, even though the patient does not take them.
(C) Cardiac disease requires medical direction by state law.
(D) Medical direction is not necessary in any EMT–Basic intervention.

20. Common side effects seen after the administration of nitroglycerin include

(A) general weakness, altered mental status, and bradycardia.
(B) nausea, dizziness, drop in blood pressure, and headache.
(C) chills, hypertension, and stupor.
(D) seizures, coma, and hypertension.

21. Contraindications to administration of nitroglycerin include all of the following EXCEPT

(A) hypotension.
(B) previous allergic reaction.
(C) nausea.
(D) field treatment of hypertension.

DIABETIC AND ALTERED MENTAL STATES

1. All of the following are metabolic causes of altered mental status EXCEPT

(A) overdose.
(B) hypothermia.
(C) CVA.
(D) diabetic emergencies.

2. The diabetic condition in which there is a rapid onset of altered mental status, which can lead to unconsciousness, seizures, and sometimes even death, is known as

   (A) hypoglycemia.
   (B) hyperglycemia.
   (C) ketoacidosis.
   (D) diabetic coma.

3. All of the following are signs of hypoglycemia EXCEPT

   (A) hunger.
   (B) agitation.
   (C) weakness.
   (D) excessive thirst.

4. Oral glucose is administered to the patient with a diabetic emergency. All of the following are indications for its administration EXCEPT

   (A) diabetic history.
   (B) altered mental status.
   (C) unconsciousness.
   (D) consciousness.

5. Treatment of the unconscious patient who is suspected of having a diabetic emergency would include all of the following EXCEPT

   (A) administration of oral glucose.
   (B) maintenance of airway and ventilation.
   (C) placement in recovery position.
   (D) requesting ALS assistance.

6. Which of the following is the appropriate treatment for a patient with seizures?

   (A) Protect the patient from injury by moving furniture and other objects out of the way of the patient.
   (B) Support ventilations and administer high-concentration oxygen.
   (C) Do not apply restraints to the seizure patient.
   (D) All of the above

7. The condition in which multiple seizures occur one after another without a lucid interval is known as

   (A) prolonged seizure syndrome.
   (B) status epilepticus.
   (C) multiple seizure disorder.
   (D) grand mal seizure.

8. You are dispatched to a 75-year-old male who is disoriented. On your arrival, the family states that the patient was complaining of a headache and then became disoriented. Your assessment reveals that the patient is confused, has unequal pupils and slurred speech, and has lost the use of his right side. Your initial assessment reveals a diagnosis of

   (A) hypoglycemia.
   (B) stroke.
   (C) seizure.
   (D) intoxication.

ALLERGIES AND ANAPHYLAXIS

1. The major difference in determining between an allergic reaction and anaphylaxis is that the patient with anaphylaxis will have

   (A) itching and hives.
   (B) had a previous reaction to a certain allergen.
   (C) signs of respiratory distress and shock.
   (D) fever and a rash.

2. You respond to an asthmatic patient who is complaining of difficulty breathing after a bee sting. On your arrival, you notice no other signs of an allergic reaction. In obtaining a patient history, which of the following questions would be the most appropriate to ask to assist you in your diagnosis between asthma and anaphylaxis in this patient?

   (A) Has the patient ever been stung by a bee before?
   (B) Has the patient taken any of his medications?
   (C) Is there a family history of allergies to bee stings?
   (D) How long ago did the difficulty in breathing start?

3. In the patient with an anaphylactic reaction (shock), which of the following is the highest priority treatment?

   (A) Administration of the patient's auto-injector of epinephrine
   (B) Airway maintenance, including adjuncts and assisted ventilations, if needed
   (C) Monitoring of vital signs every 10 minutes
   (D) Contact with medical direction for additional instructions

4. All of the following are signs and symptoms of anaphylaxis EXCEPT

   (A) itching.
   (B) respiratory distress.
   (C) fever.
   (D) throat tightness.

5. One of the most common side effects of epinephrine auto injectors is

   (A) rapid heart rate.
   (B) slow heart rate.
   (C) decreased blood pressure.
   (D) increased difficulty breathing.

POISONING AND OVERDOSE

1. All of the following are entry points into the body for poisons and toxins EXCEPT

   (A) ingestion.
   (B) inhalation.
   (C) absorption.
   (D) close proximity.

2. All of the following are important questions in obtaining a history of a poisoning EXCEPT asking

   (A) if the patient has ever taken the substance before.
   (B) when the substance was ingested.
   (C) how much of the substance was ingested.
   (D) what type of substance was taken.

3. In general, treatment of the patient with an ingested poison is directed at

   (A) preventing absorption.
   (B) inducing vomiting.
   (C) speeding up absorption.
   (D) administering antitoxins.

4. You are off from work, and your neighbor comes running over, stating that her 5-year-old son has ingested a large amount of drain cleaner. On your arrival, you find an unconscious child with foamy blood in his airway. In order to manage the airway and provide ventilations, you should

   (A) open the airway and begin mouth-to-mouth ventilations.
   (B) open the airway and begin mouth-to-mask ventilations.
   (C) attempt to dilute the poison with water.
   (D) attempt to induce vomiting by inserting your fingers into the patient's airway.

5. You have administered activated charcoal to a patient who has ingested a poison. After the administration, the patient vomits the charcoal. Your next intervention should be to

   (A) begin transport, as there is nothing more you can do.
   (B) consider that the vomiting has cleared the poison.
   (C) administer another dose of activated charcoal.
   (D) administer syrup of ipecac.

ENVIRONMENTAL EMERGENCIES

1. All of the following are ways the body can lose heat EXCEPT

    (A) conduction.
    (B) radiation.
    (C) evaporation.
    (D) absorption.

2. The first priority in treating a hypothermic patient is

    (A) management of airway and passive rewarming.
    (B) administration of warm fluids.
    (C) rapid re-warming by applying external heat.
    (D) contacting medical direction for additional instructions.

3. You are called to the scene of an unconscious patient in a factory where the temperatures have been over 100 degrees all week. The foreman states that the patient, a 37-year-old male, was complaining of dizziness and then passed out. Your assessment reveals that he has hot and dry skin, a rapid pulse, and dilated pupils. This patient is suffering from

    (A) non-emergent hyperthermia.
    (B) emergent hyperthermia.
    (C) diabetic emergency.
    (D) stroke.

4. Cold water–drowning patients should not be resuscitated if they have been submerged in water longer than 30 minutes.

    (A) True
    (B) False

5. All of the following are complications of near-drowning patients EXCEPT

    (A) massive pulmonary edema.
    (B) destruction of red blood cells.
    (C) severe hypoxia.
    (D) hyperthermia.

6. You are treating the patient with a snake bite from a pit viper. All of the following are proper treatment procedures EXCEPT

    (A) ensuring that the scene is safe and the snake is away from the area.
    (B) providing airway support for the patient.
    (C) keeping the patient comfortable and motionless.
    (D) suctioning the venom from the bite area with your mouth.

BEHAVIORAL EMERGENCIES

1. Which of the following factors may cause alterations in a patient's behavior?

   (A) Drug or alcohol abuse
   (B) Blood sugar disorders
   (C) Hypoxia
   (D) All of the above

2. The number one priority in responding to a behavioral emergency is

   (A) airway management of the patient.
   (B) safety of the rescuers.
   (C) obtaining a psychological history of the patient.
   (D) determination of a suicide attempt.

3. All of the following are situations that may lead to suicidal attempts or ideations EXCEPT

   (A) recent divorce or loss of a loved one.
   (B) high stress levels at home or work.
   (C) drug or alcohol addiction.
   (D) None of the above

4. You are called to the scene of a 35-year-old male who is extremely violent. On your arrival, the police have not yet arrived; however, the patient's family is stating that the patient is in the house and threatening to hurt himself or anyone who comes near him. Your first course of action should be to

   (A) enter the home carefully and attempt patient contact.
   (B) request police to the scene and remain in a safe area.
   (C) speak to the patient through a window, which will afford your safety.
   (D) have a family member go in and tell the patient to come outside.

5. All of the following steps should be taken while restraining a patient EXCEPT

   (A) ensuring enough personnel to facilitate a rapid and safe restraint.
   (B) informing the patient that she will be restrained and allow her a chance to come in the ambulance on her own.
   (C) having an adequate plan before approaching the patient.
   (D) allowing the patient one free arm to maintain balance.

6. While interviewing a patient during a behavioral emergency, the EMT–Basic should maintain which of the following attitudes?

   (A) A hard and in-charge approach
   (B) A caring and understanding ear
   (C) The EMT–Basic should ignore the patient's conversation, as the patient is not acting normally.
   (D) None of the above

OBSTETRICS AND GYNECOLOGICAL EMERGENCIES

1. All of the following structures are important to childbirth EXCEPT the

   (A) uterus.
   (B) umbilical cord.
   (C) placenta.
   (D) fallopian tube.

2. The first stage of labor consists of the

   (A) delivery of the placenta.
   (B) infant entering the birth canal until birth.
   (C) beginning of contractions until full cervical dilation.
   (D) cutting of the umbilical cord.

3. The second stage of labor consists of the

   (A) delivery of the placenta.
   (B) infant entering the birth canal until birth.
   (C) beginning of contractions until full cervical dilation.
   (D) cutting of the umbilical cord.

4. The third stage of labor consists of the

   (A) delivery of the placenta.
   (B) infant entering the birth canal until birth.
   (C) beginning of contractions until full cervical dilation.
   (D) cutting of the umbilical cord.

5. The best indicator for imminent delivery of an infant in the field is

   (A) when the bag of waters ruptures.
   (B) when visual inspection of the vagina is positive for crowning.
   (C) when contractions are two minutes apart.
   (D) There is no field indication for imminent birth.

6. The predelivery emergency characterized by severe abdominal pain, dark red bleeding, and a hard, rigid uterus is most likely

   (A) threatened abortion.
   (B) placenta previa.
   (C) abruptio placenta.
   (D) eclampsia.

7. The predelivery emergency that develops as the cervix dilates and separates from a low-lying placenta is called

   (A) threatened abortion.
   (B) placenta previa.
   (C) abruptio placenta.
   (D) eclampsia.

8. During an assisted delivery, you should suction the infant's airway

   (A) after the infant is fully delivered.
   (B) after the infant's head is delivered.
   (C) as soon as you can access the infant's mouth.
   (D) Suctioning should only be done at the hospital.

9. During suctioning of a newborn's airway, what is the proper order in which suctioning should occur?

    (A) Nose and then mouth
    (B) Mouth and then nose
    (C) Mouth only
    (D) Nose only

10. During your assisted delivery, you notice that the umbilical cord is twisted around the newborn's neck, and you cannot remove it. This situation is preventing the newborn from delivering. You should

    (A) begin rapid transport, as this is a true emergency.
    (B) request advanced life support to provide advanced airway skills.
    (C) clamp the cord and carefully cut it.
    (D) None of the above

11. You are preparing to deliver a newborn in the field. Upon inspection of the vagina for crowning, you notice that the umbilical cord has delivered out of the vagina. It is pulsating, and you can see the newborn's head. What intervention is most appropriate?

    (A) Clamp and cut the cord immediately
    (B) Push the cord back past the newborns head to facilitate delivery
    (C) Insert your gloved hand into the vaginal opening, creating an airway for the newborn
    (D) Administer high-concentration oxygen, touch nothing, and transport immediately

12. When dealing with a limb presentation, which of the following is not acceptable treatment?

    (A) Push the limb back in to the birth canal and try to reposition the infant
    (B) Administer high-concentration oxygen
    (C) Begin rapid transport
    (D) Elevate the pelvis of the mother

13. The diagnosis of eclampsia (in a previously diagnosed mother with pre-eclampsia) during pregnancy is predicated on the presentation of which of the following events?

    (A) Hypertension
    (B) Vomiting
    (C) Seizures
    (D) Headache

14. The most dangerous complication of vaginal bleeding in a woman of any age is

    (A) development of hypovolemic shock.
    (B) development of seizures.
    (C) rapid heart rate.
    (D) change in mental status.

ANSWER SHEET

Chapter 5: Medical

Pharmacology

1. Ⓐ Ⓑ Ⓒ Ⓓ   3. 1. Ⓐ Ⓑ Ⓒ Ⓓ   4. Ⓐ Ⓑ Ⓒ Ⓓ
2. Ⓐ Ⓑ Ⓒ Ⓓ   2. Ⓐ Ⓑ Ⓒ Ⓓ
              3. Ⓐ Ⓑ Ⓒ Ⓓ
              4. Ⓐ Ⓑ Ⓒ Ⓓ
              5. Ⓐ Ⓑ Ⓒ Ⓓ

Respiratory

1. Ⓐ Ⓑ Ⓒ Ⓓ   3. Ⓐ Ⓑ Ⓒ Ⓓ   5. Ⓐ Ⓑ Ⓒ Ⓓ   7. Ⓐ Ⓑ Ⓒ Ⓓ
2. Ⓐ Ⓑ Ⓒ Ⓓ   4. Ⓐ Ⓑ Ⓒ Ⓓ   6. Ⓐ Ⓑ Ⓒ Ⓓ   8. Ⓐ Ⓑ Ⓒ Ⓓ

Cardiac

1. Ⓐ Ⓑ Ⓒ Ⓓ   5. Ⓐ Ⓑ Ⓒ Ⓓ   9. Ⓐ Ⓑ Ⓒ Ⓓ   13. Ⓐ Ⓑ Ⓒ Ⓓ   17. Ⓐ Ⓑ Ⓒ Ⓓ   21. Ⓐ Ⓑ Ⓒ Ⓓ
2. Ⓐ Ⓑ Ⓒ Ⓓ   6. Ⓐ Ⓑ Ⓒ Ⓓ   10. Ⓐ Ⓑ Ⓒ Ⓓ   14. Ⓐ Ⓑ Ⓒ Ⓓ   18. Ⓐ Ⓑ Ⓒ Ⓓ
3. Ⓐ Ⓑ Ⓒ Ⓓ   7. Ⓐ Ⓑ Ⓒ Ⓓ   11. Ⓐ Ⓑ Ⓒ Ⓓ   15. Ⓐ Ⓑ Ⓒ Ⓓ   19. Ⓐ Ⓑ Ⓒ Ⓓ
4. Ⓐ Ⓑ Ⓒ Ⓓ   8. Ⓐ Ⓑ Ⓒ Ⓓ   12. Ⓐ Ⓑ Ⓒ Ⓓ   16. Ⓐ Ⓑ Ⓒ Ⓓ   20. Ⓐ Ⓑ Ⓒ Ⓓ

Diabetic and Altered Mental States

1. Ⓐ Ⓑ Ⓒ Ⓓ   3. Ⓐ Ⓑ Ⓒ Ⓓ   5. Ⓐ Ⓑ Ⓒ Ⓓ   7. Ⓐ Ⓑ Ⓒ Ⓓ
2. Ⓐ Ⓑ Ⓒ Ⓓ   4. Ⓐ Ⓑ Ⓒ Ⓓ   6. Ⓐ Ⓑ Ⓒ Ⓓ   8. Ⓐ Ⓑ Ⓒ Ⓓ

Allergies and Anaphylaxis

1. Ⓐ Ⓑ Ⓒ Ⓓ   3. Ⓐ Ⓑ Ⓒ Ⓓ   5. Ⓐ Ⓑ Ⓒ Ⓓ
2. Ⓐ Ⓑ Ⓒ Ⓓ   4. Ⓐ Ⓑ Ⓒ Ⓓ

Poisoning and Overdose

1. Ⓐ Ⓑ Ⓒ Ⓓ   3. Ⓐ Ⓑ Ⓒ Ⓓ   5. Ⓐ Ⓑ Ⓒ Ⓓ
2. Ⓐ Ⓑ Ⓒ Ⓓ   4. Ⓐ Ⓑ Ⓒ Ⓓ

Environmental Emergencies

1. Ⓐ Ⓑ Ⓒ Ⓓ   3. Ⓐ Ⓑ Ⓒ Ⓓ   5. Ⓐ Ⓑ Ⓒ Ⓓ
2. Ⓐ Ⓑ Ⓒ Ⓓ   4. Ⓐ Ⓑ

Behavioral Emergencies

1. Ⓐ Ⓑ Ⓒ Ⓓ   3. Ⓐ Ⓑ Ⓒ Ⓓ   5. Ⓐ Ⓑ Ⓒ Ⓓ
2. Ⓐ Ⓑ Ⓒ Ⓓ   4. Ⓐ Ⓑ Ⓒ Ⓓ   6. Ⓐ Ⓑ Ⓒ Ⓓ

Obstetrics and Gynecological Emergencies

1. Ⓐ Ⓑ Ⓒ Ⓓ   4. Ⓐ Ⓑ Ⓒ Ⓓ   7. Ⓐ Ⓑ Ⓒ Ⓓ   10. Ⓐ Ⓑ Ⓒ Ⓓ   13. Ⓐ Ⓑ Ⓒ Ⓓ
2. Ⓐ Ⓑ Ⓒ Ⓓ   5. Ⓐ Ⓑ Ⓒ Ⓓ   8. Ⓐ Ⓑ Ⓒ Ⓓ   11. Ⓐ Ⓑ Ⓒ Ⓓ   14. Ⓐ Ⓑ Ⓒ Ⓓ
3. Ⓐ Ⓑ Ⓒ Ⓓ   6. Ⓐ Ⓑ Ⓒ Ⓓ   9. Ⓐ Ⓑ Ⓒ Ⓓ   12. Ⓐ Ⓑ Ⓒ Ⓓ

ANSWERS TO CHAPTER 5

Pharmacology	Respiratory	Cardiac		Diabetic and Altered Mental States	Allergies and Anaphylaxis	Poisoning and Overdose
1. A	1. A	1. C	12. C	1. C	1. C	1. D
2. C	2. B	2. C	13. B	2. A	2. A	2. A
3.	3. D	3. B	14. C	3. D	3. B	3. A
1. D	4. C	4. C	15. A	4. C	4. C	4. B
2. E	5. B	5. B	16. A	5. A	5. A	5. C
3. A	6. A	6. B	17. D	6. D		
4. C	7. B	7. C	18. B	7. B		
5. B	8. C	8. B	19. A	8. B		
4. D		9. A	20. B			
		10. A	21. C			
		11. A				

Environmental Emergencies	Behavioral Emerciencies	Obstetrics and Gynecological Emergencies
1. D	1. D	1. D
2. A	2. B	2. C
3. B	3. D	3. B
4. B	4. B	4. A
5. D	5. D	5. B
6. D	6. B	6. C
		7. B
		8. B
		9. B
		10. C
		11. C
		12. A
		13. C
		14. A

RATIONALES FOR THE ANSWERS

Pharmacology

1. **The correct answer is (A).** The EMT–Basic may have activated charcoal, oral glucose, and oxygen, which are available on his ambulance. This availability will be based on local protocols. Regardless of local protocol, the EMT–Basic should be well aware of the indications and contraindications regarding their administration. Epinephrine is a prescription medication that is not administered by the EMT–Basic; however, the EMT–Basic may assist the patient in taking these medications if the patient has a prescribed medication and is in urgent need of it.

2. **The correct answer is (C).** Oxygen is a medication that is carried by all levels of EMS providers and may be administered to all patients who require it. The EMT–Basic can assist in the administration of epinephrine, nitroglycerin, and metered dose inhalers to patients who have a prescription for these medications. The EMT–Basic should refer to local protocols for a more comprehensive ruling as to assisted medications.

3. **Answers**

1. Intravenous	(D)	Into the vein
2. Sublingual	(E)	Under the tongue
3. Intramuscular	(A)	Into the muscle
4. Subcutaneous	(C)	Beneath the skin
5. Intraosseous	(B)	Into the bone

4. **The correct answer is (D).** When administering medications to a patient, the EMT–Basic should verify that she has the correct patient, medication, dose, and route of administration prior to administering any medication to a patient. The EMT–Basic should be familiar with any medications she may find herself assisting a patient in administering. The correct needle size is usually the correct answer in advanced EMS training; however, in the case of the EMT–Basic, all medications that she will assist in administering will either not be injectable or will be auto injectors, which have the appropriate needle attached.

Respiratory

1. **The correct answer is (A).** The proper order of the structures of the respiratory system is as follows:

   nose
   pharynx
   larynx
   trachea
   bronchi
   alveoli

2. **The correct answer is (B).** All of the above are signs of inadequate breathing. The patient who is suffering from difficulty breathing for any reason will present with some signs of inadequate breathing. The EMT–Basic must be aware that all patients may not present with the same obvious signs but with subtle signs or maybe just one symptom of difficult breathing. You must be aware of all the signs of breathing difficulties in order to properly treat the patient. In this case, an asthma attack will not usually present with unequal chest expansion.

3. **The correct answer is (D).** The medication of choice in the treatment of breathing difficulty is oxygen. The EMT–Basic should never withhold oxygen from any patient with breathing difficulty. Epinephrine, metered dose inhalers, and nitroglycerin may all help the patient who is complaining of breathing difficulty; however, they are specialized medications for the treatment of specific medical alterations in respiratory status. All patients with breathing difficulty, regardless of the cause, should receive oxygen.

4. **The correct answer is (C).** In all patients with respiratory insufficiency, the ventilations should be assisted by using a bag-valve-mask ventilator with an oxygen reservoir. This patient, in addition to having breathing difficulty, is also suffering from inadequate ventilation. Oxygenation and ventilation must be assisted by the EMT–Basic in order for this patient to receive the proper amount of oxygenation. This artificial ventilation should continue until the patient regains the ability to support his own ventilations or until the patient is transferred to another provider for additional treatments.

5. **The correct answer is (B).** The conscious patient with adequate ventilation should be allowed to sit in a position that is most comfortable to him. This position (usually leaning forward in a tripod position) will ensure that the patient can maintain adequate ventilations without assistance. The EMT–Basic should administer supplemental oxygen to all patients complaining of difficulty breathing.

6. **The correct answer is (A).** The signs of adequate air exchange are equal chest expansion, clear breath sounds bilaterally, no use of the accessory muscles of breathing, unlabored efforts at ventilation, and signs of adequate oxygenation. Any patient who exhibits anything but normal signs should be carefully evaluated for conditions that may cause breathing difficulty and should be promptly treated.

7. **The correct answer is (B).** Many children will not tolerate an oxygen mask on their face—it may be too confining, and the child will naturally try to remove it. In the event that this occurs, the EMT–Basic can hold the mask a few inches from the child's face to deliver oxygen to the patient. Efforts in restraining the child are not effective, as they will agitate the child and cause an increase in oxygen consumption by the body, causing increased difficulty in breathing. The EMT–Basic should never discontinue the administration of oxygen to a patient who requires it.

8. **The correct answer is (C).** Asthma is a disease that occurs irregularly in patients who suffer from it; therefore, it is known as episodic. Asthma attacks may range from mild breathing difficulty to patients with complete inability to exchange air. These severe patients will need the EMT–Basic to provide ventilatory assistance as well as supplemental oxygen. COPD (chronic bronchitis and emphysema) patients are usually short of breath and, in many cases, will not call for assistance unless their breathing difficulty worsens significantly for any reason (usually secondary infection). Epiglottitis is a life-threatening disease that is caused by a bacterial infection. Epiglottitis must be treated rapidly, as it may cause an airway obstruction and prevent breathing.

Cardiac

1. **The correct answer is (C).** Atherosclerosis is a major cause of many cases of chest pain. Although not the direct diagnosis, atherosclerosis is the causative factor in most cases of angina pectoris, myocardial infarction, and cardiac ischemia (angina). When calcium and fat particles begin to clog the coronary arteries, the blood flow to the heart lessens, and the heart muscle does not receive enough oxygen to its cells, causing ischemia. This condition will get progressively worse until the patient suffers from a myocardial infarction or the condition is corrected by a physician.

2. **The correct answer is (C).** Patients with angina pectoris will usually complain of an onset of pain after some type of exertion, and the pain usually subsides after rest or administration of oxygen or nitroglycerin. The pain of myocardial infarction may not be precipitated by any obvious causes, is usually not relieved by nitroglycerin or oxygen administration, and will not subside after a period of rest.

3. **The correct answer is (B).** Tachycardia is defined as a heart rate above 100 beats per minute. To be more specific, it is defined as a heart rate between 100 and 150 beats per minute, with higher heart rates being more specific in origin. A heart rate of between 60 and 100 beats per minute is considered normal, while a heart rate under 60 beats per minute is considered bradycardia.

4. **The correct answer is (C).** Bradycardia is defined as a heart rate of less than 60 beats per minute. In the case of a patient with a rate slower than 60, the EMT–Basic should be aware that many athletic persons have normal resting heart rates of below 60. This rate is no cause for alarm except when it is accompanied by symptoms of poor blood flow to the body, typically low blood pressure.

5. **The correct answer is (B).** Onset and duration are of great importance in a differential diagnosis between angina pectoris and myocardial infarction. In this case, the patient stated that the pain came on at rest, has been present for 45 minutes, and was not relieved by nitroglycerin. This information would lead to a diagnosis of myocardial infarction, based on the onset and duration alone. The non-response to medication would only serve to confirm your diagnosis of myocardial infarction.

6. **The correct answer is (B).** Although CPR and proper ventilation will prolong the window of opportunity to convert a cardiac arrest patient, the definitive treatment of a cardiac arrest patient within the first few minutes of the event is defibrillation. Multiple studies have shown that in the first few minutes of cardiac arrest, the heart is in ventricular fibrillation that can been defibrillated, prompting a normal rhythm. The AED, if available, should be attached to any pulseless patient as early as possible.

7. **The correct answer is (C).** The fully automatic defibrillator will provide hands-free full functionality without any steps needed by the user. The fully automatic AED will analyze a cardiac arrest rhythm and, if indicated, will give an all clear, charge up, and deliver the shock by itself. The semi-automatic AED will analyze and then advise the user to charge and deliver the shock. Both units will be equipped with hands-free pads that are applied to the chest.

8. **The correct answer is (B).** Different forms of ventricular tachycardia may look exactly the same on a cardiac monitor; however, one produces a pulse and one does not. The AED does not detect a pulse and, therefore, will recommend a shock for this rhythm. If this shock is delivered, it may cause great harm to the patient—to the extent of stopping the heart. To prevent this grave error, it is only advisable to attach an AED to a patient who has no pulse.

9. **The correct answer is (A).** Transport should be given high priority after a sixth shock is delivered. Current guidelines prove the need for medications after a patient has been defibrillated with no success. The EMT–Basic should consider transport as the highest priority after six unsuccessful defibrillation attempts. In regard to ALS care, if the ALS unit is en route and their ETA is longer than it would take to arrive at the nearest hospital, transport should begin to the hospital. If, for any reason, the ETA of the ALS unit should change, then arrangement can be made via the dispatcher to have the ALS unit intercept the BLS unit to provide care.

10. **The correct answer is (A).** During the analyze phase of AED use, there should be no unnecessary patient movement. Although modern AEDs will be able to decipher what is artifact and what is not, there is always a chance of a false reading and a shock indication where one is not warranted. The EMT–Basic must have a clear understanding that delivered shocks to a patient where shock is not indicated can have very serious results.

11. **The correct answer is (A).** The AED will perform a rhythm check after each shock. The treatment algorithm states that three shocks should be delivered in succession. These successive shocks may be of great benefit to the patient in cardiac arrest. If the AED does not detect a shockable rhythm, it will not deliver additional shocks.

12. **The correct answer is (C).** Whenever an AED is in analyze mode or set to shock in the back of the ambulance, the vehicle should be stopped. Movement of the vehicle may cause interference that could be incorrectly analyzed or could prevent proper analysis of the rhythm. Delivery of defibrillations in a moving vehicle can have dangerous effects, especially if the vehicle is turning during a shock and the EMT–Basic comes in contact with the patient or defibrillation pads. All AED treatments should be done while not in motion.

13. **The correct answer is (B).** After return of spontaneous circulation, the patient may need cardiorespiratory support until the heart returns to normal and perfusion status improves. The EMT–Basic should support the patient's ventilations and establish baseline vital signs. These vital signs should be reassessed frequently to monitor the condition of the patient.

14. **The correct answer is (C).** The 6-year-old drowning patient is not a candidate for AED use. Pediatric patients do not fall into the category for AED defibrillation. Since pediatric cardiac arrest is usually caused by respiratory insufficiency, it is highly unlikely that the AED will be beneficial. In addition, the AED cannot deliver a proper joule setting that is concurrent with pediatric standards.

15. **The correct answer is (A).** The defibrillator is attached and has delivered a shock, and this is a good indicator that another shock will be delivered shortly. There is no reason to delay treatment while changing monitors to deliver this shock and successive ones. The ALS crew can use their extra hands to prepare for advanced interventions after these shocks are delivered. After the third shock is delivered and there is no shock indicated, the ALS crew may switch monitors in order to confirm a non-shockable rhythm and decide on a treatment for this type of rhythm.

16. **The correct answer is (A).** The AED should be inspected prior to the beginning of each shift to ensure that it is fully charged and operational. Failure to do a shift check may result in a charge of negligence on the part of the EMT–Basic if it fails to operate at the scene of a cardiac arrest. The EMT–Basic should not take the word of the previous shift that the unit is operational and should check the unit himself. In addition, regardless of when it was charged and used, it should be tested prior to every shift. Even if a battery shows a full charge at the beginning of the previous shift, temperature conditions and other environmental factors may take a charge from a battery. A defective battery may show a charge then drop the charge in a few hours.

17. **The correct answer is (D).** Single rescuer AED procedures are similar to layperson CPR, with the exception of activating EMS. In this situation, the EMT–Basic does not leave to activate EMS but remains with the patient to begin definitive treatments. The CPR survey is done to ensure that the patient's airway is intact. After the airway is ensured, AED procedures should take precedence over any other intervention.

18. **The correct answer is (B).** When encountering a patient in a wet area, the EMT–Basic should immediately move the patient into a dry area before attaching the AED. This will ensure safety in operation of the unit. Electrical current follows the path of least resistance and may be conducted through a puddle or wet surface, injuring rescuers and bystanders. If the patient is wet, they should be rapidly dried with a towel before proceeding to defibrillate.

19. **The correct answer is (A).** Medical direction is an essential aspect of emergency medical care. The EMT–Basic should call medical direction prior to the assisted delivery of a patient's medications. There is no substitute for the experience and knowledge base of the medical control physician. In some cases, a patient may be presenting with chest pains but have hypotension, which would make nitroglycerin a contraindication. The medical director will be there to assist the field crews in their patient care.

20. **The correct answer is (B).** Common side effects of nitroglycerin include nausea, vomiting, dizziness, hypotension, headache, and bitter taste in the mouth (from the pill). These are considered common side effects. The dizziness and/or lightheadedness come from nitroglycerin's effect on dilating blood vessels, which drop blood pressure.

21. **The correct answer is (C).** Previous episodes of nausea after the administration of nitroglycerin are not a contraindication to its administration. True contraindications to the use of nitroglycerin would include hypotension, previous allergic reactions, and using it to treat hypertension in the field.

Diabetes and Altered Mental States

1. **The correct answer is (C).** Metabolic causes of altered mental states are conditions that are caused by factors outside of the central nervous system. Many of these factors are from the outside environment. CVA (cerebrovascular accident, or stroke) is considered a structural cause of altered mental status because it occurs in the central nervous system.

2. **The correct answer is (A).** Hypoglycemia is characterized by a rapid onset of alteration of mental status. Blood sugar may drop for multiple reasons, including the patient taking her insulin and then failing to eat. After insulin is taken, it converts free glucose to stored glucose, and the body cannot use it. Once glucose levels begin to drop, the patient will become disoriented. Hyperglycemia, ketoacidosis, and diabetic coma are all definitions of too much sugar in the blood.

3. **The correct answer is (D).** Signs and symptoms of hypoglycemia include hunger, agitation, weakness, alteration of mental status (rapidly deteriorating), and salivation. The onset of hypoglycemia can take just a few minutes. A patient may go from a normal mental status and then start to suffer from drastic changes from the drop in blood sugar. Excessive thirst, excessive urination, and a delayed onset of altered mental status are indicative of hyperglycemia.

4. **The correct answer is (C).** Unconscious patients should never be given anything by mouth. An unconscious patient may lose control of their ability to protect the airway and may aspirate the oral glucose, causing severe airway problems. The patient should have all three of the above indications in order to receive oral glucose.

5. **The correct answer is (A).** The unconscious patient who is having a diabetic emergency should be treated with airway and ventilatory maintenance, placed in the recovery position to guard against aspiration, and ALS assistance requested for administration of intravenous glucose and advance emergency management. As previously stated, unconscious patients should receive nothing by mouth, including glucose.

6. **The correct answer is (D).** A patient suffering from a seizure needs to be protected from injury. In addition, seizures may cause a prolonged period of apnea and can result in hypoxia. You must be alert for signs of hypoxia and treat accordingly.

7. **The correct answer is (B).** Status epilepticus is the condition where a patient suffers two or more seizures without a lucid interval. Status epilepticus is a dire emergency that requires ventilatory support as well as rapid transport or ALS intervention. The EMT–Basic should assess the patient for status epilepticus and make a decision as to rapid transport or ALS request. As always, if ALS is further away than the closest hospital, the decision to transport should be made immediately.

8. **The correct answer is (B).** This patient is showing classic signs of a stroke. Slurred speech, confusion, unequal pupils, and hemiplegia are all characteristic of a stroke. Treatment of this patient would include airway and ventilatory support, high concentration oxygen, and transportation in the recovery position to facilitate airway safety.

Allergies and Anaphylaxis

1. **The correct answer is (C).** The patient suffering from anaphylaxis will have signs of respiratory distress and shock. Allergic reactions are a much more common occurrence than are true anaphylactic emergencies. Many people will develop allergies to outside allergens without ever developing anaphylaxis. It is important that you differentiate those who have developed anaphylaxis. These patients need definitive care above and beyond those with a general allergic reaction.

2. **The correct answer is (A).** In this patient, there are two possible diagnoses. This patient is a known asthmatic and was also stung by a bee. The determining factor would be whether or not the patient has ever been stung by a bee before. Due to the fact that a patient cannot develop an allergic reaction from the first encounter with an allergen (antigen), if the patient has never been stung before, this would rule out an allergic reaction. At that point, the focus would be on the asthma attack. Additional information on the development of this particular episode would include associated signs and symptoms. Anaphylaxis usually presents with itching, hives, and generalized swelling on the body. If these signs are not present, there is a good chance that a different diagnosis should be made.

3. **The correct answer is (B).** The patient with an anaphylactic reaction (shock) will require immediate airway management. This management may need to be aggressive at best. The physical response by the body to an allergen (antigen) will cause rapid airway swelling and could place the patient in danger of death from hypoxia. Airway maintenance is always the highest priority in this type of patient.

4. **The correct answer is (C).** Patients with anaphylaxis generally do not develop fevers. The EMT–Basic must, however, remain aware that a patient with a fever who is also having an anaphylactic reaction may be on antibiotic medications. Antibiotic medications, especially penicillin derivatives, are major causes of allergic reactions and anaphylaxis.

5. **The correct answer is (A).** Epinephrine commonly increases heart rate; after the injection of epinephrine, the patient may have an increase in pulse rate. Epinephrine will also open airway passages and constrict blood vessels. This will result in increased blood pressures as well as a decrease in breathing difficulty.

Poisoning and Overdose

1. **The correct answer is (D).** The four common entry routes of poison and toxins are injection, ingestion, inhalation, and absorption. Being in close proximity to a poisonous agent or toxin may not necessarily cause a reaction; however, the EMT–Basic should be aware that certain poisons and toxins (e.g., radiation) may cause a reaction in patients who were near the object but never actually came in physical contact with it.

2. **The correct answer is (A).** When eliciting a history in a poisoning, it is not important to immediate treatment to determine if the patient has ever taken the poison before. The EMT–Basic should focus on what type of substance was taken, when it was taken, how it was taken, and how much was taken. This information is essential when contacting poison control or medical direction. In determining the amount and route of ingestion, the medical team can develop a rapid treatment plan to prevent absorption of the substance.

3. **The correct answer is (A).** The treatment of a poisoning patient is aimed at prevention of the absorption of the poison. It is not in the patient's best interest to speed up absorption, as this will increase the severity of the physical effects of the poison. The EMT–Basic will not always induce vomiting in the poisoning patient. Induced vomiting may be hazardous with certain substances. Administration of antitoxins may be indicated in special situations, but it is beyond the scope of the EMT–Basic. Airway management and prevention of absorption are the highest priority for the EMT–Basic.

4. **The correct answer is (B).** The goal of patient management in a poisoning is to support the airway. The off-duty EMT will probably not have all the essential equipment to deal with this emergency; however, the EMT–Basic should always have a pocket mask in case of an emergency. Mouth-to-mouth ventilations should never be attempted on a poisoning patient, as the poison may be absorbed into the rescuer. Dilution of poisons and induced vomiting may be indicated; however, this is an unconscious patient, and neither intervention is indicated.

5. **The correct answer is (C).** If a patient vomits up the first dose of activated charcoal, it is acceptable to administer an additional dose. Activated charcoal works in the gastrointestinal system by absorbing poisons and binding them, preventing their absorption into the body. If the patient vomits up the charcoal, it will be ineffective. Vomiting up the charcoal will usually not clear the poison from the body, and administration of ipecac in this case is not necessary since the patient is already vomiting.

Environmental Emergencies

1. **The correct answer is (D).** The body can lose heat by conduction, convection, radiation, evaporation, and respiration. It is essential that the EMT–Basic is aware of what factors may be affecting the patient's ability to maintain heat and correct them immediately. Absorption is not a process by which the body loses heat.

2. **The correct answer is (A).** Airway maintenance and passive rewarming is the highest priority in the treatment of this patient. The EMT–Basic should not administer warm fluids or rapidly rewarm a hypothermic patient. These actions could ultimately result in a poor patient outcome due to physiological changes that occur during rapid rewarming.

3. **The correct answer is (B).** Patients who have been exposed to high heat without proper ventilation and hydration will develop increased internal temperatures, resulting in hyperthermia. In this case, the patient has hot and dry skin. Hot and dry skin is an ominous sign, and the patient should be moved to a cool area and rapidly cooled if possible. This form of heat emergency is a true emergency that requires rapid transport to the hospital.

4. **The correct answer is (B).** Attempts at resuscitation of the cold water-drowning patient should be initiated immediately, regardless of submersion time (with the exception of obvious death). There are documented cases of patients surviving after long periods of submersion in cold water. The EMT–Basic should begin resuscitation efforts immediately at the scene, including drying off the patient and passive rewarming.

5. **The correct answer is (D).** It highly unusual for a drowning or near-drowning patient to be suffering from hyperthermia, as water acts to pull heat from the body. Near-drowning patients may suffer from pulmonary edema (salt water drowning), red blood cell destruction (fresh water drowning), and severe hypoxia from long submersion times.

6. **The correct answer is (D).** Snakebite patients, especially those bitten by highly venomous snakes, should be afforded airway and cardiovascular support as a high priority. In addition, the patient should be kept as still as possible to avoid rapid movement of the venom through the body. It is extremely important that the EMT–Basic understand that in no case should poison be sucked through the bite using the mouth. These are extremely harmful poisons and may cause injury to the rescuer should this be done. If suction is necessary, a proper snake bite kit should be used to remove venom from the bite area.

Behavioral Emergencies

1. **The correct answer is (D).** There are many medical causes of behavioral changes. The EMT–Basic should be aware that the behavioral emergency they are responding to may actually have a medical cause. It is not acceptable to just assume that a behavioral emergency is psychological in nature until the physical causes have been investigated.

2. **The correct answer is (B).** As with any response, the safety of rescuers is the highest priority. In behavioral emergencies, this is even more important. The EMT–Basic should assure that any scene that is entered affords protection for herself and her partner. Behavioral emergencies can become rapidly violent situations, and the EMT–Basic should be alert to the environment and proceed with caution.

3. **The correct answer is (D).** All three situations may lead to suicidal attempts or thoughts. Suicide, or thoughts of suicide, may be brought on by many factors: high stress, depression, drug or alcohol addiction, recent breakups, or deaths of close relatives and friends. It may also be brought on by severe depression. Most attempts at suicide are a cry for help. The patient may attempt to hurt himself as a sign that something is wrong. The EMT–Basic should openly accept these signs and treat the patient physically as well as emotionally.

4. **The correct answer is (B).** Scene safety is the number one concern in any emergency. The EMT–Basic should not, under any circumstances, enter a home where a patient is threatening violence. Approaching a window is just as dangerous—if a patient breaks the window, the EMT–Basic may become injured and then need treatment. This will only add to the confusion on the scene. At no time should a family member be asked to retrieve a patient, especially during a violent outbreak.

5. **The correct answer is (D).** When restraining a patient is necessary, the EMS providers should work with the police in developing a restraint plan before moving in on the patient. The patient should always be given the option of being transported on his or her own accord; however, if this approach fails, then the restraint procedure should go into effect. One rescuer should be there to talk to the patient while the restraints are being applied. The violent patient should never be allowed a free arm or limb. This could result in injury to the rescuers.

6. **The correct answer is (B).** In any patient interaction, the EMT–Basic should maintain a caring and understanding ear. Many behavioral patients are only looking for somebody to talk to. The EMT–Basic can be a major asset to the treatment of the patient if they maintain compassion. This does not mean that the EMT–Basic should feed into any delusions. In addition, the EMT–Basic may find many clues as to the patient's condition during the conversation.

Obstetric and Gynecological Emergencies

1. **The correct answer is (D).** The EMT–Basic must be familiar with all of the anatomical structures of the female reproductive system in order to assist in the delivery of an infant. These structures include the uterus, vagina, placenta, umbilical cord, amniotic sac, and the fetus. A good understanding of all of the functions of these structures is imperative to assist in the delivery of the infant. The fallopian tubes, although a structure in the female reproductive system, serve no purpose in the actual birth of the child.

2. **The correct answer is (C).** Labor can be defined in three stages. The first stage of labor is from the beginning of contractions until the cervix is fully dilated. The second stage of labor is from the time the infant enters the birth canal until the time of birth. The third stage of labor begins after delivery of the infant and ends with the delivery of the placenta.

3. **The correct answer is (B).** See rationale for question 2.

4. **The correct answer is (A).** See rationale for question 2.

5. **The correct answer is (B).** When dealing with the pregnant patient, the EMT–Basic should assess the mother for signs of imminent birth. Some of the indicators are breaking of the bag of waters, contractions that are less than two minutes apart, and the mother's urge to push. However, the best field indicator is direct vaginal visualization for crowning. Crowning is when the head of the infant is showing at the vaginal opening. This is a sure sign of imminent delivery.

6. **The correct answer is (C).** An abruptio placenta is defined as premature separation of the placenta from the uterus. This separation may be partial or complete. The signs of abruption are severe abdominal or back and flank pain, a rigid uterus, and dark red bleeding.

7. **The correct answer is (B).** Placenta previa is characterized by bright red (arterial) and painless bleeding that usually occurs during the last trimester of pregnancy. The placenta is attached to the uterine wall at a lower point than normal; when the cervix begins to dilate, the placenta begins to detach from the uterine wall, causing arterial bright red bleeding.

8. **The correct answer is (B).** The EMT–Basic who is assisting delivery of a newborn should suction the infant's airway after the head is fully delivered. Usually, the head delivers facing down and rotates as it becomes fully delivered. The EMT–Basic can assist in this rotation; however, care must be taken to avoid injury to the infant. Suctioning should commence after delivery of the head to prevent aspiration should the infant breathe spontaneously.

9. **The correct answer is (B).** The proper procedures for suctioning a newborn's airway is to suction the mouth first and then suction the nose.

10. **The correct answer is (C).** If during an assisted delivery you notice the umbilical cord is wrapped around the infant's neck, you should initially try and lift it over the head, freeing up the head and continuing delivery. If it is impossible to slip the cord over the infant's head, the EMT–Basic should clamp the umbilical cord and then cut between the clamps to facilitate delivery.

11. **The correct answer is (C).** A prolapsed cord can be a major emergency if it interferes with blood supply to the infant. If the cord gets pinched and blood flow is restricted, the infant will become hypoxic and go into distress. It is imperative that the EMT–Basic provides an open airway for the newborn. This is accomplished by inserting two gloved fingers into the vagina on either side of the newborn's nose; this way, an open airway is provided in case the infants breathing stimulus is activated due to cord compression.

12. **The correct answer is (A).** A limb presentation must be transported to a hospital immediately. There is no field treatment for this presentation, and the EMT–Basic should never try to insert her hand into the birth canal to reposition the infant. The mother should be transported immediately with her pelvis elevated and on high-concentration oxygen.

13. **The correct answer is (C).** Pre-eclampsia is a condition characterized by hypertension, headache, and sensitivity to light during pregnancy. If the hypertension continues to worsen, seizures may develop. The diagnosis of eclampsia is based on seizure activity.

14. **The correct answer is (A).** Cardiac arrest secondary to hypovolemic shock is the most serious complication of vaginal bleeding. The EMT–Basic should use sound judgment and rapid transport for any patient who has uncontrollable bleeding. When treating these patients, it is essential to remember that the EMT–Basic should never pack the vagina with dressings to prevent bleeding.

Chapter 6

TRAUMA

In this section, you will review questions based on module five of the National Standard Curriculum. Module five encompasses assessment and treatment of the trauma patient. You should attempt to answer all questions, then evaluate your performance using the answer keys and rationales. Any need for additional information on a specific subject can be found in your original course textbook in the corresponding chapter.

BLEEDING AND SHOCK

1. The type of bleeding characterized by a rapid pulsatile flow of bright red blood is known as

   (A) arterial.
   (B) venous.
   (C) capillary.
   (D) cellular.

2. The type of bleeding characterized by a steady flow of dark red blood is known as

   (A) arterial.
   (B) venous.
   (C) capillary.
   (D) cellular.

3. The type of bleeding characterized by a slow oozing of blood from an abrasion is known as

   (A) aterial.
   (B) venous.
   (C) capillary.
   (D) cellular.

4. All of the following are signs of shock due to bleeding EXCEPT

   (A) increased pulse.
   (B) decreased pulse.
   (C) decreased blood pressure.
   (D) altered mental status.

5. All of the following are steps in controlling bleeding in the field EXCEPT

   (A) direct pressure.
   (B) elevation.
   (C) pressure point.
   (D) wire tourniquet.

6. You respond to a multiple trauma patient at the scene of a motorcycle collision. On your arrival, you find a 26-year-old male with large bruises to his abdomen above the liver, a distended abdomen, bleeding from the mouth, deformity in the left lower extremity, and signs of shock. These types of findings are indicative of

   (A) severe bleeding in the head.
   (B) severe internal bleeding.
   (C) severe external bleeding.
   (D) minor internal and external bleeding.

7. The maximum time an EMT–Basic should remain on the scene with a critical trauma patient is

   (A) 10 minutes.
   (B) 20 minutes.
   (C) 60 minutes.
   (D) There is no time limit on patient care.

8. The most important intervention the EMT–Basic should make in the treatment of a patient in shock is

   (A) controlling bleeding.
   (B) maintaining an open and secure airway.
   (C) transporting the patient.
   (D) splinting any suspected fractures.

SOFT-TISSUE INJURIES

1. Which of the following is not a layer of the skin?

   (A) Muscle
   (B) Epidermis
   (C) Dermis
   (D) Subcutaneous

2. A contusion is best defined as

   (A) a collection of blood under intact skin due to an injury.
   (B) a large area of heavy bleeding under the skin.
   (C) an open area of scraping with oozing blood.
   (D) a large open wound with arterial bleeding.

3. The difference between a contusion and a hematoma is that

   (A) a hematoma is a less severe injury.
   (B) a hematoma involves a larger area of injury.
   (C) a hematoma occurs only in the brain.
   (D) There is no difference in these injuries.

4. Your patient has a long jagged cut on his right arm. Which of the following best describes this type of injury?

(A) Abrasion
(B) Contusion
(C) Laceration
(D) Avulsion

5. After falling off his bicycle, a 6-year-old patient has multiple scrapes and scratches on his arms and legs. This type of injury is known as

(A) abrasion.
(B) contusion.
(C) laceration.
(D) avulsion.

6. You are assigned to a motor vehicle collision. On your arrival, you find a 56-year-old male who was the driver of the automobile. Your findings include a flap of skin that is hanging from the man's head. This injury occurred when the man's head hit the windshield of the car during the collision. The definition of this type of injury is

(A) abrasion.
(B) contusion.
(C) laceration.
(D) avulsion.

7. You are treating a patient who has a gunshot wound to the right upper chest. The patient is complaining of difficulty breathing. On your assessment, you find that the wound makes a characteristic sucking sound when the patient breathes. The treatment of this type of injury would include all of the following EXCEPT

(A) administration of high-concentration oxygen.
(B) splinting of the chest using the patient's right arm.
(C) application of an occlusive dressing to the injury site.
(D) monitoring of breath sounds for diminished sounds on the injured side.

8. Which of the following best describes a hemopneumothorax?

(A) Air trapped in the lungs
(B) Blood trapped in the lungs
(C) Air and blood trapped in the pleural space surrounding the lungs
(D) Chest pain associated with blood in the lungs

9. Which of the following is NOT part of the treatment for an abdominal evisceration?

(A) Administration of high-concentration oxygen
(B) Application of an occlusive dressing
(C) Application of a dry sterile dressing
(D) Application of a moist sterile dressing

10. Which best describes a full thickness burn?

(A) Skin reddening after exposure to the sun
(B) Blistering of the skin after touching an open flame
(C) Charring of the skin after contact with a bare electrical wire
(D) Reddening and blistering of the skin after contact with a caustic chemical

11. Which best describes a partial thickness burn?

(A) Skin reddening after exposure to the sun
(B) Blistering of the skin after touching an open flame
(C) Charring of the skin after contact with a bare electrical wire
(D) Reddening and blistering of the skin after contact with a caustic chemical

12. Which of the following best describes a superficial burn?

(A) Skin reddening after exposure to the sun
(B) Blistering of the skin after touching an open flame
(C) Charring of the skin after contact with a bare electrical wire
(D) Reddening and blistering of the skin after contact with a caustic chemical

13. You respond to a house on fire. On your arrival, you are led to a 27-year-old woman who was pulled from the fire by the fire department. Your assessment reveals partial thickness burns on her chest and arms. You also note that there are burns to the lips and soot around the nose. You suspect

(A) possible full thickness burns to the lips.
(B) critical burns to the chest and arms.
(C) airway burns.
(D) possible fluid loss from the burns.

14. You are treating a burn patient who has full thickness burns to both arms as well as his anterior chest and abdomen. Using the rule of nines, the percent of burn area is

(A) 27 percent.
(B) 32 percent.
(C) 36 percent.
(D) 42 percent.

15. Your patient is a 6-year-old child with burns to his anterior chest and back as well as his head. Using the rule of nines for a child, what percentage of his body is burned?

(A) 36 percent
(B) 42 percent
(C) 54 percent
(D) 61 percent

16. Which of the following is classified as a critical burn?

(A) A patient with superficial burns over 40 percent of her body
(B) A child with partial thickness burns over 15 percent of his body
(C) A patient with partial thickness burns to 18 percent of his legs
(D) A patient with full thickness burns to her feet

17. Treatment for burns includes all of the following EXCEPT

(A) monitoring the patient's airway.
(B) application of moist sterile dressings.
(C) application of dry sterile dressings.
(D) maintenance of body temperature.

18. Your first priority in the treatment of the patient with an electrical burn who already has been safely removed from danger is

(A) assessing the patient for entrance and exit wounds from the electrical source.
(B) assessment and management of the patient's airway.
(C) applying sterile dressings.
(D) applying ice to the affected area.

19. You respond to the scene of a fight in a local tavern. On your arrival, you find a 23-year-old female with a knife protruding from her upper right abdominal quadrant. Treatment for this patient includes all of the following EXCEPT

(A) airway maintenance.
(B) application of a bulky dressing around the impaled object.
(C) removal of the impaled object and application of a bulky dressing over the wound.
(D) administration of high-concentration oxygen.

20. Which of the following is NOT an acceptable treatment of a patient with a partial amputation?

(A) Wrapping the affected part in dry sterile dressings and bandages
(B) Removing the remaining intact skin and placing the amputated part in a plastic bag to prevent infection
(C) Control bleeding with pressure point, if necessary
(D) Transport to an appropriate facility

MUSCULOSKELETAL CARE

1. Which of the following is NOT a part of the appendicular skeleton?

(A) Cranium
(B) Humerus
(C) Femur
(D) Acetabulum

2. All of the following are bones of the upper extremities EXCEPT

(A) humerus.
(B) ulna.
(C) metacarpal.
(D) metatarsal.

3. A closed fracture to bones may result in major internal blood loss. Of the following bones, which one can result in the most severe blood loss?

(A) Humerus
(B) Femur
(C) Pelvis
(D) Radius

4. Effective immobilization of a bone includes which of the following?

(A) Immobilizing the area above and below the fracture site
(B) Immobilizing the joint above and below the fracture site
(C) Maintaining manual stabilization throughout the transport
(D) Splinting the patient after they are placed in the ambulance to speed up transport

5. After you apply a splint, the patient complains of a tingling sensation to the immobilized extremity. This is due to

(A) nerve damage from the injury.
(B) applying the splint too loosely.
(C) applying the splint too tightly.
(D) This is a normal reaction to a splint application.

6. All of the following are contraindications to the application of a traction splint EXCEPT a

(A) pelvic fracture.
(B) knee injury.
(C) acetabular fracture.
(D) open femur fracture.

7. Your patient is complaining of pain to her hands after falling on outstretched arms. Your assessment reveals a fork-type fracture to the patient's hands. This is known as a(n)

(A) collets fracture.
(B) colles fracture.
(C) simple wrist deformity.
(D) acetabular fracture.

INJURIES TO THE HEAD AND SPINE

1. There are _____ vertebrae in the cervical spine.

(A) seven
(B) twelve
(C) five
(D) four

2. The central nervous system consists of

(A) all nerves and nerve pathways of the body.
(B) the parasympathetic nervous system.
(C) the brain and spinal cord.
(D) the twelve cranial nerves.

3. A concussion is described as

   (A) severe head injury with moderate bleeding.
   (B) mild head injury with a possible loss of consciousness.
   (C) open head injury with deep unconsciousness.
   (D) arterial bleeding of the brain.

4. Which of the following best describes an epidural hematoma?

   (A) Venous bleeding below the dura mater in the brain
   (B) Arterial bleeding below the dura mater in the brain
   (C) Venous bleeding above the dura mater in the brain
   (D) Arterial bleeding above the dura mater in the brain

5. Which of the following best describes a subdural hematoma?

   (A) Venous bleeding below the dura mater in the brain
   (B) Arterial bleeding below the dura mater in the brain
   (C) Venous bleeding above the dura mater in the brain
   (D) Arterial bleeding above the dura mater in the brain

6. Which of the following best describes an intracerebral hematoma?

   (A) Bleeding above the dura mater
   (B) Bleeding below the dura mater
   (C) Bleeding within the brain tissue
   (D) Bleeding above the brain tissue

7. The primary concern in the patient with severe facial injury is

   (A) severe blood loss.
   (B) airway compromise.
   (C) brain injury.
   (D) cervical spinal injury.

8. You are on the scene of a patient who fell from a window. The patient fell approximately 25 feet and is conscious and complaining of numbness and tingling from his neck down. You suspect

   (A) thoracic spinal injury.
   (B) cervical spinal injury.
   (C) brain injury.
   (D) concussion.

9. The Glasgow coma scale examines which of the following?

   (A) Extremity movement, mental status, sensation
   (B) Verbal response, movement, sensation
   (C) Eye opening, verbal response, motor response
   (D) Motor response, verbal response, sensation

10. Which of the following is the required airway maneuver for a patient with suspected spinal injury?

    (A) Modified jaw thrust
    (B) Head tilt–chin lift
    (C) Jaw lift
    (D) Tongue pull

11. On arrival at a motor vehicle accident, you find a patient seated in a vehicle that has severe damage to the front end. You notice that the patient has a laceration to the forehead and the windshield is cracked from where the patient hit his head. The immobilization device of choice is

(A) rapid extrication on a long spine board.
(B) a log roll.
(C) a short spine board.
(D) a cervical collar and long spine board.

12. You arrive at the scene of a rollover vehicle collision. On your arrival, the patient is standing at the scene speaking with police officers. The patient is complaining of neck pain and right-sided tingling. The immobilization technique of choice for this patient would be

(A) short spine board or KED.
(B) rapid takedown.
(C) cervical collar only; transport seated.
(D) There is no immobilization needed since the patient is already walking.

13. Helmet removal should be attempted in which of the following cases?

(A) A football player who suffered a lower back injury, is conscious, and is talking with the EMT crew
(B) A motorcycle rider who is unconscious and wearing a full face shield
(C) A motorcycle rider who is conscious and wearing a half helmet
(D) A hockey player who went head first into the boards and is complaining of dizziness

14. Your patient is a 59-year-old male who is found on the street with an altered mental status. Bystanders state that the patient was walking and just sat down and started talking and making no sense. Which of the following would be the best possible explanation for this type of behavior?

(A) Traumatic brain injury
(B) Stroke
(C) Seizure
(D) Cervical spinal injury

Questions 15–20 are based on the following scenario:

You are called to a private residence for a psychological emergency. On your arrival, you find a 28-year-old male who is acting violently. The family states that he woke up this morning and was not himself. They also state that the patient was in an accident two days ago in which he sustained a head injury but refused medical care. As you are speaking to the family, the patient collapses.

15. What should be your initial intervention?

(A) Assess breathing
(B) Open the airway with the jaw thrust maneuver and assess the airway
(C) Assess circulation
(D) Administer glucose paste to the patient

16. After your initial intervention, you should

    (A) assess breathing.
    (B) open the airway with the jaw thrust maneuver and assess the airway.
    (C) assess circulation.
    (D) administer glucose paste to the patient.

17. After your second intervention, you should

    (A) assess breathing.
    (B) open the airway with the jaw thrust maneuver and assess the airway.
    (C) assess circulation.
    (D) administer glucose paste to the patient.

18. Your findings show that the patient has a stable airway, is breathing, and has a good pulse rate. Your next intervention should be to

    (A) do a neurological assessment.
    (B) begin a secondary assessment.
    (C) immobilize the patient and begin transport.
    (D) examine the head for suspected injury.

19. Based on the history, you would suspect that this patient is suffering from which type of head injury?

    (A) A concussion
    (B) A cervical spine fracture
    (C) A subdural hematoma
    (D) An epidural hematoma

20. How should this patient be transported?

    (A) On a stretcher with head elevated
    (B) Immobilized to a long spine board with a cervical collar
    (C) Immobilized with a KED to ensure cervical spinal immobilization
    (D) On a short spine board, then transferred to the long spine board in the ambulance

ANSWER SHEET

Chapter 6: Trauma

Bleeding and Shock

1. Ⓐ Ⓑ Ⓒ Ⓓ   5. Ⓐ Ⓑ Ⓒ Ⓓ
2. Ⓐ Ⓑ Ⓒ Ⓓ   6. Ⓐ Ⓑ Ⓒ Ⓓ
3. Ⓐ Ⓑ Ⓒ Ⓓ   7. Ⓐ Ⓑ Ⓒ Ⓓ
4. Ⓐ Ⓑ Ⓒ Ⓓ   8. Ⓐ Ⓑ Ⓒ Ⓓ

Soft-Tissue Injuries

1. Ⓐ Ⓑ Ⓒ Ⓓ   6. Ⓐ Ⓑ Ⓒ Ⓓ   11. Ⓐ Ⓑ Ⓒ Ⓓ   16. Ⓐ Ⓑ Ⓒ Ⓓ
2. Ⓐ Ⓑ Ⓒ Ⓓ   7. Ⓐ Ⓑ Ⓒ Ⓓ   12. Ⓐ Ⓑ Ⓒ Ⓓ   17. Ⓐ Ⓑ Ⓒ Ⓓ
3. Ⓐ Ⓑ Ⓒ Ⓓ   8. Ⓐ Ⓑ Ⓒ Ⓓ   13. Ⓐ Ⓑ Ⓒ Ⓓ   18. Ⓐ Ⓑ Ⓒ Ⓓ
4. Ⓐ Ⓑ Ⓒ Ⓓ   9. Ⓐ Ⓑ Ⓒ Ⓓ   14. Ⓐ Ⓑ Ⓒ Ⓓ   19. Ⓐ Ⓑ Ⓒ Ⓓ
5. Ⓐ Ⓑ Ⓒ Ⓓ   10. Ⓐ Ⓑ Ⓒ Ⓓ   15. Ⓐ Ⓑ Ⓒ Ⓓ   20. Ⓐ Ⓑ Ⓒ Ⓓ

Musculoskeletal Care

1. Ⓐ Ⓑ Ⓒ Ⓓ   5. Ⓐ Ⓑ Ⓒ Ⓓ
2. Ⓐ Ⓑ Ⓒ Ⓓ   6. Ⓐ Ⓑ Ⓒ Ⓓ
3. Ⓐ Ⓑ Ⓒ Ⓓ   7. Ⓐ Ⓑ Ⓒ Ⓓ
4. Ⓐ Ⓑ Ⓒ Ⓓ

Injuries to the Head and Spine

1. Ⓐ Ⓑ Ⓒ Ⓓ   6. Ⓐ Ⓑ Ⓒ Ⓓ   11. Ⓐ Ⓑ Ⓒ Ⓓ   16. Ⓐ Ⓑ Ⓒ Ⓓ
2. Ⓐ Ⓑ Ⓒ Ⓓ   7. Ⓐ Ⓑ Ⓒ Ⓓ   12. Ⓐ Ⓑ Ⓒ Ⓓ   17. Ⓐ Ⓑ Ⓒ Ⓓ
3. Ⓐ Ⓑ Ⓒ Ⓓ   8. Ⓐ Ⓑ Ⓒ Ⓓ   13. Ⓐ Ⓑ Ⓒ Ⓓ   18. Ⓐ Ⓑ Ⓒ Ⓓ
4. Ⓐ Ⓑ Ⓒ Ⓓ   9. Ⓐ Ⓑ Ⓒ Ⓓ   14. Ⓐ Ⓑ Ⓒ Ⓓ   19. Ⓐ Ⓑ Ⓒ Ⓓ
5. Ⓐ Ⓑ Ⓒ Ⓓ   10. Ⓐ Ⓑ Ⓒ Ⓓ   15. Ⓐ Ⓑ Ⓒ Ⓓ   20. Ⓐ Ⓑ Ⓒ Ⓓ

ANSWERS TO CHAPTER 6

Bleeding and Shock	Soft Tissue Injuries		Musculoskeletal Care	Injuries to the Head and Spine	
1. A	1. A	11. D	1. A	1. A	11. C
2. B	2. A	12. A	2. D	2. C	12. B
3. C	3. B	13. C	3. C	3. B	13. B
4. B	4. C	14. C	4. B	4. D	14. B
5. D	5. A	15. C	5. C	5. A	15. B
6. B	6. D	16. D	6. D	6. C	16. A
7. A	7. B	17. B	7. B	7. B	17. C
8. B	8. C	18. B		8. B	18. A
	9. C	19. C		9. C	19. C
	10. C	20. B		10. A	20. B

RATIONALES FOR THE ANSWERS

Bleeding and Shock

1. **The correct answer is (A).** Arterial bleeding is characterized by a rapid, spurting, pulsatile flow of oxygenated blood. Arterial bleeding should be considered serious, as patients can lose a large volume of blood from an arterial bleed in a very short period of time. The EMT–Basic should apply direct pressure to stop arterial bleeding initially.

2. **The correct answer is (B).** Venous bleeding is characterized by a steady flow of dark, deoxygenated blood. This type of bleeding is common in most soft-tissue injuries. Although not as serious and life threatening as arterial bleeding, venous bleeding should be controlled immediately to prevent large amounts of blood loss.

3. **The correct answer is (C).** Capillary bleeding is a slow and oozing type of bleeding. Since blood flow in the capillaries is under low pressure, and the capillaries are very small, capillary bleeding does not pose a life threat. Applying direct pressure to the injury site easily controls capillary bleeding.

4. **The correct answer is (B).** Decreased pulse is not a sign of shock. Initial response to hypoperfusion (shock) is that the body will increase pulse rate. As bleeding continues and shock progresses, the patient will develop an altered mental status and his skin color will take on a pallor (paleness). The skin will also become cold and clammy. Decreased blood pressure is a late sign of shock. The EMT–Basic must be aware of the signs of shock. Bleeding control is the definitive treatment of patients with shock.

5. **The correct answer is (D).** Bleeding control is accomplished by first applying direct pressure; if that is unsuccessful, elevation of the injured area is applied. If bleeding control is still unsuccessful, a pressure point would be used to slow bleeding to the area. Although a tourniquet may be considered as a last resort, wire should never be used as a tourniquet, as tightening it would cause additional injury to the patient.

6. **The correct answer is (B).** This patient has classic signs of severe internal bleeding. After a major traumatic event, abdominal bruising, especially over the site of a major organ, is a definite sign of internal bleeding. A distended abdomen is another sign of internal injuries. Management of this type of injury includes rapid transport to a hospital for definitive care.

7. **The correct answer is (A).** In the case of a critical trauma patient, the patient should be transported rapidly to a trauma center for surgical intervention. It is commonly known that the patient must be delivered to a surgical facility within the first hour of her injury. This term, known as the golden hour, is an EMS golden rule. The EMT–Basic should rapidly transport all critical trauma patients at the earliest possible opportunity.

8. **The correct answer is (B).** Maintenance of the airway is the highest priority in any aspect of patient care. The EMT–Basic should always make airway management and patient oxygenation the highest priority in trauma care. Following the basics, airway, breathing, and circulation will always be helpful to the trauma patient.

Soft-Tissue Injuries

1. **The correct answer is (A).** The skin consists of three layers: epidermis, dermis, and subcutaneous. The muscle lies below the subcutaneous layer. Muscle is not considered part of the skin, as it has a different classification of tissue. The subcutaneous tissue is a fatty layer of skin that assists in the protection of underlying tissue, such as muscle.

2. **The correct answer is (A).** A contusion is usually a small isolated area of bleeding under the skin. Contusions are considered a closed wound; closed wounds are defined as an injury where the skin remains intact. Contusions are usually self-limiting; however, they may require some pre-hospital treatment. Application of cold compresses is usually indicated in the treatment of a contusion.

3. **The correct answer is (B).** A hematoma is similar to a contusion. A hematoma always involves a larger area of injury with additional tissue damage. As in a contusion, the skin remains intact; however, the area of internal injury is more widespread.

4. **The correct answer is (C).** A laceration is a cut that may have jagged edges or a fine, smooth edge. A laceration is a common injury that the EMT–Basic may encounter. Treatment of the patient with an isolated laceration would include direct pressure and elevation of the lacerated extremity. Lacerations are usually superficial and result in venous bleeding; however, they may also be deep, resulting in arterial bleeding.

5. **The correct answer is (A).** Abrasions are defined as scrapes and scratches that affect the skin superficially. Due to the superficial nature of an abrasion, the bleeding is usually slow and oozing from capillaries. These injuries usually contain small stones and dirt. The EMT–Basic should attempt to keep all injuries from becoming contaminated with foreign substances.

6. **The correct answer is (D).** An avulsion is defined as any soft-tissue injury that involves the removal of skin, or a flap of skin. Treatment of an avulsion includes folding the flap of skin back to its original position and covering it with a clean dressing.

7. **The correct answer is (B).** A sucking chest wound should be treated immediately with high-concentration oxygen, an occlusive dressing, and breath sound monitoring. The EMT–Basic should monitor the occlusive dressing and the patient's response to the treatment. In some cases, the occlusive dressing may cause increased difficulty in breathing. This is due to a developing tension pneumothorax. If increased difficult breathing develops, the EMT–Basic should release the dressing occasionally to release trapped air. Splinting of the chest using the patient's right arm is not part of the treatment.

8. **The correct answer is (C).** A hemopneumothorax is defined as air and blood trapped in the lungs. Blood in the lungs is especially dangerous, as the lungs are considered a "potential space." This means that excessive bleeding in that area can result in hypoperfusion and shock. This type of bleeding may be difficult to assess from the outside; however, detailed assessment of breath sounds will tip off the EMT–Basic that a hemothorax has developed. Breath sounds in hemothorax are usually absent, and gurgling may be heard on the affected side.

9. **The correct answer is (C).** The treatment of an abdominal evisceration includes administration of high-concentration oxygen, an occlusive dressing, and moist sterile dressings. In addition, the EMT–Basic should assess frequently for shock and transport immediately. Application of a dry sterile dressing is not part of the treatment.

10. **The correct answer is (C).** Burns are classified as superficial, partial thickness, and full thickness. Superficial burns cause reddening to the affected area, while partial thickness burns cause reddening and blistering. Full thickness burns are characterized by redness, blistering, and charring of the affected area.

11. **The correct answer is (D).** See rationale, question 10.

12. **The correct answer is (A).** See rationale, question 10.

13. **The correct answer is (C).** Whenever a patient is involved in a fire and has associated burn injury, the EMT–Basic should immediately assess the status of the patient's airway. This assessment should include a visual inspection of the area of the mouth and nose for burns and black soot. Included in this assessment should be a visual inspection of the mouth and monitoring of breath sounds for developing wheezes.

14. **The correct answer is (C).** In this patient, the rule of nines includes both arms and the anterior chest and abdomen. Each arm is 9 percent of the burn area, the chest is another 9 percent, and the abdomen is 9 percent. The total is 36 percent.

15. **The correct answer is (C).** The rule of nines for a child is different from that of an adult. This child has burns on his anterior chest and back as well as the head. The chest accounts for 18 percent, the back is another 18 percent, and the head is 18 percent. This makes the total burn area of this child 54 percent. In the child, the head accounts for a larger surface area due to the fact that the head is bigger in a child.

16. **The correct answer is (D).** Burns to the hands, feet, genitalia, and airway are always considered critical. Although they may only account for a small percentage of total body surface areas burned, these need immediate treatment.

17. **The correct answer is (B).** Application of moist sterile dressings is not recommended for the treatment of burns. The EMT–Basic should keep the area clean and apply dry sterile dressing, monitor the airway, and maintain the body temperature of the burn patient.

18. **The correct answer is (B).** Airway management is always the first priority in the care of any patient. The EMT–Basic should be aware that in an electrical burn, the patient might develop cardiac arrhythmias from the electrical current. The EMT–Basic should be alert for a patient in cardiac arrest from electrical burns. The use of the AED is indicated in the treatment of these patients.

19. **The correct answer is (C).** The EMT–Basic should never attempt to remove an impaled object from any part of the body excepting the cheek. Removal of an impaled object could result in massive bleeding that may have been prevented by the object. As we cannot know the angle of the object in most cases, removal of the object can also cause additional injury.

20. **The correct answer is (B).** The EMT–Basic should never remove a partially amputated part. The treatment of a partial amputation is to wrap the limb in dry sterile dressings and transport the patient to an appropriate treatment facility.

Musculoskeletal Care

1. **The correct answer is (A).** The appendicular skeleton consists of all the skeletal parts of the extremities, while the axial skeleton consists of the bones of the skull, spinal column, and the ribs.

2. **The correct answer is (D).** The following bones are all included in the upper extremities: humerus, radius, ulna, carpals, metacarpals, and phalanges (fingers). Metatarsals are the bones of the foot.

3. **The correct answer is (C).** While any closed fracture may result in blood loss, a fracture to the pelvis can result in a large amount of blood loss. It is not uncommon to lose one to two liters (20 to 33 percent) of blood volume due to this type of injury. Any time the EMT–Basic suspects a fracture to the pelvic area, a consideration should be made as to how much associated blood loss may be endured. The EMT–Basic should assess the patient for signs of shock and treat accordingly.

4. **The correct answer is (B).** To properly immobilize a bone, the EMT–Basic should immobilize the joints above and below the fracture site. This will ensure that no movement of the bone will be possible. Unless the patient has other critical injuries, there should be no attempt to move the patient until painful and swollen limbs have been properly immobilized.

5. **The correct answer is (C).** If, after a splint is applied, the patient suffers from any type of numbness or tingling in that extremity, the EMT–Basic should reapply the splint a second time with less pressure. Applying a splint too tightly can cause nerve and blood vessel damage.

6. **The correct answer is (D).** The traction splint is indicated for long bone fractures of the lower extremity. This includes open fractures. Injuries to the pelvis, acetabulum, and knee are not treated with traction splint application.

7. **The correct answer is (B).** Fractures due to falling on an outstretched arm are known as colles fractures. A colles fracture takes on what is called a dinner fork shape and has a classic and unique presentation. This fracture should be splinted on a position of function and the patient transported for additional medical care.

Injuries to the Head and Spine

1. **The correct answer is (A).** The cervical spine consists of seven vertebrae. Injury to higher vertebrae of the cervical spine can cause an immediate threat to the patient's life. It is of the utmost importance that the EMT–Basic identifies potential cervical spinal fractures and immobilizes them accordingly.

2. **The correct answer is (C).** The brain and spinal cord make up the central nervous system. The nerves and nerve pathways in the body are collectively known as the nervous system. The twelve cranial nerves are part of the central nervous system; however, they are not independently known as the central nervous system.

3. **The correct answer is (B).** A concussion is a mild head injury that may occur after a patient strikes her head on another object. Signs and symptoms of a concussion are headache and lethargy as well as possible loss of consciousness. Concussions may range from mild to severe based on symptoms but never result in permanent brain damage.

4. **The correct answer is (D).** Epidural hematoma is bleeding above the dura mater in the brain. This bleeding is almost always arterial in nature and can result in severe brain damage in a very short period of time. Based on the fact that the bleeding is arterial in nature, the bleeding is at high pressure and develops a rapidly expanding hematoma that may cause irreversible damage.

5. **The correct answer is (A).** Subdural hematomas always occur below the dura mater ("sub" dural) and are almost always venous in nature. A subdural hematoma can take longer to become symptomatic than an epidural hematoma. In some cases, it may take several days for a patient to develop symptoms from a subdural hematoma. Development of symptoms is directly related to the amount of internal bleeding.

6. **The correct answer is (C).** Intracerebral hematomas are defined as bleeding that occurs within the brain itself. While subdural and epidural hematomas actually occur in the protective tissues that are above the brain, the intracerebral hematoma is bleeding within the brain tissue itself.

7. **The correct answer is (B).** Any patient who suffers from severe facial injury should be monitored for airway compromise. Broken bones, blood, and teeth may endanger an open airway. The EMT–Basic must prepare to maintain the airway of a patient with facial injury using any means possible. This may include airway adjuncts and suctioning of the patient's airway at regular intervals during treatment.

8. **The correct answer is (B).** Whenever a patient complains of any loss of sensation, the EMT–Basic should suspect spinal injury above the level of the sensation loss. In this case, the patient is complaining of sensation loss from the neck down. This is a good indication that the injury to the spinal cord is in the cervical area. Treatment of this patient would include aggressive airway management and full spinal immobilization.

9. **The correct answer is (C).** The Glasgow coma scale uses a chart and numbering system to assess a patient's status. The scale uses the patient's ability to respond to commands. It measures eye opening, verbal response, and motor response.

10. **The correct answer is (A).** In all cases of suspected cervical spine injury and cases in which a patient is unconscious from an unknown cause, the EMT–Basic should open the patient's airway using the jaw thrust maneuver (modified jaw thrust). This maneuver allows opening of the airway while maintaining cervical spinal stabilization.

11. **The correct answer is (C).** Any patient with suspected cervical spinal injury should be immobilized with a short board or a KED prior to removal from a seated position in a vehicle. The EMT–Basic should take precautions not to endanger the cervical spine by omitting the use of these devices. Rapid extrication to a long board is indicated only in cases of severe trauma where the patient is critical.

12. **The correct answer is (B).** All patients involved in motor vehicle accidents where there is a rollover should be immobilized, regardless of complaint. The fact that this patient is already standing does not make a difference. The rapid takedown procedure should be used to immobilize any patient that is standing at the scene of a collision with any hint of major mechanism of injury.

13. **The correct answer is (B).** The EMT–Basic should attempt to remove a helmet only if it interferes with airway management. Most helmets today, excepting full-face guard helmets, allow the EMT–Basic to maintain an airway while securing the patient to a long board with the helmet on. Any patient who has a manageable airway and can be immobilized with a helmet on should be immobilized as such. Removal of a helmet may worsen a previously unidentified spinal injury.

14. **The correct answer is (B).** The key to diagnosis of this patient is the history of present illness. Bystanders stated that the patient was walking and just sat down. There was no report or sign of any trauma. This patient is probably suffering from a medical cause of brain injury, which can be field diagnosed as a cerebrovascular accident.

15. **The correct answer is (B).**

16. **The correct answer is (A).**

17. **The correct answer is (C).**

18. **The correct answer is (A).**

19. **The correct answer is (C).**

20. **The correct answer is (B).**

Rationale, questions 15–20

This patient is exhibiting inappropriate behavior several days after a head injury. The patient never received medical attention and went home. After the patient loses consciousness, the EMT–Basic should assist him by doing a complete primary assessment. This consists of the A, B, C's and then a neurological assessment. After the neurological assessment, the patient should be immobilized to a long spine board with a cervical collar applied. Based on the patient's delayed response to injury, the EMT–Basic should be able to effectively rule out an epidural hematoma, as they are rapid arterial bleeds. A concussion will not present with severe symptoms several days later. A cervical spinal injury will not cause inappropriate behavior if it is isolated to the cervical spine. However, a subdural hematoma, which is bleeding slowly from a venous source, can surely cause this type of behavior. A subdural hematoma may take hours or even days to develop, with neurological symptoms being delayed. Treatment for this patient includes high-concentration oxygen, airway management, and rapid transport to the hospital.

Chapter 7

INFANTS AND CHILDREN

In this chapter, the EMT–Basic will review questions based on Module 6 of the National Standard Curriculum. This module concerns infants and children. The EMT–Basic should answer the questions, then review the answers and rationales. Additional information may be accessed from your course textbook.

1. The major cause of death in children over one year of age is

   (A) respiratory disease.
   (B) trauma.
   (C) respiratory failure.
   (D) cardiovascular diseases.

2. Which pediatric age group has a fear of permanent injury or death?

   (A) Birth to 1 year
   (B) 1 to 3 years
   (C) 3 to 6 years
   (D) 6 to 12 years

3. Which pediatric age group may not cooperate with the EMT–Basic during a physical examination?

   (A) 12 to 18 years
   (B) Birth to 1 year
   (C) 6 to 12 years
   (D) 1 to 3 years

4. In a child, the proper insertion of an oropharyngeal airway is

   (A) with the tip facing the nose, then twisted, as in an adult.
   (B) with the tip facing sideways, then twisted down into the oropharynx.
   (C) with the tip facing the chin and inserted along the anatomy.
   (D) oropharyngeal airways are not used in children.

5. The major cause of cardiac arrest in the pediatric patient is

   (A) respiratory insufficiency.
   (B) congenital disorders.
   (C) sleep apnea.
   (D) heart disease.

6. The child in respiratory distress should be treated with

   (A) positive pressure ventilation.
   (B) high-concentration oxygen by mask.
   (C) blow by oxygen.
   (D) low-concentration oxygen.

7. The child in respiratory failure should be treated with

 (A) positive pressure ventilation.
 (B) high-concentration oxygen by mask.
 (C) blow by oxygen.
 (D) low-concentration oxygen.

8. Signs of compensated shock in the pediatric patient include all of the following EXCEPT

 (A) rapid pulse.
 (B) dry mucous membranes.
 (C) decreased output of urine.
 (D) decreased blood pressure.

9. The pediatric patient with an altered mental status, rapid respiratory rate, and delayed capillary refill is probably suffering from

 (A) compensated shock.
 (B) decompensated shock.
 (C) decreased blood sugar.
 (D) head injury.

10. The most common cause of seizures in an otherwise healthy child is

 (A) epilepsy.
 (B) trauma.
 (C) fever.
 (D) hypoxia.

11. Which of the following is not an appropriate treatment for a child in shock?

 (A) Elevating the legs
 (B) Maintaining body temperature
 (C) Administering fluids by mouth
 (D) Administering high-concentration oxygen

12. You respond to a private residence for an unconscious child. On your arrival, you find a child lying on the bedroom floor bleeding from the head. You complete your assessment and notice that the child has bruises in various stages of healing. You suspect

 (A) child abuse.
 (B) that bruising is normal for children.
 (C) that the child fell and has a head injury.
 (D) that the child has a medical condition that causes bruising.

13. Children with a history of child abuse will usually be outspoken and friendly.

 (A) True
 (B) False

14. In dealing with the death of a child, it is important for the EMT–Basic to

 (A) accept it as part of the job and move on.
 (B) discuss her feelings about the situation with her partner or co-worker.
 (C) spend the night out with friends at the local tavern.
 (D) go home after work, take a sleep aid, and go to bed.

ANSWER SHEET

Chapter 7: Infants and Children

Infants and Children

1. Ⓐ Ⓑ Ⓒ Ⓓ
2. Ⓐ Ⓑ Ⓒ Ⓓ
3. Ⓐ Ⓑ Ⓒ Ⓓ
4. Ⓐ Ⓑ Ⓒ Ⓓ
5. Ⓐ Ⓑ Ⓒ Ⓓ
6. Ⓐ Ⓑ Ⓒ Ⓓ
7. Ⓐ Ⓑ Ⓒ Ⓓ
8. Ⓐ Ⓑ Ⓒ Ⓓ
9. Ⓐ Ⓑ Ⓒ Ⓓ
10. Ⓐ Ⓑ Ⓒ Ⓓ
11. Ⓐ Ⓑ Ⓒ Ⓓ
12. Ⓐ Ⓑ Ⓒ Ⓓ
13. Ⓐ Ⓑ
14. Ⓐ Ⓑ Ⓒ Ⓓ

ANSWERS TO CHAPTER 7

Infants and Children

1. B	8. D
2. D	9. B
3. D	10. C
4. C	11. C
5. A	12. A
6. B	13. B
7. A	14. B

RATIONALES FOR THE ANSWERS

1. **The correct answer is (B).** Traumatic injury is the leading cause of death in children of all age groups. Trauma kills more children every year than all other causes of childhood death combined. The goal of preventing death from trauma in childhood is prevention. The EMT–Basic should become active in his community in injury prevention programs in order to reduce the number of pediatric trauma deaths.

2. **The correct answer is (D).** Children 6 to 12 years have the greatest fear of disfigurement and death. The child in this age group is impressionable and does not fully understand what is going on when she is sick or injured. She may have seen a similar injury on television or on a friend, or she may associate another type of injury with her injury. The EMT–Basic should approach children with honesty and alleviate fears that they may be expressing.

3. **The correct answer is (D).** Pediatric patients in the 1- to 3-year categories are not comfortable with being touched by strangers. The EMT–Basic should approach these patients with a calming demeanor and attempt to do an examination from toe to head. It is a good idea to have the parent hold a child in this age group to facilitate a calming atmosphere. At no time should the EMT–Basic separate the child from the parent; this will only worsen the situation.

4. **The correct answer is (C).** The oropharyngeal airway should be inserted with the tip facing the chin and then inserted along the anatomy. This is the opposite of the adult procedure in which the airway is inserted upside down and then twisted into the airway.

5. **The correct answer is (A).** The major cause of cardiac arrest in pediatric patients is due to some form of respiratory insufficiency. This can be due to respiratory infections, asthma attacks, or any other pathophysiological or structural defect causing respiratory distress. The EMT–Basic should ensure that the pediatric patient has an open airway at all times and is well oxygenated.

6. **The correct answer is (B).** Any child in respiratory distress should be treated with high-concentration oxygen. In respiratory distress, the child is still breathing sufficiently on his own. The EMT–Basic can deliver supplemental oxygen by mask. High-concentration oxygen is indicated in all cases of respiratory distress. There is no contraindication to oxygen administration in these patients.

7. **The correct answer is (A).** Children in respiratory failure should be treated with positive pressure ventilation by way of a bag-valve-mask ventilator. In respiratory failure, the child has already lost the ability to support her own ventilations. Ominous signs are grunting and head bobbing. Positive pressure ventilation with high-concentration oxygen will support the ventilations of the child until definitive care can be initiated.

8. **The correct answer is (D).** Decreased blood pressure is a late sign of shock in children and adults. The EMT–Basic should be aware of subtle signs of compensated shock in a child. Signs of dehydration are early signs of shock. The child with a history of diarrhea or vomiting should be suspect of compensated shock. Sunken fontanels in infants are also a sign of dehydration as well as compensated shock.

9. **The correct answer is (B).** The child in decompensated shock will present with alterations of mental states, and increased respiratory rates. The EMT–Basic must be aware that falling blood pressure is an ominous late sign and should be avoided at all costs. Interventions should be attempted to prevent blood pressure drop and circulatory collapse. Pediatric patients compensate for volume loss longer than an adult, but decompensation is rapid and usually irreversible.

10. **The correct answer is (C).** Pediatric patients who suffer from a seizure and have no history of seizures are usually having a response to fever. The seizure is not related to the actual temperature, but the rate at which the temperature rises. Rapid temperature increase will cause the patients to seize. This seizure will present as a tonic clonic seizure, otherwise known as a grand mal seizure. Care for this patient is airway management, cooling, and transport to the hospital. The EMT–Basic must not lose sight of the fact that the seizure may be associated with meningitis, which can also cause fever.

11. **The correct answer is (C).** The EMT–Basic should never attempt to administer fluids by mouth to any patient in shock. This can cause vomiting and airway compromise. The goal in treating the child in shock is to maintain airway, blood pressure, and body temperature. Prevention of hypothermia, even on a warm day, is essential to survival of the child. Airway and oxygenation are of greatest importance in the treatment of pediatric shock patients.

12. **The correct answer is (A).** A child who has bruises in various stages of healing, especially when the child is unconscious from a head injury, is a definite suspect for an abused child. The EMT–Basic should treat the child and withhold personal feelings toward the parents. The priority is to assist the child and get them to definitive care, not to confront the parents.

13. **The correct answer is (B).** The child with a history of abuse will usually be quiet, not cry from painful injuries, and be generally withdrawn from the situation. The EMT–Basic should treat any life-threatening injuries and transport the patient to definitive care. On arrival at the emergency department, the EMT–Basic should report all findings to the emergency department staff for investigation by the proper authorities.

14. **The correct answer is (B).** The death of a child is one of the most difficult aspects of a career in EMS. The EMT–Basic will be facing a variety of feelings after the death of a child. The best way to deal with this type of situation is to discuss it with your partner or loved ones. Alcohol and drug use will only compound the problem and add to the grief that the EMT–Basic will be feeling. At no time should you accept this or any other traumatic event as part of the job. The EMT–Basic must realize that she is human, and she will respond emotionally to emotional situations. Discussion or participation in critical incident stress debriefing is essential to healthy living in the world of EMS.

Chapter 8

OPERATIONS

In this chapter, the EMT–Basic will review questions based on Module 7 of the National Standard Curriculum. This module concerns EMS Operations. The EMT–Basic should answer the questions, and then review the answers and rationales. Additional information may be accessed from your course textbook.

AMBULANCE OPERATIONS

1. Choose the following true statement about the use of excessive speed when responding to an emergency call.

   (A) Excessive speed increases the chance of an accident.
   (B) Excessive speed is indicated in true emergencies.
   (C) Excessive speed cuts down response time.
   (D) Excessive speed is permitted, if using due regard.

2. You are responding to an emergency call down a one-way street with a passing lane, when you come upon a school bus that is loading children. Which of the following would be the correct action to take?

   (A) Make sure your sirens are on, and pass the school bus with caution.
   (B) Announce over the ambulance address system that nobody should move, then pass.
   (C) Stop your vehicle, and wait to be waved on by the bus driver.
   (D) There is no requirement on stopping for a school bus.

3. All of the following factors will affect response to an emergency call EXCEPT

   (A) construction zones.
   (B) clear, dry roads.
   (C) rain and wind.
   (D) icy conditions.

4. Which of the following pieces of information is not part of essential dispatch information given to the EMT–Basic?

   (A) Address of the call
   (B) Type of emergency
   (C) Patient's medical history
   (D) Telephone number of the caller

5. When is it appropriate to notify the receiving hospital of the patient's condition?

   (A) During the response phase
   (B) During the treatment phase
   (C) During the transport phase
   (D) During the delivery phase

6. Which of the following describes high-level disinfection?

   (A) The killing of pathogens by using a potent means of disinfection
   (B) The killing of pathogens by application of heat
   (C) The killing of pathogens by the application of a pathogenic aerosol or spray
   (D) Washing and showering after a call where the EMT–Basic was spattered with blood

7. Which of the following describes sterilization?

   (A) The killing of pathogens by using a potent means of disinfection
   (B) The killing of pathogens by application of heat
   (C) The killing of pathogens by the application of a pathogenic aerosol or spray
   (D) Washing and showering after a call where the EMT–Basic was spattered with blood

8. The written run report is prepared during which phase of response?

   (A) The transport phase
   (B) The post-run phase
   (C) The delivery phase
   (D) The treatment phase

9. When operating at the scene of a helicopter evacuation, the EMT–Basic should always approach the helicopter from

   (A) the rear.
   (B) the side.
   (C) the front.
   (D) The EMT–Basic should not approach a helicopter.

10. Which of the following is not a part of the post-run phase?

   (A) Cleaning the vehicle
   (B) Notification of availability for the next run
   (C) Equipment restocking
   (D) Patient documentation

GAINING ACCESS

1. During extrication of a patient from a motor vehicle, what is the first priority for the EMT–Basic?

   (A) Stabilizing the vehicle
   (B) Establishing if vehicle entry is safe for the rescue crew
   (C) Blocking traffic
   (D) Establishing a command sector at the incident

2. Which of the following is not a component of vehicle rescue?

   (A) Hazard management
   (B) Vehicle stabilization
   (C) Patient removal
   (D) Traffic control

3. The initial phase of vehicle extrication begins with

   (A) gaining access.
   (B) size-up.
   (C) stabilizing the vehicle.
   (D) patient packaging.

4. Which of the following best describes a complex access scene?

   (A) A motor vehicle collision in which the patient's foot is pinned
   (B) A building collapse in which a large piece of cement has a man pinned by the legs
   (C) A woman with her hand trapped in a machine
   (D) A man whose car has fallen on his arm

5. You respond to a call for a man pinned by a tractor. On your arrival, you find that the tractor has flipped over and the man's leg has been pinned under the front of the tractor. His vital signs are stable, and he is complaining of only moderate pain. This scene is known as a

   (A) simple access scene.
   (B) complex access scene.
   (C) medium access scene.
   (D) This scene is not rated.

OVERVIEWS

1. Which of the following statements best describes a disaster?

   (A) A disaster is an incident that produces more than 100 patients.
   (B) A disaster affects multiple geographic regions or damages the infrastructure of one region.
   (C) A disaster is any incident that produces multiple patients.
   (D) A disaster is only naturally occurring.

2. A mass casualty incident is best defined as

   (A) any incident that taxes the resources of a given area.
   (B) any incident that produces more than ten patients.
   (C) an incident that involves mass transportation.
   (D) a terrorist event.

3. All of the following are responsibilities of the EMT–Basic at the scene of a hazardous materials incident EXCEPT

   (A) recognizing the incident.
   (B) establishing scene control.
   (C) mitigating the hazardous material.
   (D) establishing a treatment sector.

4. On the NFPA hazardous materials classification chart, the color blue stands for

   (A) health hazard.
   (B) fire hazard.
   (C) specific hazard.
   (D) reactivity.

5. On the NFPA hazardous materials classification chart, the color red stands for

   (A) health hazard.
   (B) fire hazard.
   (C) specific hazard.
   (D) reactivity.

6. At a mass casualty incident, the incident commander is responsible for

   (A) command and control of the entire incident.
   (B) command of communications only.
   (C) command of transport only.
   (D) command of patient care only.

7. You are assigned to the treatment area at a mass casualty incident. You report directly to

   (A) the incident commander.
   (B) the triage officer.
   (C) the treatment officer.
   (D) the transportation officer.

8. Under the triage tag system, the color black refers to

   (A) a dead or unsalvageable patient.
   (B) a high-priority patient.
   (C) a low-priority patient.
   (D) a patient requiring no intervention.

9. Under the triage tag system, the color red refers to

   (A) a dead or unsalvageable patient.
   (B) a high-priority patient.
   (C) a low-priority patient.
   (D) a patient requiring no intervention.

10. At a hazardous materials incident, the hot zone refers to the

    (A) treatment area.
    (B) decontamination area.
    (C) area of the spill or event.
    (D) staging area.

ANSWER SHEET

Chapter 8: Operations

Ambulance Operations

1. Ⓐ Ⓑ Ⓒ Ⓓ
2. Ⓐ Ⓑ Ⓒ Ⓓ
3. Ⓐ Ⓑ Ⓒ Ⓓ
4. Ⓐ Ⓑ Ⓒ Ⓓ
5. Ⓐ Ⓑ Ⓒ Ⓓ
6. Ⓐ Ⓑ Ⓒ Ⓓ
7. Ⓐ Ⓑ Ⓒ Ⓓ
8. Ⓐ Ⓑ Ⓒ Ⓓ
9. Ⓐ Ⓑ Ⓒ Ⓓ
10. Ⓐ Ⓑ Ⓒ Ⓓ

Gaining Access

1. Ⓐ Ⓑ Ⓒ Ⓓ
2. Ⓐ Ⓑ Ⓒ Ⓓ
3. Ⓐ Ⓑ Ⓒ Ⓓ
4. Ⓐ Ⓑ Ⓒ Ⓓ
5. Ⓐ Ⓑ Ⓒ Ⓓ

Overviews

1. Ⓐ Ⓑ Ⓒ Ⓓ
2. Ⓐ Ⓑ Ⓒ Ⓓ
3. Ⓐ Ⓑ Ⓒ Ⓓ
4. Ⓐ Ⓑ Ⓒ Ⓓ
5. Ⓐ Ⓑ Ⓒ Ⓓ
6. Ⓐ Ⓑ Ⓒ Ⓓ
7. Ⓐ Ⓑ Ⓒ Ⓓ
8. Ⓐ Ⓑ Ⓒ Ⓓ
9. Ⓐ Ⓑ Ⓒ Ⓓ
10. Ⓐ Ⓑ Ⓒ Ⓓ

ANSWERS TO CHAPTER 8

Ambulance Operations	Gaining Access	Overviews
1. A	1. B	1. B
2. C	2. D	2. A
3. B	3. B	3. C
4. C	4. B	4. A
5. C	5. A	5. B
6. A		6. A
7. B		7. C
8. C		8. A
9. C		9. B
10. D		10. C

RATIONALES FOR THE ANSWERS
Ambulance Operations

1. **The correct answer is (A).** The use of excessive speed in response to any emergency increases the chances of an accident with another vehicle. Driving an ambulance requires sharp driving skills, and using excessive speed reduces reaction time. There is no indication for the use of excessive speed while responding to or from any emergency call.

2. **The correct answer is (C).** When responding to an emergency call, the driver of the ambulance must drive with due regard for the safety of others. Law requires that an ambulance pause for a stopped school bus and wait until waved on by the bus driver.

3. **The correct answer is (B).** The EMT–Basic will be expected to respond to calls in adverse weather conditions. Adverse weather, as well as construction and road closing, will all affect response and safety. It is a good idea to find out about planned road closings and adjust your response accordingly. Bad weather conditions call for a slower and safer response. You must remember that wet roads increase stopping distances. Careful driving is the key to safety.

4. **The correct answer is (C).** Dispatch information given to the EMT–Basic varies by region. The EMT–Basic should receive the following information for every call:

   Type of call
   Name and location of caller
   Telephone number of caller
   Number of patients
   Patient condition

In some cases, the dispatcher may advise the responding ambulance of construction closings and weather advisories during the assignment. The EMT–Basic should be aware that he might request additional information from the dispatcher by way of a call back to the address of the emergency.

5. **The correct answer is (C).** The EMT–Basic should radio the hospital with patient conditions while transporting. Earlier notice may be given in the event of a special operation, such as a mass casualty incident; however, in a single patient emergency, the notification should be transmitted while en route to the hospital. En route, the EMT–Basic has already collected vital information and can easily deliver it to the receiving hospital.

6. **The correct answer is (A).** High-level disinfection is the killing of pathogens by using a potent means of disinfection. Application of heat to kill pathogens is known as sterilization, and using a spray or aerosol to kill pathogens is defined as disinfection. The EMT–Basic should have an awareness of when each level of disinfection is appropriate and should initiate the proper levels at all times.

7. **The correct answer is (B).** Sterilization is defined as application of heat to kill pathogens. Many surfaces and contaminated equipment can be cleaned using high-level disinfection or regular disinfection. There are certain pieces of equipment that must be cleaned by sterilization. As an EMT–Basic, you should have full knowledge of which equipment must be sterilized and which equipment may be safely disinfected.

8. **The correct answer is (C).** After patient delivery to the hospital, and before the post-run phase begins, the EMT–Basic is required to complete a run sheet to document patient care. This run sheet should not be completed during the transport phase due to the fact that the EMT–Basic should be tending to the patient and not to paperwork. All documentation should be accurate and comprehensive regarding all aspects of the emergency call.

9. **The correct answer is (C).** While operating during a MEDEVAC (helicopter evacuation), you should always approach the helicopter from the front, and then only when waved on by the pilot. Helicopter blades have a great degree of tilt and may cause serious injury or even death to the unknowing EMS provider. It is always a good rule to wait for the pilot to give the all-clear signal before approaching.

10. **The correct answer is (D).** Patient documentation should always be done during the delivery phase. After delivery to the hospital and after all paperwork is complete, the EMT–Basic must clean and restock the vehicle for the next emergency call. As soon as the vehicle is ready, the dispatcher should be notified so that your unit may be assigned to another call.

Gaining Access

1. **The correct answer is (B).** In all cases of emergency response, safety of the rescuers is the highest priority. You should always ensure that the vehicle is properly stabilized, there are no hazardous materials or scene hazards that may injure you or your partner, and you are wearing the proper protective equipment. In many regions, specialized units perform vehicle rescues and other extrications. If the EMT–Basic is not trained in extrication, then he should remain clear of the extrication and await patient delivery.

2. **The correct answer is (D).** The EMT–Basic should not be involved in traffic control unless there are no police agencies on the scene and then only if traffic poses a potential risk to the operation.

3. **The correct answer is (B).** Size-up of all calls should begin as soon as the assignment is given to you. The EMT–Basic should perform a scene size-up immediately after arrival at an incident. Size-up includes determination of the number of patients, patient condition, additional resources needed, and scene hazards. A complete size-up should be done at all scenes, and the scene should be re-assessed several times during any operation.

4. **The correct answer is (B).** In cases where heavy chunks of debris or heavy machinery are involved, and the rescue will take more than the typical rescue equipment, the scene is labeled a complex access scene. A building collapse poses special hazards as well as complex access patients. Building stability and the possibility of falling debris is always a factor in the safety of the scene.

5. **The correct answer is (A).** This is a simple access scene due to the fact that the patient is pinned by his leg, and basic extrication equipment should be sufficient to safely extricate him. Treatment involves stabilization and extrication from the site.

Overviews

1. **The correct answer is (B).** A disaster may be a naturally occurring event or an event caused by man-made means. A disaster may not always produce multiple patients; in fact, it may not produce any patients. A disaster will, however, damage the area's infrastructure. Communications, basic, and even emergency services systems may be incapacitated by the results of a disaster.

2. **The correct answer is (A).** The definition of a mass casualty incident varies from region to region. In some regions, it is any incident that produces more than a given number of patients. The national definition of a mass casualty incident is an incident that produces more patients than can be handled by the initial response agency or any incident that taxes the resources of a given area.

3. **The correct answer is (C).** The job of the EMT–Basic is to provide patient care. Any and all responsibilities in regard to caring for the patient fall within that realm. Mitigation is not the job of the EMT–Basic. Hazardous materials specialists are specially trained teams of individuals that will deal with the hazard and secure it safely. The EMT–Basic in an emergency vehicle does not have the necessary equipment to handle a situation such as a hazardous materials incident.

4. **The correct answer is (A).** The NFPA (National Fire Protection Association) has developed the Hazardous Materials Classification chart to assist emergency responders in determining the hazard of a given material. Although this chart does not identify a specific substance, it can afford a rescuer the information needed to assess the severity of an incident. The color blue is for health hazards, red for fire hazards, yellow for reactivity of the agent (example: reacts violently with water), and white is a specific hazard (example: acid, alkali, etc.). Finding this placard on any material should tip off the EMT–Basic of a hazardous materials incident.

5. **The correct answer is (B).** See rationale, question 4.

6. **The correct answer is (A).** The incident commander is in command of the entire incident. Under the incident command system, sectors are set up to coordinate different activities. These sectors are triage, treatment, staging, transportation, and support. Each of these sectors reports directly to the incident commander.

7. **The correct answer is (C).** When assigned to a sector at a mass casualty incident, you would report directly to the officer of that sector. The only person who reports directly to the incident commander is the officer from each sector. This system cuts down on radio traffic by allowing face-to-face communications between sector members and radio communication to the incident commander by sector officers.

8. **The correct answer is (A).** The triage tag system (MET-TAG or other) is designed to identify patients of the highest priority. The color system is universal and is as follows:

   Black—Dead or unsalvageable
   Red—High priority
   Yellow—Low priority
   Green—Walking wounded, requires no transport

This system is accepted nationally and should be initiated when a mass casualty incident is identified.

9. **The correct answer is (B).** See rationale, question 8.

10. **The correct answer is (C).** There are three zones identified in a hazardous materials incident:

    The Hot Zone—area of the incident, spill, or dissemination of the hazardous material.
    The Warm Zone—area outside, but surrounding the hot zone.
    The Cold Zone—area that is deemed safe to operate

Decontamination is usually done in the warm zone on the border of the cold zone. The EMT–Basic should be aware of the designated sectors and remain in his assigned sector. Without protective clothing (level A or B), the EMT–Basic should never be in the hot or warm zone.

Chapter 9
EMT–BASIC SKILLS AND EVALUATION

GUIDELINES FOR TAKING A PRACTICAL SKILLS EXAMINATION

The process of certification as an EMT–Basic includes the demonstration of competence in the performance of the practical skills that will be used in the field to perform patient care. The EMT–Basic should have a good working knowledge of these skills and should have had sufficient opportunity to practice these skills during his training program. Most states do not allow a candidate to sit for a written examination until he has demonstrated competence in skills performance. This chapter will review how to develop competence in these skills and lend advice on how to pass the practical skills examination.

THE PRACTICAL SKILLS

Typically, the required practical skills for the EMT–Basic include

Patient assessment–Medical
Patient assessment–Trauma
Airway management skills–Bag valve mask ventilation
Airway management skills–Oxygen administration
Airway management skills–Suctioning
Airway management skills–Airway adjuncts
Airway management skills–Mouth to mask ventilation
Bleeding and shock–Management of bleeding and shock
Fracture management–Long bone splinting
Fracture management–Traction splinting
Fracture management–Joint injuries
Spinal immobilization–Seated patient
Spinal immobilization–Lying Patient
Cardiac arrest management–Use of the AED

Some states add additional requirements to the list of skills above.

Many of these skills are performed while at the same testing station; for example, airway skills may be performed on a continuing scenario-based testing station where all the skills would be performed at the same station. These types of practical examinations base the testing station on a single scenario, allowing the EMT–Basic to assess and manage a patient with a developing "difficult airway" problem. The EMT–Basic would be required to assess the airway, and then perform the correct interventions in order to pass the station.

It is always beneficial to learn how the testing will be performed and what will be expected of the candidate. Many training institutions will prepare their candidates for final testing by running their practice stations in the exact way that a testing station is administered.

PRACTICING SKILLS

The EMT–Basic should seek out every opportunity to practice skills. Competence in skills performance will not only help you pass the examination, but it will also help you become a more confident EMT in the field. The more proficiency that you show in the classroom, the better your confidence will be out in the field in an uncontrolled situation.

Practicing skills to a competent level is completed in several ways. In the classroom, it is difficult for all students to get a good amount of time at skills sessions. Usually, there are multiple students in a group, and the group is time controlled before they must move on to a different station. To gain proficiency, the EMT–Basic should practice in the following ways:

1. Take full advantage of practice time afforded in class. Hanging out and talking while others practice is not beneficial for you or your classmates. When it is your turn to practice a skill, take your time, perform the skills while looking at the skill sheet, and make sure that all the steps are followed as stated on the skills performance sheet. Make sure that any critique that is offered by the station instructor is noted and that you work to correct deficiencies on your next round of practice

2. If you feel you need more practice, discuss it with your senior instructor. Many institutions will set up hours for you to attend remediation sessions or allow you to show up early for additional practice time. You can usually request that an instructor be there to assist you in your proficiency.

3. If you belong to an EMS agency, ask one of the senior people there to assist you. Most times, EMS agencies will have equipment for training at the station. This can be extremely helpful, especially if you need a large amount of practice. You can spend hours practicing certain skills with senior members, who will be happy to assist you.

4. Practice your assessment skills at home. Ask a family member to allow you to practice your patient assessment skills while they are relaxing at home. All they need to do is lie down, and you can run through the steps of assessment. This approach is extremely helpful. In addition, it will give your family members insight as to what you are trying to accomplish and how difficult it may be to perform your job as an EMT–Basic. You can also ask a family member to look at the sheet as you go through the steps, advising you of missed items and omissions of intervention.

It is essential that you know the skills performance sheet in its entirety. EMS training institutions will almost always give these sheets to the students early on in the training program so that the student will have ample time to memorize them. Memorization of the sheets will guarantee that you have a firm grip on the knowledge. Once you have a sheet memorized, then, and only then, should you begin attempting to practice skills without looking at the sheet. This is best attempted with an assistant present. Your assistant can stop you when you omit a step and also reinforce good performance. Attempts at skills practice prior to memorization will serve to confuse you and possibly delay your mastery of a particular skill.

It is also advisable to get together with other candidates to compare notes. The best study partner is somebody who is also aspiring to pass the same examination. This person will be just as serious about skills performance as you are, and you may accomplish more.

If you misunderstand the theory behind a skill, consult your textbook. Most EMS textbooks will have a full explanation of skills theory as well as pictures of skills being performed. These may help you immensely in understanding the performance of the skills.

Some final advice on developing skills proficiency: Practice, practice, practice!

There is no replacement for practice time, so use it wisely.

SKILLS EXAMINATION DAY

Just as you would prepare for a written examination, you should prepare for the practical skills examination. This means that you should get plenty of rest the night before the examination. It is never a good idea to stay up all night reading the skills sheets. Reading and studying sheets should be done long before the night prior to the examination. It may be a good idea to get some practice in the night before. Using the suggestions in the practice section of this chapter, the EMT–Basic should go through the skills to smooth out rough edges. This practice session should be very light and lack the pressure and intensity of previous sessions. A review session can be very helpful, if properly executed.

When you arrive at the testing site, make sure you have all the equipment with you that you will need for the examination. Most examination sites will supply everything that you need to complete the skills examination; however, some may require you to have your personal equipment, such as a stethoscope, penlight, pocket mask, and a pair of trauma shears.

Bring your skills sheets with you to look over as you are waiting to be called upon for a station. Once again, this should be a light "going over" of the skills mentally. It is not a good idea to focus on any one skill, as you may be called to perform a different skill.

ENTERING THE SKILLS STATION

Once you enter the skills station, you need to accomplish several things. The first thing is to claim your composure. If you are stressed and nervous, it will affect your performance. Most skills examiners take nervousness into consideration. They have been in your position, so keep that in mind.

If you are nervous, take a deep breath. There is nothing better to reduce stress than a good, long cleansing breath. Take a step back and breathe in deep, hold it, then release it. Try and clear your mind and wait for the examiner to give you your instructions.

Once you have gotten your instructions, the examiner will tell you to look over all the equipment. Look at it. Is it all there? Make sure that you have everything that you need to perform the skills without stopping and asking for additional equipment. It is not a general practice to intentionally remove an essential piece of equipment during testing, but it may have been left out accidentally—so be vigilant.

All skills stations require that the student take infection control precautions. Make sure that at every station, you put on gloves. Omission of infection control precautions is usually a critical failure and will cause the student to fail the station even before they begin. WEAR GLOVES AT ALL STATIONS.

The most important aspect of the skills examination is successfully completing the skill. In mannequin demonstrations, it may be hard for the examiner to actually know what you are doing during an assessment. It is suggested that you verbalize everything that you are doing, even though it is obvious. As you begin your skill, if you are assessing, ask questions such as "I am opening the airway. Is it open?" The examiner will answer you appropriately, confirming that you have completed that part of the station. Continue verbalization throughout the examination.

If the examiner asks you a question, remain calm. It may be part of the test, or she may be giving you a hint that you missed something. Hints are usually not allowed, but they happen. Take advantage of that, and think about what you did in the last twenty seconds, trying to remember if you missed anything. If you don't think you missed anything, don't dwell on it—answer the question and move on. Dwelling on a previous question will throw you off your plan and break your concentration.

When you complete the station, state that you are complete. When the examiner releases you, leave. They will usually not give you results at the station. It is an uncommon practice because if a student fails a station and is told, it will affect their performance at other stations. Move on and finish your other stations. You will get your results soon enough.

Once you leave a station, forget it for now and concentrate on the next station. Keeping the completed station on your mind will leave less room for concentration on the new station. Take a fresh approach to each station as if it is the only station you will test on that day. Then, move on to the next.

At the end of the test, you will be given your results. Keep in mind that even if you fail a station or two, most examinations will allow you to retest only those stations you have failed. Many institutions allow retesting the same day, so you can still get another shot at testing while you're on your game.

EMT–BASIC SKILLS EVALUATION SHEETS

The Skill Sheets

The following skill sheets have been provided with permission from the New York State Department of Health, Bureau of Emergency Medical Services. These are based on the National Standard Curriculum and offer a comprehensive approach to the practical skills. Each sheet will give you a complete set of steps that you need to pass the examination and will outline the critical failures for each station. If your course is going to be using other sheets for testing, do not memorize these sheets. It will only serve to confuse you as to the proper steps required for your examination.

The National Standard Curriculum Templates are commonly used throughout the United States and are the accepted evaluation tool for the EMT–Basic.

STATION

1

PATIENT ASSESSMENT/MANAGEMENT
TRAUMA

INSTRUCTIONS TO THE CANDIDATE

This station is designed to test your ability to perform a patient assessment of a victim of multi-systems trauma and "voice" treat all conditions and injuries discovered. You must conduct your assessment as you would in the field including communicating with your patient. You may remove the patient's clothing down to shorts or swimsuit if you feel it is necessary. As you conduct your assessment, you should verbalize everything you are assessing. Clinical information not obtainable by visual or physical inspection will be given to you after you demonstrate how you would normally gain that information. You may assume that you have two EMTs working with you and that they are correctly carrying out the verbal treatments you indicate. You have 15 minutes to complete this skill station. Do you have any questions?

NOTES

NEW YORK STATE DEPARTMENT OF HEALTH
Emergency Medical Services

EMT/Certified First Responder
Practical Examination

STATION 1	PATIENT ASSESSMENT MANAGEMENT – TRAUMA	Pass _____ Fail _____

Please print.

Candidate _____

Examiner _____ Initials _____

Date _____ Start Time _____ Stop Time _____

		Points:	Possible	Awarded	Comments
SCENE SIZE-UP	Takes, or verbalizes, body substance isolation precautions		C		
	Determines the scene is safe		C		
	Determines the mechanism of injury / nature of illness		I		
	Considers stabilization of spine		C		
INITIAL ASSESSMENT	Verbalizes general impression of the patient		I		
	Determines responsiveness/level of consciousness (AVPU)		I		
	Determines chief complaint/apparent life threats		I		
	Airway and breathing — Assesses and maintains airway		C		
	Initiates appropriate oxygen therapy		C		
	Assures adequate ventilation		C		
	Manages life threats to airway/breathing		C		
	Circulation — Assesses/controls major bleeding		C		
	Assesses pulse		C		
	Assesses skin (color, temperature and condition)		C		
	Assesses airway, breathing & circulation prior to detailed physical exam		C		
	Identifies priority patients/makes transport decision		C		
	Utilized CUPS status determination		I		
FOCUSED HISTORY/ PHYSICAL EXAM/ RAPID ASSMNT.	Selects appropriate assessment (focused or rapid assessment)		I		
	Obtains, baseline vital signs — Pulse Determines rate & quality (+/- 10)		C		
	Respirations Determines rate & quality (+/- 4)		C		
	Blood Pressure systolic & diastolic (+/- 10)		C		
	Obtains S.A.M.P.L.E. history		I		
DETAILED PHYSICAL EXAMINATION	Assesses the head — Inspects and palpates the scalp and ears		I		
	Assesses the eyes		I		
	Assesses the facial area including oral and nasal areas		I		
	Assesses the neck — Inspects and palpates the neck		I		
	Assesses for JVD		I		
	Assesses for tracheal deviation		I		
	Assesses the chest — Inspects		I		
	Palpates		I		
	Auscultates		I		
	Assesses the abdomen/pelvis — Assesses the abdomen		I		
	Assesses the pelvis		I		
	Verbalizes assessment of genitalia/perineum as needed		I		
	Assesses the extremities — Inspects & palpates all 4 extremities (1 pt. ea.)		4		
	Check motor, sensory, distal circulation (1 pt. ea.)		4		
	Assesses the posterior — Assesses thorax		I		
	Assesses lumbar		I		
	Manages secondary injuries & wounds appropriately		I		
	Ongoing Assessment (verbalized) Repeats initial assessment		I		
	Repeats vital signs		I		
	Repeats focused assessment		I		
	Candidate completed station within 15 minute time limit.		C		

Note: *Candidate must complete all critical criteria and receive at least 23 points to pass this station.*

Total to pass 23   Total 33

COMMENTS:

NEW YORK STATE DEPARTMENT OF HEALTH
Emergency Medical Services

STATION
2

PATIENT ASSESSMENT/MANAGEMENT
MEDICAL

INSTRUCTIONS TO THE CANDIDATE

This station is designed to test your ability to perform a patient assessment of a patient with a chief complaint of a medical nature and "voice" treat all conditions discovered. You must conduct your assessment as you would in the field including communicating with your patient. You may remove the patient's clothing down to shorts or swimsuit if you feel it is necessary. As you conduct your assessment, you should verbalize everything you are assessing. Clinical information not obtainable by visual or physical inspection will be given to you after you demonstrate how you would normally gain that information. You may assume that you have two EMTs working with you and that they are correctly carrying out the verbal treatments you indicate. You have 15 minutes to complete this skill station. Do you have any questions?

NOTES

NEW YORK STATE DEPARTMENT OF HEALTH
Emergency Medical Services

EMT/Certified First Responder
Practical Examination

Please print.

STATION 2	PATIENT ASSESSMENT MANAGEMENT – MEDICAL	Pass _____ Fail _____

Candidate _____

Examiner _____ Initials _____

Date _____ Start Time _____ Stop Time _____

		Points: Possible	Awarded	Comments
SCENE SIZE-UP	Takes, or verbalizes, body substance isolation precautions	C		
	Determines the scene is safe	C		
	Determines the mechanism of injury/nature of illness	I		
	Considers stabilization of spine if indicated	I		
ASSESSMENT	Verbalizes general impression of the patient	I		
	Determines responsiveness/level of consciousness (AVPU)	I		
	Determines chief complaint/apparent life threats	I		
	Airway and breathing — Assesses and maintains airway	C		
	Initiates appropriate oxygen therapy	C		
	Assures adequate ventilation	C		
	Circulation — Assesses/controls major bleeding	C		
	Assesses pulse	C		
	Assesses skin (color, temperature and condition)	C		
INITIAL	Assesses airway breathing & circulation prior to focused history/physical exam	C		
	Identifies priority patients/makes transport decision	C		
	Utilized CUPS status determination	I		
	Assesses history of present illness-ask required number of questions	C		

PHYSICAL EXAM

Respiratory	Cardiac	Altered Mental Status	Allergic Reaction	Poisoning /Overdose	Environmental Emergency	Obstetrics	Behavioral
❏ Onset?	❏ Onset?	❏ Description of the episode.	❏ History of allergies?	❏ Substance?	❏ Source?	❏ Are you pregnant?	❏ How do you feel?
❏ Provokes?	❏ Provokes?	❏ Onset?	❏ What were you exposed to?	❏ When did you ingest/become exposed?	❏ Environment?	❏ How long have you been pregnant?	❏ Determine suicidal tendencies.
❏ Quality?	❏ Quality?	❏ Duration?	❏ How were you exposed?	❏ How much did you ingest?	❏ Duration?	❏ Pain or contractions?	❏ Is the patient a threat to self or others?
❏ Radiates?	❏ Radiates?	❏ Associated Symptoms?	❏ Effects?	❏ Over what time period?	❏ Loss of consciousness?	❏ Bleeding or discharge?	❏ Is there a medical problem?
❏ Severity?	❏ Severity?	❏ Evidence of Trauma?	❏ Progression?	❏ Interventions?	❏ Effects of general or local?	❏ Has water broken?	❏ Interventions?
❏ Time?	❏ Time?	❏ Interventions?	❏ Interventions?	❏ Estimated Weight?	(4)	❏ Do you feel the need to push?	(4)
❏ Interventions?	❏ Interventions?	❏ Seizures?	(4)	(5)		❏ Last menstrual period?	
(5)	(5)	❏ Fever?				(5)	
		(6)					

		Possible	Awarded	Comments
HISTORY AND	Signs / symptoms	I		
	Allergies	I		
	Medications	I		
	Past pertinent history	I		
	Last oral intake	I		
	Event leading to present illness (rule out trauma)	I		
	Performs focused physical exam. (consistent with scenario)	I		
	Vitals (obtains baseline vital signs)			
	Pulse — Determines Rate and Quality (+/- 10)	C		
	Respirations — Determines Rate and Quality (+/- 4)	C		
	Blood Pressure — Determines Systolic & Diastolic (+/- 10)	C		
FOCUSED	**TREATMENTS/INTERVENTIONS**			
	(Consistent with New York State and Regional Protocols)	I		
	Did not administer a dangerous or inappropriate intervention	C		
	Transport (re-evaluates the transport decision)	I		
	Verbalizes the consideration of completing a detailed physical examination	I		
	ONGOING ASSESSMENT (verbalized)			
	Repeats initial assessment	I		
	Repeats vital signs	I		
	Repeats focused assessment regarding patient complaint or injuries	I		
	Candidate completed station within the 15 minute time limit	C		

Note: *Candidate must complete all critical criteria and receive at least 13 points to pass this station.*

Total to pass 13   Total 19

NEW YORK STATE DEPARTMENT OF HEALTH
Emergency Medical Services

STATION
3

CARDIAC ARREST MANAGEMENT

INSTRUCTIONS TO THE CANDIDATE

This station is designed to test your ability to manage a prehospital cardiac arrest by integrating CPR skills, defibrillation, airway adjuncts and patient/scene management skills. There will be an EMT assistant in this station. The EMT assistant will only do as you instruct. As you arrive on the scene, you will encounter a patient in cardiac arrest. A first responder will be present performing single rescuer CPR. You must immediately establish control of the scene and begin resuscitation of the patient with an automated external defibrillator. At the appropriate time, the patient's airway must be controlled and you must ventilate or direct the ventilation of the patient using adjunctive equipment. You may use any of the supplies available in this room. You have 15 minutes to complete this skill station. Do you have any questions?

NOTES

NEW YORK STATE DEPARTMENT OF HEALTH
Emergency Medical Services

EMT
Practical Examination

STATION 3	CARDIAC ARREST MANAGEMENT AED

Pass _____
Fail _____

Please print.

Candidate _____

Examiner _____ Initials _____

Date _____ Start Time _____ Stop Time _____

	Points:	Possible	Awarded	Comments
ASSESSMENT				
Takes, or verbalizes, body substance isolation precautions		C		
Briefly questions the rescuer about arrest events		I		
Directs rescuer to stop CPR		I		
Verifies absence of spontaneous pulse (**skill station examiner states "no pulse"**)		C		
Directs resumption of CPR		I		
Turns on defibrillator power		I		
Attaches automated defibrillator to the patient		I		
Directs rescuer to stop CPR		I		
Ensures all individuals are clear of the patient		I		
Initiates analysis of the rhythm		I		
Delivers shock (up to three successive shocks)		C		
Verifies absence of spontaneous pulse (**skill station examiner states "no pulse"**)		I		
TRANSITION				
Directs resumption of CPR		I		
Gathers additional information about arrest event		I		
Verifies effectiveness of CPR (ventilation and compression)		I		
INTEGRATION				
Verbalizes insertion of a simple airway adjunct (oral/nasal airway)		I		
Ventilates the patient		I		
Assures high concentration of oxygen is delivered to the patient		I		
CPR continues without unnecessary/prolonged interruption		I		
Re-evaluates patient in approximately one minute		I		
Candidate verbalizes defibrillation sequence protocol		I		
TRANSPORTATION				
Verbalizes transportation of patient		I		
Candidate initiated first shock within 1 minute of arrival		C		
Assured all individuals were clear of patient before delivering each shock		C		
Directed initiation/resumption of ventilation/compressions at appropriate times		C		
Candidate completed station within the 15 minute time limit		C		

Note: *Candidate must complete all critical criteria and receive at least 13 points to pass this station.*

Total to pass 13   Total 19

COMMENTS:

STATION
4

BAG-VALVE-MASK
APNEIC WITH PULSE

INSTRUCTIONS TO THE CANDIDATE

This station is designed to test your ability to ventilate a patient using a bag-valve-mask. As you enter the station you will find an apneic patient with a palpable central pulse. There are no bystanders and artificial ventilation has not been initiated. The only patient management required is airway management and ventilatory support. You must initially ventilate the patient for a minimum of 30 seconds. You will be evaluated on the appropriateness of ventilatory volumes. I will then inform you that a second rescuer has arrived and will instruct you that you must control the airway and the mask seal while the second rescuer provides ventilation. You may use only the equipment available in this room. You have five minutes to complete this station. Do you have any questions?

NOTES

NEW YORK STATE DEPARTMENT OF HEALTH
Emergency Medical Services

EMT/Certified First Responder Practical Examination

Please print.

STATION 4	BAG-VALVE-MASK APNEIC PATIENT

Pass _____
Fail _____

Candidate _____
Examiner _____ Initials _____
Date _____ Start Time _____ Stop Time _____

Points:	Possible	Awarded	Comments
Takes, or verbalizes, body substance isolation precautions	C		
Opens the airway	I		
Inserts an airway adjunct.	I		
Selects appropriately sized mask	I		
Creates a proper mask-to-face seal	I		
Ventilates patient at no less than 800 ml volume (The examiner must witness for at least 30 seconds)	C		
Candidate ventilated patient prior to connecting supplemental oxygen	C		
Connects reservoir and oxygen	I		
Adjusts liter flow to 15 liters/minute or greater	C		
The examiner indicates arrival of a second EMT The second EMT is instructed to ventilate the patient while the candidate controls the mask and the airway	I		
Reopens the airway	I		
Creates a proper mask-to-face seal	I		
Instructs assistant to resume ventilation at proper volume per breath (The examiner must witness for at least 30 seconds)	I		
Did not interrupt ventilation for more than 20 seconds	C		
Allows for adequate exhalation	C		
Candidate must complete the station within the 5 minute time limit	C		

Note: Candidate must complete all critical criteria and receive at least 6 points to pass this station.

Total to pass 6   Total 9

COMMENTS:

NEW YORK STATE DEPARTMENT OF HEALTH
Emergency Medical Services

SPINAL IMMOBILIZATION SKILLS
SEATED PATIENT

INSTRUCTIONS TO THE CANDIDATE

This station is designed to test your ability to provide spinal immobilization on a patient using a short spine immobilization device. You and an EMT assistant arrive on the scene of an automobile crash. The scene is safe and there is only one patient. The assistant EMT has completed the initial assessment and no critical condition requiring intervention was found. For the purpose of this station, the patient's vital signs remain stable. You are required to treat the specific, isolated problem of an unstable spine using a short spine immobilization device. You are responsible for the direction and subsequent actions of the EMT assistant. Transferring and immobilizing the patient to the long backboard should be accomplished verbally. You have 10 minutes to complete this skill station. Do you have any questions?

NOTES

EMT—Basic Certification Exam

NEW YORK STATE DEPARTMENT OF HEALTH
Emergency Medical Services

EMT
Practical Examination

Please print.

| STATION 5A | SPINAL IMMOBILIZATION SEATED PATIENT | Pass _____ Fail _____ | Candidate _____ Examiner _____ Initials _____ Date _____ Start Time _____ Stop Time _____ |

	Points: Possible	Awarded	Comments
Takes, or verbalizes, body substance isolation precautions	C		
Directs assistant to place and maintain head in the neutral in-line position	C		
Reassesses motor, sensory and circulatory function in each extremity	I		
Applies appropriately sized extrication collar	I		
Positions the immobilization device behind the patient	I		
Secures the device to the patient's torso	I		
Evaluates torso fixation and adjusts as necessary	I		
Evaluates and pads behind the patient's head as necessary	I		
Secures the patient's head to the device	I		
Verbalizes moving the patient to a long board	I		
Reassesses motor, sensory and circulatory function in each extremity	C		
Did not release or order release of manual immobilization before it was maintained mechanically	C		
Patient was not manipulated or moved excessively, to cause potential spinal compromise	C		
Did not move device excessively up, down, left, right on the patient's torso	C		
Head immobilization does not allow for excessive movement	C		
Torso fixation does not inhibit chest rise, resulting in respiratory compromise	C		
Upon completion of immobilization, head is in the neutral position	C		
Immobilized the torso before the head	C		
Candidate completed station within 10 minute time limit	C		

Note: *Candidate must complete all critical criteria and receive at least 6 points to pass this station.*

Total to pass 6   Total 8

COMMENTS:

STATION
5B

SPINAL IMMOBILIZATION- SUPINE PATIENT

INSTRUCTIONS TO THE CANDIDATE

This station is designed to test your ability to provide spinal immobilization on a patient using a long spine immobilization device. You arrive on the scene with an EMT assistant. The assistant EMT has completed the scene size-up as well as the initial assessment and no critical condition was found which would require intervention. For the purpose of this testing station, the patient's vital signs remain stable. You are required to treat the specific problem of an unstable spine using a long spine immobilization device. When moving the patient to the device, you should use the help of the assistant EMT and the evaluator. The assistant EMT should control the head and cervical spine of the patient while you and the evaluator move the patient to the immobilization device. You are responsible for the direction and subsequent action of the EMT assistant. You may use any equipment available in this room. You have 10 minutes to complete this skill station. Do you have any questions?

NOTES

NEW YORK STATE DEPARTMENT OF HEALTH
Emergency Medical Services

EMT/Certified First Responder
Practical Examination

Please print.

| STATION **5B** | SPINAL IMMOBILIZATION SUPINE PATIENT | Pass _____ Fail _____ | Candidate _____ Examiner _____ Initials _____ Date _____ Start Time _____ Stop Time _____ |

	Points: Possible	Awarded	Comments
Takes, or verbalizes, body substance isolation precautions	C		
Directs assistant to place and maintain head in the neutral in-line position	C		
Reassesses motor, sensory and circulatory function in each extremity	I		
Applies appropriately sized extrication collar	I		
Positions the immobilization device appropriately	I		
Directs movement of the patient onto the device without compromising the integrity of the spine	C		
Applies padding to voids between the torso and the board as necessary	I		
Secures the patient's torso to the device	I		
Secures the patient's legs to the device	I		
Secures the patient's head to the device	I		
Secures the patient's arms	I		
Reassesses motor, sensory and circulatory function in each extremity	C		
Did not release or order release of manual immobilization before it was maintained mechanically	C		
Patient was not manipulated or moved excessively, to cause potential spinal compromise	C		
Did not move device excessively up, down, left, right on the patient's torso	C		
Head immobilization does not allow for excessive movement	C		
Upon completion of immobilization, head is in the neutral position	C		
Immobilized the torso before the head	C		
Candidate completed station within 10 minute time limit.	C		

Note: *Candidate must complete all critical criteria and receive at least 6 points to pass this station.*

Total to pass 6   Total 8

COMMENTS:

STATION
6A

IMMOBILIZATION SKILLS – LONG BONE

INSTRUCTIONS TO THE CANDIDATE

This station is designed to test your ability to properly immobilize a closed, non-angulated long bone injury. You are required to treat only the specific, isolated injury to the extremity. The scene size-up and initial assessment have been completed and during the focused assessment a closed, non-angulated injury of the _____ (radius, ulna, tibia, fibula) was detected. Ongoing assessment of the patient's airway, breathing and central circulation is not necessary. You may use any equipment available in this room. You have 10 minutes to complete this skill station. Do you have any questions?

NOTES

NEW YORK STATE DEPARTMENT OF HEALTH
Emergency Medical Services

EMT/Certified First Responder
Practical Examination

Please print.

| STATION **6A** | IMMOBILIZATION SKILLS LONG BONE INJURY | Pass _____ Fail _____ | Candidate _____ Examiner _____ Initials _____ Date _____ Start Time _____ Stop Time _____ |

	Points: Possible	Awarded	Comments
Takes, or verbalizes, body substance isolation precautions	C		
Directs application of manual stabilization of the injury	I		
Assesses motor, sensory and circulatory function in the injured extremity	C		
Note: The examiner acknowledges "motor, sensory and circulatory function are present and normal"			
Measures the splint	I		
Applies the splint	I		
Immobilizes the joint above the injury site	C		
Immobilizes the joint below the injury site	C		
Secures the entire injured extremity	I		
Immobilizes the hand/foot in the position of function	I		
Reassesses motor, sensory and circulatory function in the injured extremity	C		
Note: The examiner acknowledges "motor, sensory and circulatory function are present and normal"			
Candidate did not grossly move the injured extremity	C		
Candidate must complete station within 10 minute time limit	C		

Note: *Candidate must complete all critical criteria and receive at least 4 points to pass this station.*

Total to pass 4   Total 5

COMMENTS:

NEW YORK STATE DEPARTMENT OF HEALTH
Emergency Medical Services

IMMOBILIZATION SKILLS – JOINT INJURY

INSTRUCTIONS TO THE CANDIDATE

This station is designed to test your ability to properly immobilize a non-complicated shoulder injury. You are required to treat only the specific, isolated injury to the shoulder. The scene size-up and initial assessment have been accomplished on the victim and during the focused assessment a shoulder injury was detected. Ongoing assessment of the patient's airway, breathing and central circulation is not necessary. You may use any equipment available in this room. You have 10 minutes to complete this skill station. Do you have any questions?

NOTES

NEW YORK STATE DEPARTMENT OF HEALTH
Emergency Medical Services

EMT/Certified First Responder
Practical Examination

STATION 6B	IMMOBILIZATION SKILLS JOINT INJURY	Pass _____ Fail _____

Please print.

Candidate _____

Examiner _____ Initials _____

Date _____ Start Time _____ Stop Time _____

	Points: Possible	Awarded	Comments
Takes, or verbalizes, body substance isolation precautions	C		
Directs application of manual stabilization of the shoulder injury	I		
Assesses motor, sensory and circulatory function in the injured extremity	C		
Note: The examiner acknowledges "motor, sensory and circulatory function are present and normal"			
Selects the proper splinting material	I		
Immobilizes the site of the injury	I		
Immobilizes the bone above the injured joint	C		
Immobilizes the bone below the injured joint	C		
Reassessed motor, sensory and circulatory function in the injured extremity	C		
Note: The examiner acknowledges "motor, sensory and circulatory function are present and normal"			
Joint is supported so that the joint does not bear distal weight	C		
Candidate completed station within the 5 minute time limit	C		

Note: *Candidate must complete all critical criteria and receive at least 2 points to pass this station.*

Total to pass 2   Total 3

COMMENTS:

NEW YORK STATE DEPARTMENT OF HEALTH
Emergency Medical Services

IMMOBILIZATION SKILLS – TRACTION SPLINTING

INSTRUCTIONS TO THE CANDIDATE

This station is designed to test your ability to properly immobilize a mid-shaft femur injury with a traction splint. You will have an EMT assistant to help you in the application of the device by applying manual traction when directed to do so. You are required to treat only the specific, isolated injury to the femur. The scene size-up and initial assessment have been accomplished on the victim and during the focused assessment a mid-shaft femur deformity was detected. Ongoing assessment of the patient's airway, breathing and central circulation is not necessary. You may use any equipment available in this room. You have 10 minutes to complete this skill station. Do you have any questions?

NOTES

EMT—Basic Certification Exam

NEW YORK STATE DEPARTMENT OF HEALTH
Emergency Medical Services

EMT
Practical Examination

Please print.

STATION 6C	IMMOBILIZATION SKILLS TRACTION SPLINTING

Pass _____
Fail _____

Candidate _____
Examiner _____ Initials _____
Date _____ Start Time _____ Stop Time _____

Points:	Possible	Awarded	Comments
Takes, or verbalizes, body substance isolation precautions	C		
Directs application of manual stabilization of the injured leg	I		
Candidate assesses motor, sensory and circulatory function in the injured extremity	C		
Note: The examiner acknowledges "motor, sensory and circulatory function are present and normal"			
Directs the application of manual traction	I		
Prepares/adjusts splint to the proper length	I		
Applies the splint to the injured leg	I		
Applies the proximal security device (e.g….ischial strap)	I		
Applies the distal securing device (e.g….ankle hitch)	I		
Applies mechanical traction	I		
Positions/secures the support straps	I		
Re-evaluates the proximal/distal security devices	I		
Candidate reassesses motor, sensory and circulatory function in the injured extremity	C		
Note: The examiner acknowledges "motor, sensory and circulatory function are present and normal"			
Note: The examiner must ask the candidate how he/she would prepare the patient for transportation			
Verbalizes securing the torso to the long board to immobilize the hip	I		
Verbalizes securing the splint to the long board to prevent movement of the splint	I		
Traction is maintained throughout application of splint	C		
The foot was not excessively rotated or extended after the splint was applied	C		
Secured the ischial strap before applying mechanical traction	C		
Final immobilization supported the femur and prevented rotation of the injured leg	C		
Applied mechanical traction before securing the leg to the splint	C		
Candidate completed the station within the 10 minute time limit	C		

Note: If the Sagar splint or the Kendricks Traction Device is used without elevating the patient's leg, application of manual traction is not necessary. The candidate should be awarded one point as if manual traction were applied.
Note: If the leg is elevated at all, manual traction must be applied before elevating the leg. The ankle hitch may be applied before elevating the leg and used to provide manual traction.

Note: Candidate must complete all critical criteria and receive at least 7 points to pass this station.

Total to pass 7   Total 11

COMMENTS:

NEW YORK STATE DEPARTMENT OF HEALTH
Emergency Medical Services

STATION
6D

BLEEDING CONTROL/SHOCK MANAGEMENT

INSTRUCTIONS TO THE CANDIDATE

This station is designed to test your ability to control hemorrhage. This is a scenario-based testing station. As you progress through the scenario, you will be given various signs and symptoms appropriate for the patient's condition. You will be required to manage the patient based on these signs and symptoms. A scenario will be read aloud to you and you will be given an opportunity to ask clarifying questions about the scenario, however, you will not receive answers to any questions about the actual steps of the procedures to be performed. You may use any of the supplies and equipment available in this room. You have five minutes to complete this skill station. Do you have any questions?

NOTES

NEW YORK STATE DEPARTMENT OF HEALTH
Emergency Medical Services

EMT/Certified First Responder
Practical Examination

Please print.

STATION 6D	BLEEDING CONTROL/ SHOCK MANAGEMENT

Pass _____
Fail _____

Candidate _____
Examiner _____ Initials _____
Date _____ Start Time _____ Stop Time _____

	Points: Possible	Awarded	Comments
Takes, or verbalizes, body substance isolation precautions	C		
Applies direct pressure to the wound	I		
Elevates the extremity	I		
Note: The examiner must now inform the candidate that the wound continues to bleed			
Applies an additional dressing to the wound	I		
Note: The examiner must now inform the candidate that the wound still continues to bleed. The second dressing does not control the bleeding.			
Locates and applies pressure to appropriate arterial pressure point	I		
Note: The examiner must now inform the candidate that the bleeding is controlled			
Bandages the wound	I		
Candidate controlled hemorrhage appropriately	C		
Note: The examiner must now inform the candidate the patient is now showing signs and symptoms indicative of hypoperfusion			
Properly positions the patient	I		
Applies high concentration oxygen	C		
Initiates steps to prevent heat loss from the patient	I		
Indicates the need for immediate transportation	C		
Candidate did not apply a tourniquet before attempting other methods of bleeding control	C		
Candidate completed the station within the 5 minute time limit	C		

Note: *Candidate must complete all critical criteria and receive at least 5 points to pass this station.*

Total to pass 5   Total 7

COMMENTS:

NEW YORK STATE DEPARTMENT OF HEALTH
Emergency Medical Services

STATION
6E

UPPER AIRWAY ADJUNCTS AND SUCTION

INSTRUCTIONS TO THE CANDIDATE

This station is designed to test your ability to properly measure, insert and remove an oropharyngeal and nasopharyngeal airway as well as suction a patient's upper airway. This is an isolated skills test comprised of three separate skills. You may use any equipment available in this room. You have five minutes to complete this station. Do you have any questions?

NOTES

NEW YORK STATE DEPARTMENT OF HEALTH
Emergency Medical Services

EMT/Certified First Responder
Practical Examination

Please print.

STATION	UPPER AIRWAY		
6E	**ADJUNCTS**	Pass _____	Candidate _____
	& SUCTION	Fail _____	Examiner _____ Initials _____
			Date _____ Start Time _____ Stop Time _____

	Points: Possible	Awarded	Comments

OROPHARYNGEAL AIRWAY

	Possible	Awarded	Comments
Takes, or verbalizes, body substance isolation precautions	C		
Selects appropriately sized airway	I		
Measures airway	I		
Inserts airway without pushing the tongue posteriorly	I		
Note: The examiner must advise the candidate that the patient is gagging and becoming conscious			
Removes the oropharyngeal airway	I		

SUCTION

	Possible	Awarded	Comments
Note: The examiner must advise the candidate to suction the patient's airway			
Turns on/prepares suction device	I		
Assures presence of mechanical suction	I		
Inserts the suction tip without suction	I		
Applies suction to the oropharynx/nasopharynx	I		
Candidate demonstrated acceptable suction technique	C		

NASOPHARYNGEAL AIRWAY

	Possible	Awarded	Comments
Note: The examiner must advise the candidate to insert a nasopharyngeal airway			
Selects appropriately sized airway	I		
Measures airway	I		
Verbalizes lubrication of the nasal airway	I		
Fully inserts the airway with the bevel facing toward the septum	I		
Candidate did not insert any adjunct in a manner dangerous to the patient	C		
Candidate completed the station within the 5 minute time limit	C		

Note: *Candidate must complete all critical criteria and receive at least 8 points to pass this station.*

Total to pass 8   Total 12

COMMENTS:

NEW YORK STATE DEPARTMENT OF HEALTH
Emergency Medical Services

STATION
6F

MOUTH-TO-MASK WITH SUPPLEMENTAL OXYGEN

INSTRUCTIONS TO THE CANDIDATE

This station is designed to test your ability to ventilate a patient with supplemental oxygen using a mouth-to-mask technique. This is an isolated skills test. You may assume that mouth-to-barrier device ventilation is in progress and that the patient has a central pulse. The only patient management required is ventilator support using a mouth-to-mask technique with supplemental oxygen. You must ventilate the patient for at least 30 seconds. You will be evaluated on the appropriateness of ventilatory volumes. You may use any equipment available in this room. You have five minutes to complete this station. Do you have any questions?

NOTES

NEW YORK STATE DEPARTMENT OF HEALTH
Emergency Medical Services

**EMT/Certified First Responder
Practical Examination**

Please print.

STATION **6F**	MOUTH-TO-MASK WITH SUPPLEMENTAL OXYGEN

Pass _____

Fail _____

Candidate _____

Examiner _____ Initials _____

Date _____ Start Time _____ Stop Time _____

Points:	Possible	Awarded	Comments
Takes, or verbalizes, body substance isolation precautions	C		
Connects one-way valve to mask	I		
Opens patient's airway or confirms patient's airway is open (manually or with adjunct)	I		
Establishes and maintains a proper mask to face seal	I		
Ventilates the patient at the proper volume and rate (800-1200 ml per breath/10-20 breaths per minute)	I		
Candidate ventilated patient prior to connection of supplemental oxygen	C		
Connects the mask to high concentration of oxygen	I		
Adjusts flow rate to at least 15 liters per minute	C		
Continues ventilation of the patient at the proper volume and rate (800-1200 ml per breath/10-20 breaths per minute)	I		
Note: the examiner must witness ventilations for at least 30 seconds			
Candidate provided proper volume per breath (Cannot accept more than 2 ventilations per minute below 800 ml)	C		
Candidate provided 10-20 breaths per minute	C		
Candidate allowed for complete exhalation	C		
Candidate completed the station within the 5 minute time limit	C		

Note: *Candidate must complete all critical criteria and receive at least 4 points to pass this station.*

Total to pass 4   Total 6

COMMENTS:

NEW YORK STATE DEPARTMENT OF HEALTH
Emergency Medical Services

STATION
6G

SUPPLEMENTAL OXYGEN ADMINISTRATION

INSTRUCTIONS TO THE CANDIDATE

This station is designed to test your ability to correctly assemble the equipment needed to administer supplemental oxygen in the prehospital setting. This is an isolated skills test. You will be required to assemble an oxygen tank and a regulator and administer oxygen to a patient using a non-rebreather mask. At this point, you will be instructed to discontinue oxygen administration by the non-rebreather mask and start oxygen administration using a nasal cannula because the patient cannot tolerate the mask. Once you have initiated oxygen administration using a nasal cannula, you will be instructed to discontinue oxygen administration completely. You may use only the equipment available in this room. You have five minutes to complete this station. Do you have any questions?

NOTES

NEW YORK STATE DEPARTMENT OF HEALTH
Emergency Medical Services

EMT/Certified First Responder Practical Examination

Please print.

STATION 6G	SUPPLEMENTAL OXYGEN ADMINISTRATION

Pass _____   Fail _____

Candidate _____
Examiner _____ Initials _____
Date _____ Start Time _____ Stop Time _____

	Points: Possible	Awarded	Comments
Takes, or verbalizes, body substance isolation precautions	C		
Assembles the regulator to the tank	I		
Opens the tank	I		
Checks for leaks	I		
Checks and verbalizes tank pressure	I		
Attaches non-rebreather mask to oxygen	I		
Prefills reservoir	C		
Adjusts liter flow to 12 liters per minute or greater	C		
Applies and adjusts the mask to the patient's face	I		
Note: The examiner must advise the candidate that the patient is not tolerating the non-rebreather mask. The medical director has ordered you to apply a nasal cannula to the patient.			
Attaches nasal cannula to oxygen	I		
Adjusts liter flow to 6 liters per minute or less	C		
Applies nasal cannula to the patient	I		
The examiner must advise the candidate to discontinue oxygen therapy			
Removes the nasal cannula from the patient	I		
Shuts off the regulator	I		
Relieves the pressure within the regulator	I		
Candidate assembles the tank and regulator without leaks	C		
Candidate completed the station within the 5 minute time limit	C		

Note: *Candidate must complete all critical criteria and receive at least 8 points to pass this station.*

Total to pass 8   Total 11

COMMENTS:

Chapter 10

TAKING THE WRITTEN EXAMINATION

TAKING THE EXAMINATION

The certification examination is the final test of the ability of a candidate to meet the performance objectives to become an EMT–Basic. There are many ways to prepare for this examination. This chapter will outline strategies for preparation as well as provide helpful hints on taking examinations in general. It will also outline the structure of a typical examination question. This outline will assist the candidate in choosing a correct answer. You should read through this chapter thoroughly. Some of the information included will add insight to passing your certification examination.

THE EXAMINATION

An examination is an evaluation tool. Like the practical skills examination evaluates the competence of the candidate to perform the skills necessary to become an EMT–Basic, the written examination evaluates the candidate's aptitude for knowledge retention. The EMT–Basic should follow a hard and fast rule of progressive study. As the course begins to run full steam, the amount of study time should increase. There are modules in the EMT–Basic curriculum that will require many hours of self-study. As these courses are usually condensed into a short period of time, it is expected that the candidate will reserve several hours of personal time per week to study for her examination.

STUDY HABITS

Developing good study habits is essential to retaining information and passing the examination. The common scene of the student "cramming" into the night comes to mind. Studies have shown that cramming information reduces retention. In fact, it may confuse the student to attempt to retain too much information at any given time. Learning to study properly is just as important as the material you are trying to study.

Refer to the study tips below and keep them in mind as you prepare for the exam. You will find that by following these few tried and true rules, your study time may decrease, while your retention increases.

1. Never study when you are tired.
   Studying when you are tired will almost always be a fruitless search for information. There comes a time each day when your body needs to rest. Attempts at studying—especially difficult technical information—are usually weak at best. You should allow time for ample rest.

2. Choose a time when you are usually most awake, and make that your study time.

   All people are different: some are more alert in the morning, and some are more alert in the evening. The best judge of your inner clock is yourself. You know when you are most alert. If you wake up in the morning and are at your best, then choose that time as your study time. Try to put at least 45 minutes a day aside at that time. You may just find that 45 minutes of studying at your peak times is much more efficient than two hours when you're tired.

3. Find a quiet and comfortable place.

   It is essential to be comfortable when you are studying. You should find a place in your home or study area that provides quiet and comfort. The temperature of the room should be set to a temperature that is good for you. It is a good idea not to make the room too hot. Heat tends to make a person sleepy or uncomfortable. Silence is another factor. It is always better to have a quiet area. Attempting to study with the television on or the stereo playing is planning to fail. It may relax you to have music playing in the background; however, the brain will be distracted since it will have to retain your studies as well as process the background music. Studying in a room with other people is also not suggested. Constant disruptions will throw you off your concentration and create confusion with topics.

4. Never study when you're hungry.

   Hunger is a great distracter. If you are hungry, you will think about food and not about your studies. So if you are hungry, eat prior to beginning your studies. Try to avoid snacks that are high in sugar and caffeine, as they will serve to provide a temporary rush and then crash you. Fruits, salads, and vegetables are a good food group to study with.

5. Study in short time blocks.

   Professional studies have shown that retention is better when a student studies in shorter blocks of time. The average maximum study time should be about 45 minutes. The brain gets tired after 45 minutes of retention and needs a break. Study for 45 minutes, take a break, rest your eyes, go for a walk. While you are in your resting phase, try to go over in your head the things that you have just studied—this will help your retention. Go back to studying only when your head feels clear again.

Simply following these suggestions will help you to retain more information. As you develop good study habits, you will notice other things that help you study better. Incorporate what you've learned about your own study habits into my suggestions above to develop an effective study plan that is right for you.

DIRECTED STUDY

It is essential to find a direction in your studies. People tend to study subjects they are comfortable with and avoid subjects they find difficult. For example, the student who is well-versed in cardiac emergencies will tend to spend more time studying cardiac emergencies. This is due to that fact that they have an understanding of the topic and that they are not confused. The problem with this is that weaker areas are never approached. This may lead to poor scores and failure of the examination.

There are many ways to direct your study. One of the best ways is to keep a record of your quiz and examination scores in each topic. As you find a trend toward weaker areas, focus on them; study a topic where you have not done well. This will strengthen your knowledge and make you a well-rounded provider. You may also ask your instructor. Many EMS instructors provide an item analysis for class final examinations (which you are sure to have before the certification examination). Ask your instructor to share your item analysis with you. This will identify your weaker areas and let you know what areas to practice. Most EMS instructors will be happy to assist you in this area. Some even assign homework based on a student's item analysis, in order to strengthen them for the upcoming certification examination.

STUDY GUIDES

Many EMS instructors have written study guides at all levels of EMS provision (you are reading one now). The candidate should find one or two study guides that they feel comfortable with and stick with them. It is not necessary to purchase the bookstore's entire stock of EMT–Basic study guides in order to pass your examination. A good review guide, coupled with your course textbook and workbook, as well as some guidance from your course instructor, is all you need to prepare for the examination.

PREPARATION FOR YOUR EXAMINATION
The Night Before

The night before your examination could very well set the tone for the entire examination. Below are several do's and don'ts of how to prepare on the night before the examination.

1. DON'T stay up all night cramming.
   This is the absolute worst thing you can do. All-night cramming will have one effect on you: It will make you tired and easily confused. The candidate who remains up all night will tend to confuse facts on the examination. There is a saying in EMS (and I am sure everywhere else) that goes, "If you don't know it by now, you wont learn it in one night." Simply put, if you have studied throughout your course, you should spend the final night reviewing key terms and concepts.

2. DON'T use drugs or alcohol to help you sleep.
   Although it may appear to help you sleep, most people who drink alcohol or take drugs to assist sleep are being fooled. Alcohol and drugs do not provide a restful sleep. As a matter of fact, alcohol will put you to sleep, only to wake you up in an hour or two, preventing restful sleep. Key tip—don't do it.

3. DO plan on getting your required amount of sleep—no more, no less.
Most people know exactly how much sleep they need to function properly.
If you need eight hours of sleep to get a good jump on your day, then plan
on getting that much sleep. If you sleep too much or too little, it could have
a detrimental effect on your performance. Too much sleep can be just as bad
as not enough sleep.

4. DO avoid stressful situations.
You should avoid all stress the night before the examination. Personal
issues, especially sensitive ones, should be avoided the night before your
examination. They will only serve to distract you, preventing sleep and study
retention.

EXAMINATION DAY

Well, you made it to examination day. Examination day can be as stressful as
any other important day in your life, including your wedding day. Some
candidates build up so much stress that they arrive at the examination site in a
cold sweat. This can wear on your ability to answer questions. Some of the tips
below are professional tips for examination day.

1. Plan on arriving early.
If your examination starts at 9:00 a.m., plan to be there at 8:00 a.m. There is
nothing worse than showing up at an examination late or leaving with just
enough time to find no parking spaces or be delayed by an accident on the
road.

2. Eat light.
It is advisable to eat something; however, a full course 16-ounce steak will
probably work against you. When we eat large amounts of food, the body
moves blood from the vital organs to the gut in order to digest the food.
This makes you tired and inefficient. My suggestions are a light snack, fruit,
vegetables, or salad. Just eat enough to hold you over for the examination.
After the examination, you can go feast.

3. Avoid high sugars and caffeine.
Food and drinks with large amounts of caffeine and sugar will work for a
short period of time, then leave you extremely tired as they wear off. This
can affect your ability to answer questions or comprehend a scenario. In
addition, coffee and tea (iced tea as well) will also act as a diuretic. This
effect will cause problems with concentration if you must keep leaving your
seat to go to the rest room. Orange juice or any other fruit juices are
exceptional ways to keep hydrated while taking an examination. And, of
course, water is also an excellent way to remain hydrated during the
examination.

4. Sit in a well-lit and comfortable area.
This tip is good if you are familiar with the classroom layout. Most
examinations are administered in the same room in which you took your
course. If you are familiar with the layout, find a seat that is comfortable.
This is usually the seat you were in during the course. Sitting near an open
window or under the air conditioning or heat diffuser can be very distracting. Size up the examination room, and pick a good seat. This is another
reason why early arrival is beneficial.

ANSWERING EXAMINATION QUESTIONS

When you take an examination, you will find that most examinations are multiple-choice questions. There are many concepts on examination taking, several of which are listed here.

1. Read the whole question and all of the answer choices before choosing the correct answer.
   When taking the examination, read the entire question, including the answers, before choosing a response. You may find that there was a distracting statement in the question, and the answer you choose may be incorrect.

2. Look for key words in your questions.
   Questions with words in bold or italics are keys to what the question is looking for. Words like except, if, and, and which are clues to specific findings in the answer choices. Make sure you locate the keys in each question.

3. Read scenario questions carefully.
   Most examinations have scenarios with several questions related to it. Read the scenario carefully and completely—don't jump to the questions until you are confident that you understand the scenario. Answer one question at a time, and go back to the scenario if you must. In some cases, a question that has an unclear answer will be answered in the next question, so be vigilant.

4. Take your time but not too much time.
   Most examinations are timed events, so make sure that you do not spend an excessive amount of time on any one question. Do some quick math to figure out approximately how much time you need per question, then begin your test. Examination proctors will usually make "time remaining" announcements. Judge your speed accordingly. In addition, this is not a race. Do not rush through an examination to be the first one done—there are no extra points for this honor.

5. If you find a question difficult, move on and come back later.
   As stated before, some questions are answered later on in the test. You can use this to your advantage when dealing with a difficult question. Move on and come back to it. Just make sure that you also skip the space on the answer sheet.

6. When you are done, go back and check your answers.
   It is always good practice to spot-check your answers. If you complete the examination and there is time left, go back and look over the examination again. There is no law that says once your done, you cannot look at the examination booklet. Read the questions, answer them again, then check your new answer against the one on the answer sheet. They should match; if they do not, read the question and try to reevaluate it, then choose the answer that seems most correct to you.

ANATOMY OF A QUESTION

A question is an evaluation tool—nothing more. It is designed to extract a fact from you, to see if you can comprehend it and relate it to a proper answer. Most examination questions are multiple choice, so we will dissect a multiple-choice question below.

Which of the following is a late sign of shock?

(A) Alteration of mental status
(B) Decreased blood pressure
(C) Hypoperfusion
(D) Increased pulse rate

The correct answer is (B).

In every multiple-choice question, there are usually four answer choices. Only one of them is the correct answer. The other three are there for effect. One of the three is called a distracter. A distracter is an answer choice that may appear to be correct, but for one reason or another, it is incorrect. In the question above, it is quite clear that decreased blood pressure is the correct answer, until you start thinking about hypoperfusion. Hypoperfusion is the definition of shock; however, under the stress of an examination, you may start thinking, "Is hypoperfusion the definition of late shock or early shock?" Hence, it is a distracter. The other answer choices are called throw-aways. They are useless fill-ins that are usually easily distinguished as incorrect answers.

A good rule to follow is that if you do not know the correct answer, find the answers that you know are not correct, and throw them away. We know in the question above that alteration of mental status and increased pulse rate are early signs of shock. So, we throw them away. Now, we only have to choose between two answers. Even if you have to guess, it increases your chances of correctly answering the question.

In closing, if you follow the hints in this chapter, you should find yourself adding a few additional points to your examination grade. Remember, the best way to pass an examination is to study during your course and not the night before the examination. Good study habits and a sharp eye on the examination will assist you in realizing your dream of becoming an EMT–Basic.

Chapter 11

GOING TO WORK

PREPARING A PROPER RESUME

Once you have passed your examination and are certified or licensed to work as an EMT–Basic, you should prepare a proper resume and send it to the agencies that you aspire to work for.

A proper resume should include your career goal as well as past employment and training. It should also list any certifications and expiration dates, so that the employer is aware of your expertise in the field of emergency medical services.

Many EMS provider agencies that deliver emergency care to a specific service area (911 employers) may not hire newly certified EMT–Basic personnel until they gain some experience on an ambulance. This is not a reason to become discouraged. If you cannot gain employment with one of these agencies, you may want to apply with a proprietary provider of EMS (private ambulance). Proprietary providers do routine transports as well as high-risk transports. They may also offer additional specialty training to help you gain experience.

Another way to gain experience is to volunteer with a local ambulance company. Volunteer agencies usually provide 911 services to their community and are a great way to gain experience and connect with people who have the same interests as you. Many EMT–Basics who move on to a paid EMS provider position retain their position in their volunteer agency because it offers good experience in emergency medical care and gives them a chance to serve their community.

The following page offers a sample resume that you may feel free to use as a model for your own resume.

A note on resumes:

Your resume should be concise but comprehensive. Proper resumes should be only one page in length and list several years of work experience, even if it is not in the field for which you are now applying. Long-winded resumes that are several pages long are usually not attractive to employers. You may also consider using a fancier paper for your resume, but keep the type easy to read. Fancy script fonts are difficult to read and may add a non-professional look to your resume. When it comes to resumes, clear and to the point says it best.

Sample Resume

Joseph B. EMT
304 Pleasant Lane
Anywhere, USA 99999
555-555-5555

Objective: A career in Emergency Medical Services where the application of my professional knowledge and skills will assist sick and injured patients to access emergency medical care in a timely and professional fashion.

Experience: December 1995 — Present
Franks Oxygen Service
Anywhere, USA

Duties: Deliver oxygen to health-care facilities, fire departments, and EMS stations. Ensure safety measures are in place. Facilitate safe and efficient delivery of bottled gases, according to state and local law.

Education: Anywhere High School
Anywhere, USA

Graduated 1995

Anywhere USA EMS Academy
Anywhere, USA

EMT–Basic Certification

Certifications: Anywhere State EMT–Basic Provider,
380076, Expires 3/30/03
Prehospital Trauma Care course
Prehospital Pediatric Care course

Interests: Computers, ice hockey, and science fiction

INTERVIEWING FOR A POSITION

Interviewing for any position can be a stressful moment. Even the most experienced people in the workforce can be nervous at an interview. The secret to a successful interview is to remain calm and to talk positively about yourself. Negative comments are simply that, negative, and will not help you gain employment. Any negative experiences from a previous employer should be left out of your interview.

On the day of your interview, prepare to be there early, dress appropriately (suit and tie or dress), and bring a copy of your resume. It should also be noted that it is helpful to have a few letters of recommendation from recent employers or your EMS instructor that outline your drive and dedication to the profession. A recommendation letter can go a long way, especially if your new employer knows the person who wrote the letter.

When you arrive at your interview site, be patient and polite. Sit down with your potential employer, and answer questions slowly and calmly. Try to remain on the topic, and stay away from personal feelings about any issues that may come up. Discuss your good qualities and your work ability. Ask questions that are pertinent to the position, and clarify any questions you may have. Eye contact is important—keeping direct eye contact while making a point is always helpful. Do not stare at the floor or a wall the entire time. Look at the person who is interviewing you. Eye contact makes a statement of confidence; MAKE THAT STATEMENT.

When the interview is over, shake hands and tell the interviewer thank you for her time. Ask if it is okay to call back in a few days just to touch base and see how things are going. Do not say, "Well, do I have the job?" Some employers will hire on the spot, but most will call in a few days after they have conducted several interviews. If you are called back for a second interview, approach it as if it were your first. Repeat your good qualities, and answer any questions honestly and concisely.

Don't get discouraged if the first employer does not hire you. Just keep trying, and eventually you will break into a rewarding and exciting career in Emergency Medical Services.

TYPES OF EMS PROVIDER AGENCIES

There are multiple types of EMS provider agencies with which you may seek employment. Listed below are several types of agencies that may provide Emergency Medical Services in your area.

Volunteer Agency

A volunteer EMS agency is made of area residents who are EMS providers. They are community-minded people who provide a needed and appreciated service to the sick and injured of their community. This is a great place to start even before you are an EMT, as these agencies will usually sponsor people in EMS courses. In most cases, you won't get paid for being there, but you will certainly gain much needed experience in the field of EMS.

Municipal Agency

A municipal agency is usually a city-, state- or town-run EMS provider agency. You will come in contact with municipal systems in larger cities and towns. Employment with these agencies will usually require a written examination, and once hired, you will probably attend their EMS academy for additional training. These are good agencies to work for, and many offer civil service positions and benefits as well as a career ladder.

Hospital-Based Agency

Many hospitals have their own ambulance services that cover a specific area around the hospital. In many areas, EMS systems were developed by hospital-based ambulances and grew into municipalities. Hospital-based agencies are similar agencies to municipal agencies and, in some cases, work in the same areas with municipal agencies to deliver emergency medical care.

Proprietary Agency

Proprietary agencies are also called private ambulance companies. Private ambulance companies transport high- and low-risk specialty patients. They are specialized crews that are assigned to a specific hospital or area and work by contract with that hospital to provide transport. Many proprietary agencies also provide 911 services to contracted service areas. There are many large proprietary agencies nationwide that will offer many different positions in EMS provision, including air medical transport.

Other Agencies

Some other EMS agencies to consider are first-response agencies, which provide first-responder units to emergency calls; air medical transports, which provide helicopter and fixed-wing aircraft for patient transport; and specialty assignments like movie sets and shipboard EMS. Overseas employers routinely advertise for EMS providers in the national EMS journals.

As an EMS provider, there are many opportunities to provide patient care in a number of different settings. Keep your options open, and find the one that best suits your needs or interests.

Good luck!

Chapter 12

PRACTICE FINAL WRITTEN EXAMINATION WITH RATIONALES

In this final section, you will take a practice 100-question examination. The amount of questions from each module is based on the number of objectives per module. You should time yourself when taking this examination. Usually for a 100-question examination, you will be allowed no more than 2.5 hours. Take the entire examination, and then upon completion, score your answers. Consider 75 percent to be a passing score. When you are completed, you can go back and check you answers and identify weak areas that need further study before your final examination.

Good luck!

1. Upon your arrival at any emergency scene, your number one priority is

   (A) scene survey.
   (B) crew safety.
   (C) patient assessment.
   (D) need for resources.

2. The responsibility for all patient care delivered by the EMT–Basic lies directly with which of the following?

   (A) The EMT–Basic alone
   (B) An Advanced Life Support provider
   (C) The medical director
   (D) The ambulance service

3. All of the following are appropriate statements by the EMT–Basic to a family who has lost a loved one EXCEPT

   (A) an offer to contact other family members.
   (B) advising the family that the patient has died.
   (C) stating, "I know how you feel."
   (D) offering to contact a priest, rabbi, or other religious person to assist them in their grief.

4. Which of the following is NOT an acceptable way to reduce stress?

   (A) Eat properly
   (B) Practice relaxation techniques
   (C) Drink alcohol to help you sleep after a bad call
   (D) Discuss bad calls with your partner or a loved one

5. Which of the following is the best example of expressed consent?

   (A) An unconscious patient who is treated by an EMS crew with the assumption that if he were conscious, he would agree to treatment
   (B) A conscious patient who, after receiving an explanation of treatment, agrees to treatment and transport
   (C) A child who is treated at school in the absence of the parents
   (D) A psychiatric patient who is restrained by police and transported to the hospital

6. You are on the scene of a stabbing in which the patient is stable. On the radio, the dispatcher is looking for a crew for a forthwith response to a pedestrian struck. You leave your patient with a first responder fire company and take the new call. You may be found guilty of

   (A) negligence.
   (B) assault.
   (C) battery.
   (D) abandonment.

7. While operating at a crime scene, which of the following is NOT an appropriate action?

   (A) Touching only what you need to provide patient care
   (B) Keeping a mental note of items or people at the scene that may assist the police later on in an investigation
   (C) Touching and moving items in the area, regardless of their necessity to patient care
   (D) Bringing as little as possible of necessary equipment into the crime scene

8. "Gurgling" breath sounds usually indicate

   (A) narrowing of the bronchioles.
   (B) upper airway obstruction.
   (C) end expiratory noise.
   (D) fluid in the airway.

9. "Wheezing" breath sounds indicate

   (A) narrowing of the bronchioles.
   (B) upper airway obstruction.
   (C) end expiratory noise.
   (D) fluid in the airway.

10. Airway obstruction, fluid in the lungs, and lung collapse will cause all of the following EXCEPT

   (A) labored breathing.
   (B) increased respiratory effort.
   (C) change in breath sounds.
   (D) decreased heart rate.

11. The difference between auscultation and palpation of a blood pressure is that auscultation will provide

   (A) only a systolic pressure.
   (B) only a diastolic pressure.
   (C) both a systolic and diastolic pressure.
   (D) Blood pressure can only be palpated.

12. Which of the following is NOT a component of the SAMPLE history?

   (A) Symptoms
   (B) Systolic blood pressure
   (C) Allergies
   (D) Medications

13. All of the following are examples of pertinent past history items EXCEPT

   (A) hypertension.
   (B) heart disease.
   (C) stroke.
   (D) gall bladder surgery fifteen years ago.

14. Which of the following is NOT a symptom?

   (A) Chest pain
   (B) Nausea
   (C) Dilated pupils
   (D) Headache

15. Lifting with your legs, proper foot position, and communication are all characteristics of

   (A) good body mechanics.
   (B) emergency moves.
   (C) power lifts.
   (D) speed lifts.

16. An emergency move is performed on all of the following patients EXCEPT

   (A) an unconscious patient with a head injury after a car accident.
   (B) a patient who is inside a car that is on fire.
   (C) a patient who is exposed to a possible life hazard.
   (D) a patient requiring airway management who is trapped under another patient.

17. You are assigned to a motor vehicle collision in which a patient is unconscious with an unsecured airway. Which of the following devices is most appropriate for patient extrication?

   (A) Cervical collar, KED, long board
   (B) Cervical collar, KED, scoop stretcher
   (C) Cervical collar, long board, rapid extrication
   (D) Cervical collar, short board, long board, rapid extrication

18. When performing mouth-to-mask ventilations with supplemental oxygen, the oxygen should be delivered at _____ liters per minute.

    (A) 6
    (B) 8
    (C) 10
    (D) 15

19. When ventilating using a bag-valve-mask ventilator, the EMT–Basic should deliver at least _____ milliliters of air with each ventilation.

    (A) 500
    (B) 600
    (C) 700
    (D) 800

20. When attached to an oxygen supply, what percentage of oxygen will the bag-valve-mask with reservoir device deliver?

    (A) 50 percent
    (B) 60 percent
    (C) 90 percent
    (D) 100 percent

21. Which of the following techniques should be used to open a patient's mouth prior to inserting an oropharyngeal airway?

    (A) Head tilt–chin lift technique
    (B) Cross-fingered technique
    (C) Jaw thrust technique
    (D) Jaw pull technique

22. The indications for use of an oropharyngeal airway include all of the following EXCEPT when

    (A) the patient has a gag reflex.
    (B) the patient is unconscious.
    (C) the patient cannot support his own airway.
    (D) the patient needs to be ventilated via a bag-valve-mask.

23. The laryngoscope blade that is designed to fit into the vallecula and lift the epiglottis is known as which of the following?

    (A) Macintosh blade
    (B) Miller blade
    (C) Nantucket blade
    (D) Straight blade

24. Endotracheal tubes used in the adult patient differ from those used in the pediatric patient. The adult endotracheal tube is

    (A) cuffed.
    (B) uncuffed.
    (C) thinner.
    (D) more supple.

25. You have performed endotracheal intubation on a patient in respiratory arrest; you assess lung sounds and find that you have only lung sounds on the right side. What is this is a common indication of?

    (A) This is normal, as the air will travel down only one lung.
    (B) The endotracheal tube is inserted too deeply and in the right mainstem bronchus.
    (C) The endotracheal tube is in the esophagus.
    (D) The ventilations are being performed incorrectly.

26. After determining that the endotracheal tube has been inserted too deeply, the first course of action would be to

    (A) remove the endotracheal tube, ventilate, and attempt intubation again.
    (B) attempt intubation around the endotracheal tube already in place.
    (C) slowly back the tube out of the trachea while monitoring breath sounds until bilateral breath sounds are heard.
    (D) contact advanced life support for additional assistance.

27. Your partner has inserted an endotracheal tube, and you are assessing breath sounds. While listening, you hear no breath sounds on either side, but you hear gurgling sounds in the epigastric area. This is a sign of

    (A) right mainstem intubation.
    (B) esophageal intubation.
    (C) collapsed lung from intubation.
    (D) inadequate lung volumes.

28. Determination of the mechanism of injury, scene safety, resource needs, and patient counts are all done during which phase of patient care?

    (A) Initial assessment
    (B) Scene size-up
    (C) Detailed physical examination
    (D) Communications

29. Which of the following is NOT one of the steps in initial assessment?

    (A) Assessment of mental status
    (B) Past history assessment
    (C) Airway assessment
    (D) Breathing assessment

30. Of the following, choose the patient with the highest priority condition.

    (A) Large leg laceration with bleeding controlled by direct pressure
    (B) Chest pain with no circulatory compromise
    (C) Chest pain with decreased blood pressure
    (D) A patient stung by a bee

31. On the AVPU scale, the U stands for

    (A) undetermined.
    (B) unresponsive.
    (C) under the influence of mind-altering substances.
    (D) understands commands.

32. On your arrival at a patient's home, the patient states that she called the ambulance because she was having chest pain that did not go away after she took her medication. This part of the patient interaction is known as

(A) patient history.
(B) chief complaint.
(C) initial assessment.
(D) on-going assessment.

33. You arrive at the scene of a pedestrian struck by a motorcycle. On your arrival, you find a 35-year-old male lying supine on the ground and unresponsive. Your findings also indicate that the patient has signs of internal bleeding and is breathing at eight breaths per minute. What is your classification of this patient?

(A) Low priority
(B) High priority
(C) Airway priority
(D) Bleeding priority

34. In the trauma patient, the detailed physical examination should be performed

(A) immediately upon arrival on the scene.
(B) before you perform any interventions.
(C) after the initial examination and critical interventions.
(D) always en route to the hospital.

35. The questions relating to onset, provocating factors, quality, radiation, and severity of pain all lead to information gathering for which part of the assessment process?

(A) Chief complaint
(B) History of present illness
(C) Past medical history
(D) Chest pain history

36. A detailed physical examination on the trauma patient differs from that performed on a medical patient. Which of the following statements best describes why?

(A) The trauma patient will always receive a detailed physical examination, while the medical patient will receive an examination based on body system involvement of his chief complaint.
(B) The medical patient will always receive a detailed physical examination, whereas a trauma patient may only receive a detailed physical examination based on obvious injury.
(C) The trauma and medical patients will both get a detailed physical examination.
(D) The detailed physical examination is done at the judgment of the EMT–Basic.

37. Which of the following is NOT a component of the on-going assessment?

(A) Initial assessment is repeated.
(B) Vital signs are reassessed.
(C) Primary interventions are begun.
(D) Focused assessment is repeated.

38. Which of the following pieces of information is NOT transmitted over the radio?

    (A) Age
    (B) Mechanism of injury
    (C) Name and address
    (D) Treatments and response

39. A good rule to follow when communicating with a small child is to

    (A) always remain standing when addressing the child so that they identify you as an adult.
    (B) bring yourself down to the level of the child by sitting or kneeling; this will reduce fear.
    (C) talk to the parents or caretakers, not with the child.
    (D) always communicate with a small child away from the parents, so the child does not get distracted by them.

40. Which of the following comments is NOT considered appropriate for the patient care report?

    (A) The patient was drunk and belligerent on our arrival.
    (B) The patient was found lying supine.
    (C) The patient stated that chest pain started 30 minutes prior to our arrival.
    (D) The patient states that he always takes his medication.

41. Which of the following medications are NOT carried on an ambulance staffed by the EMT–Basic?

    (A) Syrup of ipecac
    (B) Epinephrine
    (C) Oxygen
    (D) Activated charcoal

42. Of the following prescribed medications, which one is the EMT–Basic not trained to assist in its delivery?

    (A) Nitroglycerin
    (B) Epinephrine
    (C) Insulin
    (D) Prescribed inhaler

43. An action of a drug other than the desired action is known as a(n)

    (A) indication.
    (B) contraindication.
    (C) side effect.
    (D) allergic reaction.

44. Which of the following is NOT a sign of respiratory distress?

    (A) Noisy breathing
    (B) Cyanotic skin color
    (C) Decreased pulse rate
    (D) Accessory muscle use

45. An acute, episodic disease that causes bronchoconstriction, affects patients of all ages, and causes severe respiratory distress is known as

(A) bronchitis.
(B) asthma.
(C) emphysema.
(D) pneumonia.

46. The patient who suffers from a chronic disease that causes mucous plugging and increased work of breathing is diagnosed as having

(A) bronchitis.
(B) emphysema.
(C) asthma.
(D) pneumonia.

47. You respond to the scene of a 65-year-old man complaining of chest pain. When asked during the assessment, the patient states that he has chest pain in the middle of his chest, which radiates through his jaw and down his left arm. He has taken his medication, and it has not helped. He states that this has been going on for about 45 minutes now. You suspect

(A) respiratory distress secondary to asthma.
(B) angina.
(C) myocardial infarction.
(D) cardiogenic shock.

48. Your patient is a responsive 66-year-old male having a myocardial infarction. Which of the following treatments or interventions is NOT indicated for this patient?

(A) Assisted administration of nitroglycerin
(B) Oxygen administration
(C) Application of the AED
(D) Transport in a position of comfort

49. In treating a cardiac arrest patient with the AED, as long as the AED states a shock is indicated, how many initial shocks are delivered?

(A) 1
(B) 2
(C) 3
(D) 4

50. You are treating a cardiac arrest patient. After delivering your initial shocks, the AED states that no shock is indicated; however, the patient is still pulseless. You should

(A) turn the AED off and back on, then reassess the patient.
(B) continue CPR and consider beginning transport.
(C) request advanced life support assistance.
(D) request another AED to the scene because yours has malfunctioned.

51. You are treating a 6-year-old patient in cardiac arrest from an unknown cause. All of the following treatments should be initiated EXCEPT

(A) airway management with bag-valve-mask ventilation.
(B) cardiopulmonary resuscitation with a 5:1 ratio.
(C) rapid transport to the hospital.
(D) application of the AED.

52. You are called to the scene of an unconscious patient. On your arrival, you find a 29-year-old male lying on the bathroom floor unconscious. The patient has a strong pulse and is breathing on his own. The family states that he was fine a few minutes ago and then became sweaty and collapsed. You find a medication vial labeled insulin in the bathroom. You suspect

(A) myocardial infarction.
(B) a diabetic emergency, low blood sugar.
(C) a diabetic emergency, high blood sugar.
(D) stroke.

53. The patient in question 52 starts to become responsive; treatment of this patient would include all of the following EXCEPT

(A) high-concentration oxygen.
(B) administration of glucose paste.
(C) request for advanced life support assistance.
(D) assisted medication with the patient's insulin.

54. You are assigned to a schoolyard to assist a teacher who was stung by a bee. On your arrival, the patient is complaining of respiratory distress and itching. You notice hives on the patient's arms, and the patient looks slightly cyanotic. The diagnosis of this patients condition would be

(A) asthma attack.
(B) anxiety from a bee sting.
(C) allergic reaction.
(D) myocardial infarction.

55. The patient in question 54 states that she has an epi-pen that she keeps on her person in the case of allergic reactions. Because she is responsive, you should

(A) administer the epi-pen immediately.
(B) contact medical control for permission to administer the medication.
(C) not administer the medication, as the patient is not in shock.
(D) transport the patient and have an advanced life support intercept for additional treatment.

56. A 6-year-old child drinks a bottle of window washer fluid from the cabinet. This is an example of poisoning by

(A) injection.
(B) ingestion.
(C) inhalation.
(D) absorption.

57. An odorless, colorless, and tasteless gas that can be deadly to patients is known as

    (A) carbon dioxide.
    (B) carbon monoxide.
    (C) propane.
    (D) methane.

58. You are called to a house in the middle of the winter. On your arrival, you notice that it is very cold in the house, and the windows are open. The patient is a 72-year-old man who has an altered mental status, dilated pupils, and muscular rigidity. This patient is suffering from

    (A) mild hypothermia.
    (B) moderate hypothermia.
    (C) severe hypothermia.
    (D) stroke.

59. Your patient has been working in a warehouse during a heat wave. He is complaining of severe cramps in his arms and legs. His skin is cool and extremely moist. This condition is known as

    (A) heat cramps.
    (B) heat exhaustion.
    (C) heat stroke.
    (D) heat seizure.

60. You are assisting a drowning patient on a lake in about 5 feet of water. You are extricating the patient from the water. When would it be most appropriate to establish an airway?

    (A) Immediately, even in the water
    (B) Once aboard the rescue boat
    (C) As soon as the patient has been transferred to your stretcher
    (D) En route to the hospital.

61. While attempting to resuscitate a near-drowning patient, you feel a resistance to ventilation efforts. You should

    (A) suction the airway in case water has entered the airway.
    (B) gently press on the abdomen to help expel swallowed water.
    (C) contact advanced life support for gastric tube placement.
    (D) transport while providing forced ventilations.

62. Drug and alcohol abuse, as well as deficiencies in blood sugar, may cause a patient to act inappropriately, giving the impression of a behavioral emergency.

    (A) True
    (B) False

63. You are at the home of a 54-year-old male who is sitting in the corner of the room, withdrawn. The family states that he has been that way since the death of his wife several weeks ago. Recently, the patient has not been able to sleep, has expressed feelings of guilt and hopelessness, and has verbalized the ideation of suicide. The most probable diagnosis for this condition would be

(A) a situational reaction.
(B) depression.
(C) a suicide attempt.
(D) a medically caused behavioral problem.

64. Your patient is presenting with tense muscles, a loud angry voice, and is expressing threats of violence. You should

(A) approach the patient and try to speak with him calmly.
(B) try and speak to the patient from a safe distance and convince him to come with you to the hospital.
(C) request police assistance and do not attempt to diffuse the situation until assistance arrives.
(D) request advanced life support for assistance.

65. You are treating a pregnant patient for dizziness; she claims that she is near term and that she has had painless bright red vaginal bleeding since the morning. This is a common complaint for the condition known as

(A) placenta previa.
(B) abruptio placenta.
(C) pre-eclampsia.
(D) eclampsia.

66. You are assisting an emergency delivery of a baby and notice that there is a greenish-colored fluid discharging vaginally after the bag of waters breaks. Based on the color of the fluid, it is likely to be

(A) normal-colored amniotic fluid.
(B) meconium-stained fluid.
(C) placental discharge due to infection.
(D) Any of the above

67. What would be the highest priority during the delivery of the newborn in question 66?

(A) Full delivery, suction, oxygenation
(B) Suction as soon as the head delivers and before the first breath
(C) Drying and warming, then suction
(D) Clamp and cut the cord, suction and oxygen

68. After childbirth, at what time intervals is APGAR scoring performed?

(A) 5 then 10 minutes
(B) 4 then 8 minutes
(C) 2 then 4 minutes
(D) 1 then 5 minutes

69. Your patient is a 22-year-old male who fell from a roof. He has a large open laceration to the upper left leg with deformity and pulsating, bright red blood coming from the wound. This type of injury is classified as

(A) a suspected femur fracture with arterial bleeding.
(B) a laceration with venous bleeding.
(C) a suspected femur fracture with venous bleeding.
(D) an avulsion with arterial bleeding.

70. You are assigned to a local park for injuries after a fight. A young woman was struck in the abdomen with a baseball bat. She is lying on the ground and holding her abdominal section. Inspection reveals a large area of bruising on the right upper quadrant. This type of bruising is indicative of which type of injury?

(A) Rib fracture
(B) Internal injury with bleeding
(C) Evisceration
(D) Pelvic fracture

71. All of the following are signs of shock EXCEPT

(A) restlessness.
(B) increased heart rate.
(C) hypertension.
(D) cool, clammy skin.

72. Treatment of the patient in shock includes all of the following EXCEPT

(A) high-concentration oxygen.
(B) transport in the shock position.
(C) administration of fluids by mouth.
(D) keeping the patient warm.

73. Which of the following is not an open soft-tissue injury?

(A) Abrasion
(B) Laceration
(C) Avulsion
(D) Contusion

74. Your patient was stabbed in a knife fight. On inspection of the abdomen, you see an area of bowel protruding from the wound. This type of injury is known as

(A) puncture wound.
(B) laceration.
(C) evisceration.
(D) contusion.

75. The definition of a full thickness burn is

(A) reddening of the affected area.
(B) reddening and blistering of the affected area.
(C) charring of the affected area.
(D) loss of limb secondary to a burn.

76. An open chest wound should be treated with

(A) dry sterile dressings.
(B) an occlusive dressing.
(C) sterile tape to seal the hole.
(D) a gloved finger.

77. You respond to a factory for a man who has fallen. On your arrival, you find a 36-year-old male who fell on some pipes. A pipe is impaled in his abdomen and is sticking out about six inches; the correct treatment of this injury would be to

(A) bandage the area, administer oxygen, and remove the object immediately.
(B) request advanced life support assistance to remove the pipe.
(C) secure the impaled object with bulky dressings, treat for shock, and transport.
(D) immobilize the patient and request a field surgeon, as the patient cannot be moved until the object is removed.

78. You are treating an electrical lineman who was shocked with a high-voltage line. The patient has entrance and exit wounds from the electrical current from the left arm through the right arm and is in cardiac arrest. After performing your initial assessment, your priority in the treatment of this patient would be

(A) rapid transport to a trauma center.
(B) application of the AED to analyze the cardiac rhythm.
(C) ventilation with a bag-valve-mask and CPR.
(D) All of the above

79. A painful, deformed extremity with an area of contusion is a sign of a closed injury.

(A) True
(B) False

80. When splinting an extremity, which of the following is the proper way to secure a splint?

(A) The splint should be secured above and below the injury site.
(B) The splint should be secured at the joint above and below the injury.
(C) A traction splint may be used for lower extremity injuries.
(D) A traction splint may be used for pelvic fractures.

81. A sprain is defined as the

(A) stretching or tearing of ligaments.
(B) stretching or tearing of muscle.
(C) overexertion of muscle.
(D) overexertion of tendons.

82. The trauma patient exhibiting battle signs, clear fluid leaking from the ears, and alteration of mental status is most likely suffering from which of the following injuries?

    (A) Skull fracture with associated brain injury
    (B) Facial fractures
    (C) Spinal injury
    (D) Scalp injury

83. In the spinal column, there are _____ cervical vertebrae.

    (A) seven
    (B) twelve
    (C) five
    (D) four

84. Paralysis of the extremities is one of the most reliable signs of

    (A) brain injury.
    (B) spinal injuries.
    (C) nervous system dysfunction.
    (D) bleeding in the brain.

85. The device most commonly used to immobilize the spine of a seated patient is a

    (A) Kendrick extrication device.
    (B) long spine board.
    (C) scoop stretcher.
    (D) Reeves stretcher.

86. When doing a rapid takedown of the standing patient, where should the tallest rescuer be positioned?

    (A) On the side of the patient
    (B) In front of the patient
    (C) To the rear of the patient
    (D) Any of the above

87. Your patient has been involved in a motor vehicle accident; the patient is still in the car and is unconscious with a large amount of blood coming from her mouth. The extrication method of choice on this patient would be

    (A) a cervical collar, KED, and long board.
    (B) a cervical collar, short board, and long board.
    (C) a cervical collar and long board only.
    (D) the physical removal of the patient and transfer to a long board after she is extricated.

88. A child in a car seat has been involved in a motor vehicle collision. Which of the following methods is most appropriate for extrication and immobilization of this child?

    (A) KED
    (B) Short board with arm board to protect the spine
    (C) Extrication to a long board by turning the seat on its back
    (D) Immobilization in the seat itself by applying a collar and padding around the child

89. Any patient who has impacted the windshield of the car should be suspected of having

(A) facial trauma.
(B) spinal trauma.
(C) brain injury.
(D) All of the above

90. Due to the fact that the pediatric bones are softer, blunt trauma to the rib cage will cause which of the following?

(A) Less injury because the soft ribs will absorb the impact
(B) Severe injury to the heart and lungs, as the ribs will not protect them
(C) Easily broken ribs with no underlying damage
(D) Any of the above

91. A pediatric patient with an isolated head injury may show signs of hypovolemic shock.

(A) True
(B) False

92. Your pediatric patient is an infant who has an obstructed airway. According to AHA standards, what is the proper procedure for attempting to clear the airway?

(A) Abdominal thrusts, blind finger sweep
(B) Back blows, chest thrusts, blind finger sweeps
(C) Back blows, chest thrusts, finger sweeps at visible objects
(D) Any variation of the procedures above is acceptable.

93. All of the following are steps in management of pediatric shock EXCEPT

(A) administering high-concentration oxygen.
(B) elevating the legs.
(C) maintaining body temperature.
(D) remaining on the scene for advanced life support personnel to establish intravenous lines for fluid resuscitation.

94. Driving on icy roads, excessive speeds, and disregard for traffic control devices are all aspects of

(A) EMS response.
(B) response-time factors.
(C) unsafe driving conditions.
(D) safe response practices.

95. Your patient is not officially transferred to the emergency department staff until

(A) the paperwork is signed.
(B) the emergency department staff has received a full report on the patient's condition.
(C) the patient has been placed in an emergency department bed, regardless of report being given.
(D) you wheel the patient into the hospital.

96. Which of the following equipment is cleaned by sterilization?

    (A) Ambulance stretchers
    (B) Laryngoscope blades
    (C) Extrication equipment
    (D) Suction units

97. The patient who is pinned under a pile of rubble from a building collapse is considered to be a complex access patient.

    (A) True
    (B) False

98. In a motor vehicle collision, when the EMT–Basic can gain access to a patient without tools, it is considered

    (A) simple access.
    (B) complex access.
    (C) extrication.
    (D) disentanglement.

99. During a hazardous materials incident, the EMT–Basic who has no hazardous materials specialty training should be stationed

    (A) in the hot zone.
    (B) in the warm zone.
    (C) in the cold zone.
    (D) wherever the commander stations her.

100. Command and control, the establishment of sectors and resources, and communications at large-scale incidents is known as

    (A) preplanning.
    (B) size-up.
    (C) incident command system.
    (D) mass-casualty incidents.

ANSWER SHEET

Chapter 12: Practice Final Written Examination
With Rationales

1. Ⓐ Ⓑ Ⓒ Ⓓ
2. Ⓐ Ⓑ Ⓒ Ⓓ
3. Ⓐ Ⓑ Ⓒ Ⓓ
4. Ⓐ Ⓑ Ⓒ Ⓓ
5. Ⓐ Ⓑ Ⓒ Ⓓ
6. Ⓐ Ⓑ Ⓒ Ⓓ
7. Ⓐ Ⓑ Ⓒ Ⓓ
8. Ⓐ Ⓑ Ⓒ Ⓓ
9. Ⓐ Ⓑ Ⓒ Ⓓ
10. Ⓐ Ⓑ Ⓒ Ⓓ
11. Ⓐ Ⓑ Ⓒ Ⓓ
12. Ⓐ Ⓑ Ⓒ Ⓓ
13. Ⓐ Ⓑ Ⓒ Ⓓ
14. Ⓐ Ⓑ Ⓒ Ⓓ
15. Ⓐ Ⓑ Ⓒ Ⓓ
16. Ⓐ Ⓑ Ⓒ Ⓓ
17. Ⓐ Ⓑ Ⓒ Ⓓ
18. Ⓐ Ⓑ Ⓒ Ⓓ
19. Ⓐ Ⓑ Ⓒ Ⓓ
20. Ⓐ Ⓑ Ⓒ Ⓓ

21. Ⓐ Ⓑ Ⓒ Ⓓ
22. Ⓐ Ⓑ Ⓒ Ⓓ
23. Ⓐ Ⓑ Ⓒ Ⓓ
24. Ⓐ Ⓑ Ⓒ Ⓓ
25. Ⓐ Ⓑ Ⓒ Ⓓ
26. Ⓐ Ⓑ Ⓒ Ⓓ
27. Ⓐ Ⓑ Ⓒ Ⓓ
28. Ⓐ Ⓑ Ⓒ Ⓓ
29. Ⓐ Ⓑ Ⓒ Ⓓ
30. Ⓐ Ⓑ Ⓒ Ⓓ
31. Ⓐ Ⓑ Ⓒ Ⓓ
32. Ⓐ Ⓑ Ⓒ Ⓓ
33. Ⓐ Ⓑ Ⓒ Ⓓ
34. Ⓐ Ⓑ Ⓒ Ⓓ
35. Ⓐ Ⓑ Ⓒ Ⓓ
36. Ⓐ Ⓑ Ⓒ Ⓓ
37. Ⓐ Ⓑ Ⓒ Ⓓ
38. Ⓐ Ⓑ Ⓒ Ⓓ
39. Ⓐ Ⓑ Ⓒ Ⓓ
40. Ⓐ Ⓑ Ⓒ Ⓓ

41. Ⓐ Ⓑ Ⓒ Ⓓ
42. Ⓐ Ⓑ Ⓒ Ⓓ
43. Ⓐ Ⓑ Ⓒ Ⓓ
44. Ⓐ Ⓑ Ⓒ Ⓓ
45. Ⓐ Ⓑ Ⓒ Ⓓ
46. Ⓐ Ⓑ Ⓒ Ⓓ
47. Ⓐ Ⓑ Ⓒ Ⓓ
48. Ⓐ Ⓑ Ⓒ Ⓓ
49. Ⓐ Ⓑ Ⓒ Ⓓ
50. Ⓐ Ⓑ Ⓒ Ⓓ
51. Ⓐ Ⓑ Ⓒ Ⓓ
52. Ⓐ Ⓑ Ⓒ Ⓓ
53. Ⓐ Ⓑ Ⓒ Ⓓ
54. Ⓐ Ⓑ Ⓒ Ⓓ
55. Ⓐ Ⓑ Ⓒ Ⓓ
56. Ⓐ Ⓑ Ⓒ Ⓓ
57. Ⓐ Ⓑ Ⓒ Ⓓ
58. Ⓐ Ⓑ Ⓒ Ⓓ
59. Ⓐ Ⓑ Ⓒ Ⓓ
60. Ⓐ Ⓑ Ⓒ Ⓓ

61. Ⓐ Ⓑ Ⓒ Ⓓ
62. Ⓐ Ⓑ
63. Ⓐ Ⓑ Ⓒ Ⓓ
64. Ⓐ Ⓑ Ⓒ Ⓓ
65. Ⓐ Ⓑ Ⓒ Ⓓ
66. Ⓐ Ⓑ Ⓒ Ⓓ
67. Ⓐ Ⓑ Ⓒ Ⓓ
68. Ⓐ Ⓑ Ⓒ Ⓓ
69. Ⓐ Ⓑ Ⓒ Ⓓ
70. Ⓐ Ⓑ Ⓒ Ⓓ
71. Ⓐ Ⓑ Ⓒ Ⓓ
72. Ⓐ Ⓑ Ⓒ Ⓓ
73. Ⓐ Ⓑ Ⓒ Ⓓ
74. Ⓐ Ⓑ Ⓒ Ⓓ
75. Ⓐ Ⓑ Ⓒ Ⓓ
76. Ⓐ Ⓑ Ⓒ Ⓓ
77. Ⓐ Ⓑ Ⓒ Ⓓ
78. Ⓐ Ⓑ Ⓒ Ⓓ
79. Ⓐ Ⓑ
80. Ⓐ Ⓑ Ⓒ Ⓓ

81. Ⓐ Ⓑ Ⓒ Ⓓ
82. Ⓐ Ⓑ Ⓒ Ⓓ
83. Ⓐ Ⓑ Ⓒ Ⓓ
84. Ⓐ Ⓑ Ⓒ Ⓓ
85. Ⓐ Ⓑ Ⓒ Ⓓ
86. Ⓐ Ⓑ Ⓒ Ⓓ
87. Ⓐ Ⓑ Ⓒ Ⓓ
88. Ⓐ Ⓑ Ⓒ Ⓓ
89. Ⓐ Ⓑ Ⓒ Ⓓ
90. Ⓐ Ⓑ Ⓒ Ⓓ
91. Ⓐ Ⓑ
92. Ⓐ Ⓑ Ⓒ Ⓓ
93. Ⓐ Ⓑ Ⓒ Ⓓ
94. Ⓐ Ⓑ Ⓒ Ⓓ
95. Ⓐ Ⓑ Ⓒ Ⓓ
96. Ⓐ Ⓑ Ⓒ Ⓓ
97. Ⓐ Ⓑ
98. Ⓐ Ⓑ Ⓒ Ⓓ
99. Ⓐ Ⓑ Ⓒ Ⓓ
100. Ⓐ Ⓑ Ⓒ Ⓓ

ANSWERS TO CHAPTER 12

Practice Final Written Examination

1. B	21. B	41. B	61. B	81. A
2. C	22. A	42. C	62. A	82. A
3. C	23. A	43. C	63. B	83. A
4. C	24. A	44. C	64. C	84. B
5. B	25. B	45. B	65. A	85. A
6. D	26. C	46. A	66. B	86. C
7. C	27. B	47. C	67. B	87. C
8. D	28. B	48. C	68. D	88. D
9. A	29. B	49. C	69. A	89. D
10. D	30. C	50. B	70. B	90. B
11. C	31. B	51. D	71. C	91. A
12. B	32. B	52. B	72. C	92. C
13. D	33. B	53. D	73. D	93. D
14. C	34. C	54. C	74. C	94. C
15. A	35. B	55. B	75. C	95. B
16. A	36. A	56. B	76. B	96. B
17. C	37. C	57. B	77. C	97. A
18. D	38. C	58. B	78. D	98. A
19. D	39. B	59. A	79. A	99. C
20. D	40. A	60. A	80. B	100. C

RATIONALES FOR THE ANSWERS

1. **The correct answer is (B).** Safety of the crew is the primary concern at any emergency call. The scene survey will determine if the scene is safe or not. The EMT–Basic should complete a comprehensive scene survey on arrival to determine whether or not it is safe to begin operations.

2. **The correct answer is (C).** The system medical director holds the responsibility for all patient care activity. The EMT–Basic works under the license of the medical director, even when administering care under standing orders.

3. **The correct answer is (C).** Although it seems like an appropriate statement, telling a person that you know how they feel after the loss of a family member may be taken the wrong way. It may appear that you are trying to downplay their grief and tell them that they are not the only ones to whom this happens. While in effect this is a true statement, at the time of severe grief, people may not want to accept that as a fact. The job of the EMT–Basic is to assist the family in their needs and to make sure that everybody else on the scene is stable and safe.

4. **The correct answer is (C).** The use of alcohol and drugs is the worst thing that the EMT–Basic can do to relieve stress. Proper eating, relaxing, and discussion with partners and loved ones are all good ways to reduce stress. Alcohol and drugs only serve to increase stress levels on the body and reduce healthy recovery from a stressful event.

5. **The correct answer is (B).** Expressed consent is defined as consent given by a conscious and alert patient who is of sound mind. This consent is given after the EMT–Basic explains his findings and treatment plan, including the hospital that will receive the patient. Choices (A) and (C) define implied consent, and the patient in choice (D) is transported after a decision by the police department that he poses a risk to himself or others.

6. **The correct answer is (D).** Whenever patient contact is made, regardless of whether or not the patient is stable, the EMT–Basic must stay with the patient until one of the following happens:

    1. The patient is transported to the hospital and received properly by the hospital.
    2. The EMT–Basic hands over care to a provider of equal or higher certification.
    3. The patient refuses medical care, and the refusal process is completed legally.

    There are no other options in this matter. If you leave the patient with a first-response crew, they have neither the means of transport nor the means to help the patient should her condition worsen.

7. **The correct answer is (C).** When operating at a crime scene, patient care is the highest priority. The EMT–Basic should do whatever is possible to assist the patient; however, at the same time, an EMT–Basic should assist in the preservation of evidence that may be at the scene. Move only what you have to, and bring only whatever equipment is necessary. If certain equipment is not needed, leave it outside the scene.

8. **The correct answer is (D).** Gurgling sounds during respiration indicate the presence of fluid in the airway. This may be a sign of pulmonary edema and may be an ominous sign. Narrowing of the bronchioles causes wheezing, while upper airway obstruction causes stridor.

9. **The correct answer is (A).** Wheezing indicates the narrowing of the bronchioles. In most cases, wheezes are indicative of asthma exacerbations. The patient who is wheezing should be treated with high-concentration oxygen and assisted with her asthma medications as necessary.

10. **The correct answer is (D).** Airway problems and problems of respiration and ventilation will all cause changes to respiratory rate and quality, such as labored breathing, increase in respiratory effort, changes in breath sounds from wheezes, and gurgling and stridor to silent chest from lung collapse. The heart rate will increase, not decrease, in response to the decrease in oxygen in the body.

11. **The correct answer is (C).** Auscultation of a blood pressure with a stethoscope is the only way to obtain a complete blood pressure reading in the field. Palpation is done in severe emergencies where a baseline systolic blood pressure is needed and there is no time to auscultate a blood pressure.

12. **The correct answer is (B).** Systolic blood pressure is not a component of the SAMPLE history. SAMPLE stands for signs/symptoms, allergies, medications, past history, last meal eaten, and events leading to illness or injury. Blood pressure is obtained under the vital signs part of the assessment.

13. **The correct answer is (D).** There are many items that fall into the category of pertinent past medical history: hypertension, heart disease, diabetes, seizures, and stroke, to name a few. Gall bladder surgery that was performed many years in the past is not pertinent to an emergency patient. It would be pertinent to a patient history if it were very recent and the patient was bleeding, having difficult breathing, etc. The EMT–Basic may document the old surgery; however, it is not pertinent to a diagnosis in an emergency.

14. **The correct answer is (C).** A symptom is defined as something a patient complains of but cannot be seen by the EMT–Basic. A sign is a physical finding that the EMT–Basic will document during an assessment For example, pupil size, cool moist skin, wheezes, and hives are all signs.

15. **The correct answer is (A).** Good body mechanics are essential to the health and safety of the EMT–Basic as well as the patient. The EMT–Basic should size up a lift to ascertain whether or not he may need assistance or any special lifting process or equipment may be needed. Good communication between partners as well as proper foot placement and lifting with the legs will prevent injury to all parties involved.

16. **The correct answer is (A).** A patient with a head injury, regardless of mental status, should not be removed from a vehicle unless he is still in danger of additional injury. Emergency moves are reserved for situations when the patient is in danger of additional injury from an unsafe area.

17. **The correct answer is (C).** Patients with unmanageable airways are considered unstable and must be rapidly extricated from a vehicle. The use of a cervical collar and a long board is acceptable for rapid extrication. Stable patients should be removed using a properly applied extrication device, such as a KED or a short board. The scoop stretcher should never be used as a spinal immobilization device.

18. **The correct answer is (D).** Mouth-to-mask ventilation requires a liter flow of 15 liters a minute. The EMT–Basic should use a pocket mask with a one-way valve and an oxygen inlet to provide the proper amount of oxygen and provide a safe means of ventilating that avoids contact with blood or other body fluids. A one-way valve will protect the EMT–Basic from bodily fluids.

19. **The correct answer is (D).** Using the bag-valve-mask ventilator, at least 800 milliliters of air must be delivered to a patient to ensure adequate ventilations. Most modern bag-valve-mask devices deliver more than 1,000 milliliters of air when properly used. It is essential that the EMT–Basic become proficient in the use of the bag-valve-mask device.

20. **The correct answer is (D).** The bag-valve-mask with reservoir can deliver oxygen percentages up to 100 percent when attached to an oxygen supply. Percentages this high are essential when ventilating a patient with a bag-valve-mask device. Most patients who are being ventilated artificially are hypoxic from the inability to support their own ventilations. The bag-valve-mask device will deliver much-needed oxygen and ventilatory volumes to a hypoxic patient.

21. **The correct answer is (B).** Insertion of an oropharyngeal airway requires that the EMT–Basic open the mouth using a cross-fingered technique. This is a safe technique that allows the EMT–Basic to keep her fingers out of the patient's mouth—therefore, out of danger. Any technique to open the mouth that involves placing fingers in the mouth is not to be used.

22. **The correct answer is (A).** Oropharyngeal airways are contraindicated in patients with an intact gag reflex. Because of the angle of insertion and where the oropharyngeal airway sits in the airway, it will elicit a gag reflex in all patients who still have an intact gag reflex. It is indicated in deeply unconscious patients who have an absent gag reflex, cannot support their own airway or ventilations, and who are going to need ventilatory support via bag-valve-mask.

23. **The correct answer is (A).** The Macintosh blade is inserted into the vallecula, a structure that is defined as the area where the base of the tongue meets the epiglottis. The blade is inserted and upward pressure is exerted, lifting the epiglottis and allowing visualization of the vocal cords.

24. **The correct answer is (A).** Adult endotracheal tubes have inflatable cuffs to form a seal in the trachea. This seal prevents air leakage and allows for forceful ventilations directly into the trachea. Pediatric endotracheal tubes are uncuffed. The cricoid ring of the pediatric airway is the narrowest part of the airway, and when the proper tube size is used, it forms a natural seal.

25. **The correct answer is (B).** When an endotracheal tube is inserted too deeply into the right mainstem, the EMT–Basic will hear only breath sound in the right lung. This is due to the fact that the right mainstem has less of an acute angle and that the endotracheal tube will naturally follow the lesser of the angles.

26. **The correct answer is (C).** A right mainstem intubation is corrected by slowly backing the tube out of the trachea while monitoring breath sounds. When bilateral breath sounds are auscultated, the EMT–Basic can secure the endotracheal tube and continue ventilations.

27. **The correct answer is (B).** Absence of breath sounds after intubation indicates that the endotracheal tube was improperly inserted and is in the esophagus. The tell-tale signs of esophageal intubation are absence of breath sounds and chest rise as well as noises from the epigastrum.

28. **The correct answer is (B).** On arrival at the scene of any emergency, the EMT–Basic should do a complete assessment of the scene; this is called the scene size-up. Scene size-up includes determination of the mechanism of injury, patient count, and determining whether or not additional resources are be needed. The most important part of the scene size-up is that the EMT–Basic will make a determination of scene safety that will allow the EMT–Basic to proceed to the next steps of patient care.

29. **The correct answer is (B).** The initial assessment consists of six steps in the evaluation of a patient's status. These steps include general impression, mental status, airway, breathing, circulatory status, and prioritizing the patient's illness or injury. Patient history is not a part of the initial assessment and is gathered later on in the call.

30. **The correct answer is (C).** The patient with chest pain and decreased blood pressure is a high-priority patient and needs immediate care and transportation. This patient may be in shock and will need medication therapy in the emergency department.

31. **The correct answer is (B).** The AVPU scale is a scale designed to determine the patient's mental status. The scale is defined as follows: A=Alert, V=Voice responsive, P=Pain responsive, and U=Unresponsive.

32. **The correct answer is (B).** The chief complaint is the reason that the patient has called the ambulance. The chief complaint should be described in the patient's own words. This statement can usually be elicited right after the EMT–Basic asks, "Why was the ambulance called today?" This should be documented exactly as stated, in the patient's own words.

33. **The correct answer is (B).** This patient, based on mental status, breathing assessment, and circulatory status, is critical and should be classified as a high-priority patient. High-priority patients should be transported immediately to the area receiving hospital that is trained to care for them—in this case, a trauma center.

34. **The correct answer is (C).** The detailed physical examination should be performed on all trauma patients after the initial assessment as critical interventions are completed. This examination, which will solidify findings on the initial assessment as well as uncover previously hidden injuries, should be done en route to the hospital when a patient is high priority; however, it may be done on the scene on low-priority patients or in the case of delayed transport.

35. **The correct answer is (B).** The history of present illness will help the EMT–Basic assess different aspects of the onset of the present complaint—namely the onset of the event, factors that provoke the pain or discomfort, quality, radiation and pain severity, and the duration of the onset. All of these factors add up to a presumptive diagnosis of the history of present illness.

36. **The correct answer is (A).** Trauma patients always receive a detailed physical examination due to the fact that there may be a hidden injury that was not uncovered in the initial assessment. Medical patients are given "vectored" examinations that focus in on areas that may be causing the patient's illness.

37. **The correct answer is (C).** The on-going assessment is designed as a tool to reassess the patient's complaints, vital signs, and any physical examinations and results of any interventions. Primary interventions are not performed here; instead, they should be performed after the initial assessments and history. Although additional assessments may be initiated after the on-going assessment, it is designed as a re-evaluation tool to confirm that all interventions are keeping the patient stable.

38. **The correct answer is (C).** The patient's personal information should never be given over the radio frequencies. This is confidential information and has no bearing on the treatment that will be given at the receiving hospital.

39. **The correct answer is (B).** It is always helpful to communicate with a child face to face. Children will fear a large adult that is going to touch them, especially a stranger. The best results may be obtained by getting down to the child's level, playing for a few minutes (if the child is stable), and then beginning your assessment.

40. **The correct answer is (A).** Documentation of intoxication as well as demeanor is not appropriate on the call report. Many patients with medical conditions appear as though they are intoxicated. Some patients are even abusive to the crew due to their illness. Documenting that a patient is drunk is not an objective finding and is not recommended.

41. **The correct answer is (B).** Although the EMT–Basic is trained to assist the patient in taking epinephrine in the case of an allergic reaction, this must be the patient's medication. Epinephrine is not carried on the EMT–Basic ambulance.

42. **The correct answer is (C).** The EMT–Basic is not trained to administer insulin to any patient. Regardless of the fact that the patient has a prescription for insulin, the EMT–Basic is not trained in its use and the dangers associated with its administration.

43. **The correct answer is (C).** Side effects are reactions and other responses to a medication that may cause signs and symptoms in a patient. Some side effects are expected, and others are not. It is important to know that the side effect is not the desired action of a medication and is not a determinant factor that it is working.

44. **The correct answer is (C).** All patients who are suffering from difficulty breathing will show signs and symptoms of their distress. Some of the signs are accessory muscle use, cyanotic skin color, tripod positioning, and intercostals retractions. Symptoms include shortness of breath and anxiety. Decreased pulse rate in respiratory distress is not a normal finding, as the pulse rate increases with hypoxia. In the pediatric patient, however, decreased pulse rate secondary to respiratory distress is an ominous sign. Be alert for changes in the pediatric patient's status while she is having breathing difficulties.

45. **The correct answer is (B).** Asthma is a disease that exacerbates in acute onsets of attacks. These attacks cause the bronchioles to constrict, trapping air in the lungs and forcing the patient to work to exhale. Typical signs of an asthma attack are tripod positioning and audible wheezing. This disease is usually reversible by assisting the patient in taking his inhaler medication and oxygen administration.

46. **The correct answer is (A).** Chronic bronchitis is caused by long-term lung damage from smoking or other irritational exposures. These exposures enlarge mucous glands, and they over-secrete mucous, causing plugs. This increases the patient's work of breathing and causes respiratory distress. As this is a chronic condition, the treatment lies in oxygenation and transportation to a medical facility for definitive care.

47. **The correct answer is (C).** This patient is suffering from classic signs and symptoms of myocardial infarction. The diagnosis of angina may also be considered; however, nitroglycerin and rest usually relieve angina. This patient's pain has been persistent for 45 minutes. The treatment of choice would be high-concentration oxygen and assisted medication delivery of additional nitroglycerin, provided that the patient's blood pressure remains stable.

48. **The correct answer is (C).** The AED (automatic external defibrillator) is not indicated in responsive patients under any conditions. The application of the AED is reserved for the unconscious patient who is pulseless. There are cardiac rhythms that may present with and without pulses that would indicate that a shock is required. For that reason, the AED is never applied to a responsive patient.

49. **The correct answer is (C).** The American Heart Association recommends that the initial electrical therapy for "shocks indicated" cardiac arrests is three successive shocks. The EMT–Basic should deliver three shock is rapid succession, provided that the AED confirms that a shock is indicated.

50. **The correct answer is (B).** In some cases of cardiac arrest, the heart will not be in a rhythm that is correctable by electrical current. It is in these cases that the shock is not indicated. The EMT–Basic should request ALS assistance immediately upon arrival to a cardiac arrest call. If no shock is indicated, continue CPR and begin transport.

51. **The correct answer is (D).** Children under 12 years of age and under 90 pounds are not candidates for electrical countershocks in the field. In most cases, the arrest is caused by another medical problem, and the cardiac rhythm will not be a "shockable" rhythm. It is best to continue basic life support and transport rapidly to a receiving hospital.

52. **The correct answer is (B).** This patient has the textbook signs of a hypoglycemic event. A rapid onset of unconsciousness in a known diabetic is almost always associated with a drop in blood sugar. In the field, all unconscious diabetics should be treated as if they are hypoglycemic, regardless of the rate of onset. Patients with high blood sugar usually have a delayed onset from hours to days before they become unconscious. A rapid onset is indicative of low blood sugar.

53. **The correct answer is (D).** The EMT–Basic should never assist a patient in administration of his own insulin. Treatment of this patient is oxygen, glucose, and transport. It is always advisable to request advanced life support when a patient is unresponsive. This patient luckily started becoming responsive, so oral glucose was indicated. If the patient remained unconscious, administration of oral glucose would not be indicated.

54. **The correct answer is (C).** This patient is having an allergic reaction to a bee sting. Bee stings are one of the most common causes of allergic reactions. The patient will develop respiratory distress, hives, itching, alteration of mental status, unconsciousness, and, finally, cardiovascular collapse and death. Rapid intervention and assisted medication administration will greatly assist the patient's chances of survival.

55. **The correct answer is (B).** When assisting in the administration of medications, the EMT–Basic should contact medical control for permission and guidance in the proper administration of assisted medication. Anaphylaxis is a true emergency, and seconds count. Not treating this patient can lead to irreversible shock and death.

56. **The correct answer is (B).** Poisons may enter the body from four different paths: injection, ingestion, inhalation, and absorption (through skin). Taking the window washer fluid in by mouth is an example of poisoning by ingestion.

57. **The correct answer is (B).** Carbon monoxide poisonings are extremely common, especially in the winter. One of the by-products of combustion is carbon monoxide gas. This colorless and odorless gas will attach to the hemoglobin faster and more efficiently than oxygen, causing death by hypoxia. Treatment of these patients includes removing the patient from the affected area and administration of high-concentration oxygen.

58. **The correct answer is (B).** This patient has the symptoms of moderate hypothermia. In mild hypothermia, the patient is relatively alert and awake. The body begins shivering to produce heat. Moderate hypothermia sees the patient stop shivering and muscle rigidity sets in, pupils dilate, and mental status drops. Severe hypothermia sets in, and the patient becomes unresponsive. In severe hypothermia, the patient may develop ventricular fibrillation and, subsequently, die.

59. **The correct answer is (A).** Heat cramps are the first stage of the reaction to excessive environmental heat by the body. The patient will complain of muscular cramping and may even be rigid and unable to move his extremities. Left untreated, the patient will develop heat exhaustion and then progress to heat stroke.

60. **The correct answer is (A).** Establishment of an airway is the highest priority in any emergency. The EMT–Basic should establish a patent airway as soon as it is possible to do so. This includes while still in the water.

61. **The correct answer is (B).** When you encounter resistance while treating the near-drowning patient, this is due to pressure in the stomach caused by swallowed water. The EMT–Basic should gently push down to expel the water through the patient's mouth. The EMT–Basic should have a suction unit ready to keep the airway clear at all times.

62. **The correct answer is (A).** There are multiple medical and toxicological causes that may present themselves as a psychological emergency. Before the diagnosis of a behavioral emergency can be made, the EMT–Basic should try to rule out medical causes of the event.

63. **The correct answer is (B).** This patient has some of the classic signs of depression with a suicidal ideation. The loss of a loved one can lead to severe depression and, sometimes, attempted suicide. The EMT–Basic can never take a discussion about suicide lightly. These patients should never be allowed to refuse medical attention, and all must be transported for further evaluation.

64. **The correct answer is (C).** Whenever the EMT–Basic is faced with a threat of violence, the concept of crew safety should be the first priority. In this situation, it is best to take a step back and request police assistance to restrain this patient prior to transport. Even if the patient calms down, there is no guarantee that he will not develop another violent episode during transport.

65. **The correct answer is (A).** Placenta previa is a premature separation of the placenta prior to birth. It is characterized by bright red vaginal bleeding that causes no pain. Treatment of this emergency is oxygen and rapid transport to the emergency department.

66. **The correct answer is (B).** Whenever the amniotic fluid has a greenish color, it is assumed that there is meconium staining and that the infant may be in danger of meconium aspiration. The EMT–Basic should prepare to suction the infant immediately after the delivery of the newborn's head.

67. **The correct answer is (B).** The newborn with meconium-stained amniotic fluid must be suctioned prior to the full delivery. This means that as soon as the head delivers, the newborn should be suctioned thoroughly. Do not begin to stimulate respirations until the newborn is suctioned thoroughly.

68. **The correct answer is (D).** The APGAR score is a generalized report on the newborn's health after birth. It may advise the emergency department of the type of stress encountered during childbirth. It is essential that the APGAR score be performed in the field at the required time intervals.

69. **The correct answer is (A).** This patient has a deformity as well as bright red pulsating bleeding. This is most likely a long bone fracture of the leg with arterial injury and bleeding. The EMT–Basic should be aware that this type of bleeding can be life threatening and attempts to control the bleeding should be made immediately after securing the airway and stabilizing breathing.

70. **The correct answer is (B).** All of the potential answers to this question have a possibility of occurring secondary to a blow by a blunt instrument; however, the area of bruising is indicative of internal organ injury—in this case, the liver.

71. **The correct answer is (C).** Hypertension is not a sign of shock. Internal and external bleeding causes blood pressure to decrease. Initially, the body compensates by constricting blood vessels, and then the blood vessels begin to dilate, causing hypotension and, eventually, irreversible shock. The EMT–Basic should be alert for signs of shock and treat accordingly to prevent end-stage organ failure (irreversible shock).

72. **The correct answer is (C).** The EMT–Basic should never administer fluids by mouth to a patient in shock. A shock patient may complain of thirst; however, the blood is shunted away from the gastrointestinal system during shock to perfuse the vital organs. Administration of fluid by mouth may cause vomiting and airway management complications.

73. **The correct answer is (D).** A contusion is an example of a closed soft-tissue injury and is characterized by an area of bruising. A laceration is a jagged- or smooth-edged injury. An abrasion is a scraping of the skin that oozes blood, and an avulsion is a flap of skin that is torn loose.

74. **The correct answer is (C).** An evisceration is defined as any injury in which bowel protrudes from the wound. Treatment of this type of injury is essential because the sterility of the bowel has been broken and severe infection can develop. The area should be covered with a moist sterile dressing and an occlusive dressing over that.

75. **The correct answer is (C).** A full thickness burn (third degree) involves the upper layers of skin as well as the sub-dermal layers. It is characterized by charring of the tissue and is usually painless, due to severe nerve damage. There may be areas of blistering and reddening around the full thickness burn, as most full thickness burns have partial thickness burns in the same vicinity.

76. **The correct answer is (B).** Any open chest wound, regardless of whether or not it is a sucking chest wound, should be covered with an occlusive dressing. This will seal the hole and prevent air movement in and out of the wound. Air movement in this area may develop into a tension pneumothorax and cause decreased cardiac output and hypoxia.

77. **The correct answer is (C).** Impaled objects are never to be removed in the field, unless they are impaled in the patient's cheek. An impaled object may be preventing bleeding, and its removal may cause massive bleeding. The treatment is to stabilize them with a bulky dressing and transport immediately to the emergency department.

78. **The correct answer is (D).** In this situation, there are a few priorities; ventilation and CPR are a high priority. In electrical injuries, electrical current stops the heart, and the application of the AED is indicated to analyze for a shockable rhythm. If shock is advised, the same treatment algorithm is utilized, as if the patient were a medical arrest.

79. **The correct answer is (A).** Closed musculoskeletal injuries are usually extremely painful, deformed, and swollen; there may be an area of contusion and sensitivity to touch. Distal pulses should be checked before the splint is applied to assess for arterial involvement in the injury.

80. **The correct answer is (B).** When splinting, the splint is applied and secured to immobilize the joint above and below the injury site. This prevents movement of the injured bones and decreases the amount of pain involved in the movement of the injury site. After the application of the splint, distal pulses and neurological function should be assessed to assure that there is no impairment in blood flow or nerve impulse transmission.

81. **The correct answer is (A).** A sprain is the stretching or tearing of a ligament. Ligaments are tissues that connect bones to other bones. Any excessive stretch on a ligament can tear it or stretch it out of place, causing a painful and swollen injury. In the field, it may be difficult to differentiate between a ligament injury and a fracture, so splinting is the treatment of choice.

82. **The correct answer is (A).** Battle signs, clear fluid from the ears, and altered mental status are obvious signs of skull fracture and associated brain injury. This patient needs aggressive airway management, immobilization, and rapid transport to the nearest trauma center.

83. **The correct answer is (A).** The spinal column consists of seven cervical vertebrae. Injuries to the cervical spine can be severe and life threatening because much of the innervation to the respiratory system and the other vital organs is in the area of the first two vertebrae. A fracture in this area can cause death from respiratory failure.

84. **The correct answer is (B).** All of the nerves that innervate the body originate from the spinal cord. If the spinal cord is damaged, nerve function below the area of the injury is impaired or lost. Usually, this damage is irreparable, and the patient suffers permanent injury. It is essential to identify possible areas of injury and immobilize the patient to prevent further injury.

85. **The correct answer is (A).** The Kendrick extrication device is used to immobilize the patient with suspected spinal injuries. After the patient has a cervical collar applied, the KED is then applied and the patient moved to a long board. Distal pulses and neurological function are assessed throughout the application of the device to maintain that no additional injury has been incurred. It is important to mention that this device should not be used on critical trauma patients who require rapid transport, as it takes time to apply the device.

86. **The correct answer is (C).** The rapid takedown requires that cervical spine immobilization is maintained from behind the patient until the patient is secured to the board and brought down to the ground. This position requires a tall person with a good reach. Therefore, the tallest rescuer should be positioned behind the patient in this maneuver.

87. **The correct answer is (C).** The critical trauma patient should be rapidly extricated with the cervical collar and long board only. Treatment of uncontrolled bleeding, especially if it involves the airway, is essential for survival of the patient. Time is wasted applying complicated extrication devices, and their use is saved for non-critical patients.

88. **The correct answer is (D).** Child car seats may also double for an extrication device. The child can have a cervical collar applied, and then padding can be placed around the child and taped down. It not only serves as a good device, but it also provides access to the airway and vascular access, if necessary.

89. **The correct answer is (D).** Impacts with windshields are signs that leave a high index of suspicion. The EMT–Basic should suspect facial trauma, spinal trauma, and serious brain injury after a patient impacts a windshield. Precautionary immobilization should be applied, including the KED, unless the patient is critical.

90. **The correct answer is (B).** The softness of the pediatric patient's rib cage makes it unable to protect the organs of the thoracic cavity. This will lead to serious chest trauma and massive internal bleeding.

91. **The correct answer is (A).** The pediatric cranial cavity is larger in proportion to the adult; therefore, blood loss in that area may lead to hypovolemic shock and decreased blood pressure. This is the exact opposite of the adult, who will develop hypertension secondary to the isolated head injury.

92. **The correct answer is (C).** American Heart Association guidelines for infant foreign body airway obstruction states that the patients should receive alternating back blows and chest thrusts, with finger sweeps only utilized to remove visible objects. Blind finger sweeps are not indicated, as they may push the object deeper inside the airway.

93. **The correct answer is (D).** The EMT–Basic should never remain on the scene for the advanced life-support providers in any case of shock. Immediate transport to the emergency department is the best possible chance of patient treatment. Advanced life-support field procedures may maintain the patient's circulatory status initially; however, it will not repair the internal damage causing the shock in the first place. So, transport as soon as you are ready and try for an advanced life-support intercept on the way to the emergency department.

94. **The correct answer is (C).** Driving at excessive speeds, on icy roads, and disregarding traffic control devices are all considered unsafe driving conditions. The primary concern of the EMT–Basic is to crew safety. Placing yourself in danger by driving unsafely is not an acceptable practice.

95. **The correct answer is (B).** The patient is not transferred to emergency department care unless the staff has received a full report, the patient is transferred to a bed, and the paperwork for transfer is signed. The EMT–Basic who leaves the patient before any of these factors are complete may be guilty of abandonment.

96. **The correct answer is (B).** Any equipment that is used for invasive procedures should be sterilized using heat processes. The ambulance stretcher, extrication equipment, and suction units may be cleaned with high-level disinfection. Most suction units have disposable parts that eliminate the need for disinfection. To prevent the spread of disease, the EMT–Basic should practice good cleaning techniques.

97. **The correct answer is (A).** Any patient who requires extrication with other than typical extrication equipment is considered a complex extrication. Building collapses have a whole range of complicating factors and will result in long and complex extrication procedures.

98. **The correct answer is (A).** Simple access is defined as gaining access to a patient with no specialized tool, while complex access requires specialized tools to gain access to a patient.

99. **The correct answer is (C).** EMS personnel with no specialty training in hazardous materials should never venture into the hot zone; only personnel with specialty training and protective equipment should operate in the hot zone. All medical treatment should occur after decontamination and in the cold zone

100. **The correct answer is (C).** The incident command system was designed to break down different responsibilities at large incidents into sectors that are responsible for different activities. Each sector has a commander, and each commander reports to the overall incident commander. This system, when operated efficiently, will streamline patient care and movement, leading to the successful completion of the incident.

APPENDICES

Appendix A

AVAILABILITY OF TRAINING

EMS training is widely available in every state. Most states offer training that is easily accessible to interested parties. Fire and Rescue departments may offer EMS programs. In addition, some states may have dedicated EMS training facilities.

Each state has an EMS division within the state Department of Health. Providers who are interested should contact the Department of Health in their home state for additional information. The following pages contain the address, phone numbers, and Web sites (if applicable) of EMS offices within the fifty states:

Alabama

Alabama Department of Public Health
Emergency Medical Services Division
RSA Tower, Suite 750
201 Monroe Street
Montgomery, Alabama 36104
Telephone: 334-206-5383
Fax: 334-516-5132
Web: http://www.alapubhealth.org/ems

Alaska

Community Health and Emergency Medical Services
410 Willoughby, Suite 109
P.O. Box 110616
Juneau, Alaska 99811-0616
Telephone: 907-465-3141
Fax: 907-465-4101
Web: http://www.hss.state.ak.us/dph/EMS/CHEMS.HTM

Arizona

Arizona Department of Health Services
Emergency Medical Services Office
1651 East Morton, Suite 120
Phoenix, Arizona 85020
Telephone: 602-861-1188
Fax: 602-861-1122
Web: http://www.state.az.us/health.htm

Arkansas
Arkansas Department of Health
EMS and Trauma Systems
Freeway Medical Tower
5800 West 10th Street, Suite 800
Little Rock, Arkansas 72204
Telephone: 501-661-2262
Web: http://health.state.ar.us/

California
California EMS Authority
1930 9th Street
Sacramento, California 95814
Telephone: 916-322-4336 (Main)
916-323-9875 (Paramedic Licensure)
Fax: 916-324-2875
Web: http://www.emsa.ca.gov/default.htm

Colorado
Colorado Department of Public Health and Environment
Prehospital Care Program
4300 Cherry Creek Drive South
Denver, Colorado 80246-1530
Telephone: 303-692-2995
Fax: 303-691-7720
Web: http://www.cdphe.state.co.us/em/emhom.html

Connecticut
Connecticut Department of Public Health
Office of Emergency Medical Services
410 Capitol Avenue
MS #12 EMS, P.O. Box 340308
Hartford, Connecticut 06134-0308
Telephone: 860-509-8000
Web: http://www.state.ct.us/dph/BRS/NewBRS/emsco.htm

District of Columbia
Department of Health
Emergency Health and Medical Services
800 9th Street SW, 3rd Floor
Washington, DC 20024
Telephone: 202-645-5628
Fax: 202-645-0526
Web: http://www.dchealth.com/ehms/welcome.htm

Delaware

State of Delaware
Office of EMS
Blue Hen Corporate Center, Suite 4H
655 South Bay Road
Dover, Delaware 19901
Telephone: 302-739-4710

Florida

Bureau of Emergency Medical Services
Florida Department of Health
2002-D Old St. Augustine Road
Tallahassee, Florida 32301-4881
Telephone: 850-489-1924
Fax: 850-487-2911
Web: http://www.doh.state.fl.us

Georgia

Georgia Division of Public Health
Emergency Medical Services
47 Trinity Avenue, Suite 104
Atlanta, Georgia 30334-5600
Telephone: 404-657-6700
Fax: 404-657-4255
Web: http://www.ph.dhr.state.ga.us/programs/ems/index.shtml

Hawaii

Program Manager
State Emergency Medical Services System
3627 Kilauea Avenue, Room 102
Honolulu, Hawaii 96816-2317
Telephone: 808-733-9210
Fax: 808-733-8332
E-mail: emss@camhmis.health.state.hi.us

Idaho

Idaho EMS Bureau
P.O. Box 83720
Boise, Idaho 85705
Telephone: 208-334-4000
Fax: 208-334-4015
Web: http://www.pte.state.id.us/

Illinois

Illinois Department of Public Health
Division of EMS and Highway Safety
525 W. Jefferson Street, 5th Floor
Springfield, Illinois 62761-0001
Telephone: 217-785-2080
Fax: 217-785-0253
Web: http://www.idph.state.il.us/about/ohcr.htm

Indiana

State Emergency Management Agency
Department of Fire and Building Services
Public Safety Training Institute
Indiana Government Center South
402 West Washington Street, Room E239
Indianapolis, Indiana 46204
Telephone: 800-666-7784 (toll-free)
Fax: 317-233-6545
Web: http://www.state.in.us/sema/ems.html

Iowa

Iowa Department of Public Health
Lucas State Office Building
321 East 12th Street
Des Moines, Iowa 50319-0075
Telephone: 515-281-4951
Fax: 515-281-4958
Web: http://www.idph.state.ia.us/pa/ems

Kansas

State of Kansas Board of Emergency Medical Services
109 SW 6th Street
Topeka, Kansas 66603-3826
Telephone: 785-296-7403
Fax: 785-296-6212
Web: http://www.ksbems.org/

Kentucky

Cabinet For Health Services
Department For Public Health
Emergency Medical Services Branch
Health Services Building
1st Floor East
275 East Main Street
Frankfort, Kentucky 40621
Telephone: 502-564-8963
Fax: 502-564-6533
Web: http://cfc-chs.chr.state.ky.us/ems.htm

Louisiana
Louisiana Department of Health and Hospitals
Bureau of Emergency Medical Services
P.O. Box 94215
Baton Rouge, Louisiana 70804
Telephone: 504-342-4881
Fax: 504-342-4876
Web: http://www.dhh.state.la.us/OPH/progsvc.htm

Maine
Maine Emergency Medical Services
16 Edison Drive
Augusta, Maine 04330
Telephone: 207-287-3953
Fax: 207-287-6251
Web: http://janus.state.me.us/dps/ems/homepage.htm

Maryland
The Maryland Institute for Emergency Medical Services Systems
653 W. Pratt Street, Room 105
Baltimore, Maryland 21201-1536
Telephone: 410-706-3666
Fax: 410-706-2367
Web: http://miemss.umab.edu/Home.htm

Massachusetts
Office of Emergency Medical Services
470 Atlantic Avenue, 2nd Floor
Boston, Massachusetts 02210
Telephone: 617-753-8300
Fax: 617-753-8350
Web: http://www.state.ma.us/dph/oems

Michigan
Michigan State Government
Department of Consumer and Industry Services
Bureau of Health Services
P.O. Box 30195
Lansing, Michigan 48909
Telephone: 517-335-8570
Fax: 517-335-8582
Web: http://www.commerce.state.mi.us/bhser/

Minnesota
Minnesota Emergency Medical Services Regulatory Board
2829 University Avenue Southeast, Suite 310
Minneapolis, Minnesota 55414-3222
Telephone: 612-627-5404
Fax: 612-627-5442
Web: http://www.emsrb.state.mn.us/

Mississippi

Mississippi EMS Program
P.O. Box 1700
Jackson, Mississippi 39215-1700
Telephone: 601-987-3880
Fax: 601-987-3993
Web: http://www.msdh.state.ms.us/ems/index.htm

Missouri

Missouri Department of Health
Bureau of Emergency Medical Services
P.O. Box 570
Jefferson City, Missouri 65102
Telephone: 573-751-6356
Fax: 573-751-6348
Web: http://www.health.state.mo.us/AbouttheDepartment/DS6.html

Montana

Montana Department of Public Health and Human Services
Emergency Medical Services and Injury Prevention
1400 Broadway Street
Helena, Montana 59620
Telephone: 406-444-3895
Fax: 406-444-1814
Web: http://www.dphhs.state.mt.us/hpsd/pubheal/healsafe/ems/index.htm

Nebraska

Nebraska Department of Health and Human Services
EMS Division
301 Centennial Mall South
Lincoln, Nebraska 68509-5007
Telephone: 402-471-0120
Fax: 402-471-0169
Web: http://www.hhs.state.ne.us/ems/emsindex.htm

Nevada

Bureau of Licensure and Certification
Emergency Medical Services
1550 E. College Parkway, Suite 158
Carson City, Nevada 89706
Telephone: 775-687-3065
Web: http://health2k.state.nv.us/

New Hampshire
Emergency Medical Services
Northern New Hampshire EMS
55 Maynesboro Street
Berlin, New Hampshire 03570
Telephone: 603-752-7531
Fax: 603-752-5103
Web: http://www.state.nh.us/

New Jersey
New Jersey Department of Health and Senior Services
Office of Emergency Medical Services
50 East State Street
P.O. Box 360
Trenton, New Jersey 08625-0360
Telephone: 609-633-7777
Fax: 609-633-7954
Web: http://www.state.nj.us/health/ems/hlthems.htm

New Mexico
New Mexico Injury Prevention and EMS Bureau
P.O. Box 2610
Santa Fe, New Mexico 87501
Telephone: 505-476-7000 Ext. 107
Fax: 505-476-7010
Web: http://www.health.state.nm.us/

New York
New York State Department of Health
Bureau of Emergency Medical Services
433 River Street, Suite 303
Troy, New York 12180-2299
Telephone: 518-402-0996
Fax: 518-402-0985
Web: http://www.health.state.ny.us/nysdoh/ems/main.htm

North Carolina
The North Carolina Office of EMS
Division of Facility Services
P.O. Box 29530
Raleigh, North Carolina 27626-0530
Telephone: 919-733-2285
Fax: 919-733-7021
Web: http://www.ncems.org/

North Dakota
North Dakota Department of Health
600 East Boulevard Avenue, Department 301
Bismarck, North Dakota 58505-0200
Telephone: 701-328-2388
Fax: 701-328-1890
Web: http://www.health.state.nd.us/ndhd/resource/dehs/dehs.htm

Ohio
Ohio Department of Public Safety
Emergency Medical Services
1970 West Broad Street
P.O. Box 7167
Columbus, Ohio 43218-2073
Telephone: 614-466-9447
Fax: 614-466-9461
Web: http://www.state.oh.us/odps/division/ems/default.htm

Oklahoma
Oklahoma State Department of Health
State EMS Office
1000 NE 10th
Oklahoma City, Oklahoma 73117
Telephone: 405-271-4027
Fax: 405-271-3986

Oregon
Oregon Health Division
Emergency Medical Services and Systems
Portland State Office Building
800 NE Oregon Street, Suite 607
Portland, Oregon 97232
Telephone: 503-731-4011 Ext. 634
Fax: 503-731-4077
Web: http://www.ohd.hr.state.or.us/cehs/ems/welcome.htm

Pennsylvania
Pennsylvania Department of Health
Emergency Medical Services Office
P.O. Box 90
Harrisburg, Pennsylvania 17108
Telephone: 717-787-8740
Fax: 717-772-5085
Web: http://www.health.state.pa.us

Rhode Island
Rhode Island Department of Health
Emergency Medical Services
3 Capitol Hill
Providence, Rhode Island 02908
Telephone: 401-222-2401
Fax: 401-222-3352
Web: http://www.health.state.ri.us/index.html

South Carolina
Department of Health and Environmental Control
Emergency Medical Services Section
2600 Bull Street
Columbia, South Carolina 29201
Telephone: 803-737-7276
Fax: 803-737-7212
Web: http://www.state.sc.us/dhec/NewEMS/index.htm

South Dakota
Emergency Medical Services
South Dakota Department of Health
600 E. Capitol
Pierre, South Dakota 57501-5070
Telephone: 605-773-3915
800-738-2301 (toll-free)
Fax: 605-773-5904
Web: http://www.state.sd.us/doh/EMS/index.htm

Tennessee
Tennessee Department of Health
Division of Emergency Medical Services
1st Floor, Cordell Hull Building
425 Fifth Avenue North
Nashville, Tennessee 37247-0701
Telephone: 615-741-2584
Fax: 615-741-4217
Web: http://www.state.tn.us/health/ems

Texas
Texas Department of Health
Bureau of Emergency Management
1100 West 49th Street
Austin, Texas 78756-3199
Telephone: 512-834-6700
Fax: 512-834-6736
Web: http://www.tdh.state.tx.us/hcqs/ems/emshome.htm

Utah

Utah Department of Health
Bureau of Emergency Medical Services
288 North 1460 West, 2nd Floor
Salt Lake City, Utah 84114-2852
Telephone: 801-538-6287
Fax: 801-538-6808
Web: http://hlunix.hl.state.ut.us/ems/

Vermont

Vermont Department of Health
Division of Health Protection
EMS and Injury Prevention
108 Cherry Street, Box 70
Burlington, Vermont 05402
Telephone: 802-863-7310
Fax: 802-863-7577
Web: http://www.state.vt.us/health/ems/index.htm

Virginia

Virginia Department of Health
Office of Emergency Medical Services
1528 East Parham Road
Richmond, Virginia 23228
Telephone: 804-371-3500
Fax: 804-371-3543
Web: http://www.vdh.state.va.us/oems/index.htm

Washington

Washington State Department of Health
Office of Emergency Medical and Trauma Prevention
P.O. Box 47853
Olympia, Washington 98504-7853
Telephone: 360-705-6716
Fax: 360-705-6706
Web: http://www.doh.wa.gov/hsqa/emtp/default.htm

West Virginia

West Virginia Department of Health
Bureau of Public Health
Office of Community and Rural Health Services
1411 Virginia Street East
Charleston, West Virginia 25301-3013
Telephone: 304-558-3956
Fax: 304-558-1437
Web: http://www.wvdhhr.org/ocrhs/ems.htm

Wisconsin
EMS Systems Section
P.O. Box 2659
Madison, Wisconsin 53701-2659
Telephone: 608-266-0472
Fax: 608-261-6392
Web: http://www.dhfs.state.wi.us/dph%5Femsip/index.htm

Wyoming
Wyoming Office of Emergency Medical Services and Injury Control
Hathaway Building, Room 526
2300 Capitol Avenue
Cheyenne, Wyoming 82002
Telephone: 307-777-7955
Fax: 307-777-5639
Web: http://wdhfs.state.wy.us/ems

Appendix B

PROFESSIONAL EMS ORGANIZATIONS AND JOURNALS

The EMS provider should be aware that there are numerous professional organizations and journals that are dedicated to the field of Emergency Medical Services. These organizations and publications promote professional EMS standards for education. The EMT–Basic should review the objectives and mission statements for each organization and publication and become a member or subscriber of those that would suit her needs for continued education. The following list identifies the most widely recognized organizations and journals:

National Association of Emergency Medical Technicians
408 Monroe Street
Clinton, Mississippi 39056-4210
Telephone: 800-34-NAEMT (toll-free)
Web: http://www.naemt.org/

National Registry of Emergency Medical Technicians
Rocco V. Morando Building
6610 Busch Boulevard
P.O. Box 29233
Columbus, Ohio 43229
Telephone: 614-888-4484
Web: http://www.nremt.org

National Association of EMS Educators
230 McKee Place, Suite 500
Pittsburgh, Pennsylvania 15213
Telephone: 412-578-3219
Fax: 412-578-3241
Web: http://www.naemse.org

National Association of EMS Physicians

P.O. Box 15945-281
Lenexa, Kansas 66285-5945
Telephone: 913-492-5858
800-228-3677(toll-free)
Fax: 913-541-0156
Web: http://www.naemsp.org

Emergency Medical Services Magazine

Summer Communications Inc.
7626 Densmore Avenue
Van Nuys, California 91406-2042
Telephone: 818-786-4367
800-224-4367 (toll-free)
Fax: 818-786-9246
Web: http://www.emsmagazine.com/

Journal of Emergency Medical Services (JEMS)

JEMS Communications
P.O. Box 2789
Carlsbad, California 92018
Telephone: 760-431-9797
Fax: 760-431-8176
Web: http://www.jems.com/

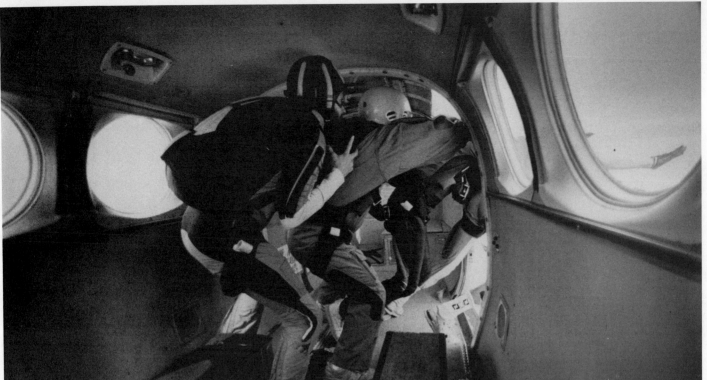

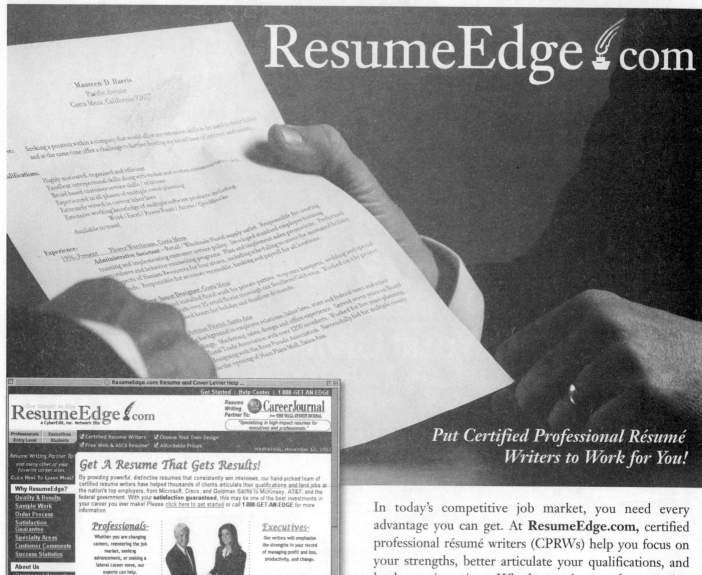